The Zondervan Church and Nonprofit Organization Tax & Financial Guide

For 1999 Tax Returns

2000 EDITION

Dan Busby, CPA

ZondervanPublishingHouse
Grand Rapids, Michigan

A Division of HarperCollins*Publishers*

THE ZONDERVAN CHURCH AND NONPROFIT ORGANIZATION TAX AND FINANCIAL GUIDE: 2000 EDITION

For information write to:
Zondervan Publishing House
Grand Rapids, Michigan 49530

Publisher's note: This guide is published in recognition of the need for clarification of tax and other laws for churches and nonprofit organizations. Every effort has been made to publish a timely, accurate, and authoritative guide. The publisher, author, and the reviewers do not assume any legal responsibility for the accuracy of the text or any other contents.

Readers are cautioned that this book is sold with the understanding that the publisher is not rendering legal, accounting, or other professional service. Organizations with specific tax problems should seek the professional advice of a tax accountant or lawyer.

References to IRS forms and tax rates are derived from preliminary proofs of 1999 forms or 1998 forms. Some adaptation for changes may be necessary. These materials should be used solely as a guide in filling out 1999 tax and information returns. To obtain the final forms, schedules, and tables for filing returns and forms, contact the IRS or a public library.

ISBN 0-310-22886-7

Printed in the United States of America

99 00 01 02 03 04 05 / DC / 10 9 8 7 6 5 4 3 2 1

Contents . . .

SPECIAL INDEX
FOR CHURCH TREASURERS

A guide within a guide

Financial records of the church

Charitable contributions

Insurance for the church

Key laws that apply to churches

Sample Board Resolutions

CAUTION: You may need to consult with a tax or legal professional before adapting these resolutions to the specific needs of your organization.

Sample Charitable Contribution Letters and Forms

INTRODUCTION

Yes, you can understand the tax rules for churches and other nonprofit organizations. It is easier than ever with this year's edition of the Guide.

Taxes and finances can be very unpleasant aspects of your organization. You do not have time or the interest to master thousands of pages of complex tax laws and regulations. But you want a basic understanding of tax and financial reporting requirements and strategies.

This book is the one for you—written in plain English—clearly explained advice you can act on, with icons in the margins to direct your attention to the most important provisions in the book.

Tip This marks strategy recommendations for saving tax dollars for your organization and your employees.

Planning Idea This alerts you to ideas for tax, compensation, or administrative planning steps.

Key Issue These are the most basic provisions in the tax law that impact churches and other nonprofit organizations.

Remember This is a friendly reminder of information to review that you will definitely want to remember.

Action Steps This highlights easy-to-follow steps to structure your tax and financial planning.

Caution This marks subjects that you should carefully study to achieve the best tax and financial treatment.

Warning! This alerts you to some of the most serious tax mistakes sometimes made by churches and other nonprofit organizations.

Cross Reference This is a reminder that more material on a topic appears in the companion guide, the 2000 edition of *The Zondervan Minister's Tax and Financial Guide.*

1999 Recent Developments

In 1999, a number of court decisions, IRS rulings, and regulations of importance to churches and other nonprofit organizations were announced.

1999 standard mileage rates

The optional standard mileage rates for employees, self-employed individuals, and other taxpayers to use in computing the deductible costs paid in 1999 in connection with the operation of a passenger automobile for business, charitable, medical, or moving expense purposes are as follows:

Type of Expense	1999 Rate (per mile)
Business	
January 1-March 31	32.5 cents
April 1 and later	31 cents
Charitable	14 cents
Moving/Medical	10 cents

1999 per diem rates

Nonprofit employers that help their employees cover business travel expenses have two basic options: (1) The employer can pay employees the precise amount of their expenses, or (2) the employer can opt for convenience and pay a set "per diem" allowance for each day of business travel.

Per diem allowances that stay within IRS-approved rates satisfy the tax law's tough accountable plan requirements almost automatically. All the employer has to do is get records of when, where, and why the employee made the trip. The employee does not have to account for actual dollars spent or keep receipts.

Employers can opt for a two-tier set of "high-low" reimbursement rates, or they can tie tax-free travel allowances to the amount the federal government provides to its employees for travel to a particular location. An employer must pick one method or the other for each employee.

Employers can provide tax-free allowances of up to $185 ($42 for meals and $143 for lodging) for each day of travel to any of 52 high-cost destinations and up to $115 per day ($34 for meals and $81 for lodging) for travel to any other location in the contiguous 48 states.

1999 transportation and parking limits

For 1999, a church can sell transit passes and tokens to ministers and other employees at discounts of up to $65 per month tax-free. Or, a church can just give cash of up to $65 for passes and tokens tax-free. Also, if a church gives an employee a parking space near its premises, it is tax-free to the employee up to a value of $175 per month. It is also tax-free up to $175 per month if the employee rents a space near the church's premises and is reimbursed. The cost of a parking space located at the employee's residence is taxable to the employee regardless of its proximity to the employer's premises.

1999 retirement plan limits

The maximum amount employees can contribute on a tax-deferred basis to a 401(k) plan is $10,000 for 1999. The maximum amount of employee voluntary salary reduction contributions to 403(b) plans (tax-sheltered annuities) is also $10,000 per year. This limit does not apply to pension plan contributions made by a church to a denominational pension plan on behalf of a minister. Other limits apply to these payments.

1999 token limitations

Charities can give slightly more to contributors before the donors must trim their deductions. Donations are fully deductible when benefits to donor are small and part of a fund-raiser and the charity says those benefits are insubstantial. Examples of these benefits might include mugs, key chains, posters, shirts, tote bags, and so on.

The value of the benefit to the donor cannot exceed the lesser of 2% of the gift or $72.00 (1999 inflation-adjusted amount). The donor can get a token item (T-shirt, for example) bearing the name or logo of the charity and costing $7.20 or less for contributions that exceed $36.00.

1999 social security taxable earnings limit

The maximum amount of taxable and creditable annual earnings subject to the social security and self-employment income tax increased to $72,600 in 1999, up from $68,400 in 1998. There is no maximum wage base for Medicare.

1999 highly compensated employee definition

The "highly compensated employee" definition is important in determining whether certain fringe benefits are taxable to employees that fall within that category. Examples of fringe benefits that may trigger additional compensation based on favoring highly compensated employees include: qualified tuition and fee discounts, educational assistance benefits, dependent care plans, group-term life benefits, and self-insured medical plans.

Employees who have compensation for the previous year in excess of $80,000 (1999 limit) and, if an employer elects, were in the top 20% of employees by compensation meet the definition.

For example, Pastor Smith received gross pay of $60,000. The church established a dependent care plan to pay for the child care of two of Pastor Smith's children. The dependent care benefit is not provided to other employees of the church. Even though the plan is clearly discriminatory, Pastor Smith does not meet the highly compensated employee definition since the gross pay is less than $80,000. Therefore, the dependent care benefit is tax free.

Fund-raising expenses

There is heightened concern about amounts paid to professional solicitation companies. State regulators are starting to publicize how much of the money raised by professional solicitation companies actually goes to charity. There are no state or federal minimums for how much professional solicitors must pass to charities.

According to the most recent annual reports in Vermont, Washington and California, charities only received about 40% of what was raised by professional solicitors. Watch for an increasing number of states to provide this information.

Outsourcing the processing of donation receipts

Some nonprofits use a third party vendor to process mail, fulfill orders and premiums, process gift income, issue receipts, perform data entry for accounting purposes, and prepare bank deposits.

In some cases, all income is deposited directly into the account of the charity and the vendor bills the charity for their services. Given adequate controls, this may be a wise use of a nonprofit's resources.

In other instances, fund-raisers may offer these services as a means of insuring payment for their services, or as a way to overcome a charity's concern about up-front costs of a fund-raising effort. This can be presented as a guaranteed no-loss effort where the fund-raiser agrees to limit its expense to no more than what actually comes in. In these cases, funds are placed directly in the account of the fund-raiser (or in a joint account with the charity) and only the income in excess of the fund-raiser's costs are forwarded to the charity. In some agreements, the charity's donor list becomes available to the fund-raiser to rent or sell to provide additional income to the fund-raiser. These situations are problematic.

Matching grants

Many nonprofits use matching grants to raise additional money for their ministry. Properly used, it is a valuable fund-raising tool.

For a matching grant to be legitimate, the matching grant(s) should be at risk. Matches constituted from internal funds are not true matching grants. Nonprofits should solicit matching grants with integrity. Example: Donor has already promised to donate $10,000 to your ministry. It would be inappropriate to ask the donor to recast the gift as a matching grant. The donor is going to give your ministry the $10,000 whether or not you raise another $10,000, so you have nothing at risk.

Soliciting funds via the Internet

Many nonprofits with Web sites are dedicating special areas of their sites to solicit visitors for gifts. These range from providing offline donation information to providing secure, online forms for making credit card contributions.

If you are accepting donations online, provide a secure Web site (symbolized by the closed padlock in the lower left-hand corner of the screen) through your own server or contracted through an outside server. If you contract for this service, be sure the funds are electronically deposited directly to your organization's bank account and not to the bank account of the service provider.

Nonprofits who are not ready to accept contributions online are providing a variety of donation-related information on their Web sites. Some charities ask donors to make their contribution by calling a toll-free number or faxing a form. In some instances, donors are asked to fill out their names and addresses and then wait to be contacted by the charity.

Gifts or grants from unrelated for-profit companies associated with Internet sales

For-profit product sales organizations promising to donate a portion, often in terms of a percentage, of their profit to charities are springing up on the Web. The buyer of products from these companies can select from a list of charities. Or, in some cases, the buyer of products can ask that another charity be added to the list of possible recipients.

So, your charity may receive a gift or a grant from one of these Internet sales companies without any effort on your part. Due diligence on the part of the recipient charity might include determining if the products sold are inconsistent with the mission of your organization.

Affinity programs

Charities are frequently presented with creative marketing opportunities that may lead to additional revenue for the charity. Some of these concepts may come near or go beyond the boundaries of traditional marketing programs. A proposed marketing program may involve recommending or promoting

- ✓ equipment, from photocopiers or other office equipment to vehicles,
- ✓ services, from household moving services to long-distance telephone services,
- ✓ or a combination of products and services.

While these marketing endeavors generally do not involve the solicitation of charitable gifts, they often include contact by the charity or a third party with the charity's donor base, members or other constituents. The contact often results in the expenditure of money to obtain a product or service. There is generally, but not always, a direct or indirect financial benefit to the charity as a result of the transaction.

Here are some basic principles to apply in evaluating potential marketing programs for your organization:

- ✓ Your donors, members and other constituents are a highly valuable resource from God.
- ✓ All marketing materials should be clear and transparent. Expectations of donors should match the reality of the marketing service or activity.
- ✓ If you are partnering with a third party, carefully consider your motivation and their motivation to engage in the relationship. The sole motivation of your organization should be to further your ministry objectives.
- ✓ Understand the risks for your ministry before entering into a marketing relationship with a third party. Do not put your organization at undue risk.
- ✓ The products or services offered should be consistent with the standards of your ministry.
- ✓ Good stewardship of ministry resources is always an important criteria.

Donations of used cars

Many nonprofits are turning to used cars as a source of operating revenue. Organizations are aggressively advertising for donations of used cars, providing charitable receipts, and then converting those vehicles to cash on the used car market or selling them for scrap.

The practice of soliciting such donations raises a variety of legal and regulatory concerns. These include state licensing requirements applicable to car wholesalers and dealers, state and federal laws applicable to mileage tampering and odometer disclosure and state and federal laws requiring charitable receipts.

California has enacted a new law requiring that a nonprofit organization and a commercial fundraiser must provide the donor with a receipt for the donation within 90 days from the date of the donation. The receipt must describe the vehicle in terms of its model age, mileage and condition, and must indicate whether a visual inspection indicated that there were any defects which would affect the value of the vehicle. The receipt must also indicate whether the vehicle was operable or inoperable. If the vehicle is sold to a dismantler, the receipt must state the amount that was paid for the vehicle.

Many donors claim values listed in guidebooks, such as the Kelley bluebook or the NADA Used Car Guide for charitable contribution purposes. In Service Center Advice, the IRS recently concluded that car sales that occur within a few days of the contribution are an indication of the value of the donated cars. Second, the fair market value of cars must be determined on a case-by-case basis and, in some instances, may have little or no relation to the amount the donee organization received upon disposing of the car.

Simplified procedures for 1999 Forms W-2 and W-3

The IRS has already issued the 1999 version of Forms W-2 and W-3. Here are some of the changes for 1999:

- ✓ The due date for employers that file 1999 Forms W-2 with the Social Security Administration electronically is March 31, 2000. This extended deadline does not apply to magnetic media or paper filers.
- ✓ You're no longer required to separately report the taxable fringe benefits that you include in Box 1 of the W-2, except for the annual lease value of vehicles your organization provides to employees. You must report the annual lease value of vehicles in Box 12 of the W-2 or on a separate statement to employees.
- ✓ If you issue a 1999 W-2 printed with a wrong employee address, you don't have to issue another, corrected W-2. You can simply place the W-2 with the incorrect address in an envelope bearing the correct employee address, and mail it to the employee.

Regulations approve use of mileage allowance for leased autos

IRS regulations now allow taxpayers to use the mileage allowance deduction and reimbursement method for autos that are leased as well as those that are owned. Under the old rules, it was not clear whether the mileage allowance rate could be used if an employee leased his or her car (Reg 1.162-2T(e)(2)).

Group-term life insurance premium table revised

The IRS has issued proposed regulations to revise the uniform premium table, effective July 1, 1999, used to calculate the cost of employer-provided group-term life insurance coverage. The new table reduces the cost of coverage and the amounts included in an employee's compensation (Reg. 209103-89).

IRS releases advice on pure trusts

The IRS has made available Significant Service Center Advice on the filing requirements and tax status of "pure trusts" (also referred to as constitutional trusts or common law trusts or contract trusts). There is no organization classified as a "pure trust" or "pure trust organization" under the Internal Revenue Code or regulations.

The Service advised that the filing requirements depend on the entity's tax classification. A pure trust that is classified as a trust must file Form 1041 and have an EIN. A pure trust that is classified as a trust but is wholly owned by the grantor, neither files Form 1041 nor needs an EIN.

The IRS has rescinded a 1996 letter that states that a pure trust has no tax requirements and that an EIN is not required. This new advice is the result of promoters of various abusive trust schemes taking the rescinded letter out of context and are concluding that neither the owner nor the trust is liable for any tax in order to promote their abusive trust schemes (SCA 1998-006).

Disclosure regulations finalized

If Christians wanted to know how much money their favorite ministry took in last year, or how much its top officers made, it hasn't been easy for them to find out. They had to show up at the charity's office in person or make a written request to the IRS and wait months for a response. If the organization was an ECFA member, they could obtain a copy of the annual audit from the charity. But audits don't include salary data.

But this all changed on June 8, 1999. Anyone with an interest in a nonprofit organization's finances is now able to obtain Form 990 information with as little effort as sending an e-mail request. The Form 990 is the annual information return which must be filed each year with the IRS by many nonprofits.

For additional explanation of the public disclosure rules, see pages 45-46.

Intermediate sanction regulations

The proposed intermediate sanction regulations were issued in 1998, but it does not appear that the final regulations will be issued until 2000.

Prior to the issuance of these regulations, the IRS could only apply the "death penalty" of revoking the exempt status of an organization. Now the IRS can impose intermediate sanctions to punish disqualified persons and organization managers who participate in or acquiesce to excess benefit transactions.

Intermediate sanctions, in the form of excise taxes, generally are intended to be the sole sanction for excess benefit transactions. But if excess benefit transactions occur repeatedly or are of an unusually large size or scope, revocation is still an option.

Nonprofits have two challenges in dealing with the new regulations—first, in setting compensation and related benefits for disqualified persons. Compensation must be reasonably set and accurately reported. This shouldn't represent anything new if your board has been approaching this as a serious responsibility.

The second area involves other financial transactions with disqualified persons. The easiest advice on limiting liability in this area is to avoid these types of transactions entirely. Although the new regulations do not ban these transactions, why take the risk? If your organization chooses to enter into transactions with a disqualified person, you must ensure that the transaction does not contribute to the personal enrichment of the insider.

What is an excess benefit transaction? It is any transaction in which the charity provides an economic benefit to a disqualified person that has a greater value than what it receives from the person. This includes payment of excessive compensation, certain revenue-sharing arrangements and sales, leases, loans, or royalty arrangements with disqualified persons in which the terms of the transaction unduly favor the disqualified person.

Who is a disqualified person? This is someone who was in a position to exert substantial influence over the nonprofit at any time during the five years preceding an excess benefit transaction.

What are the penalties? There is a two-tiered tax structure. The first, 25% of the excess benefit, is imposed on disqualified persons who receive an excess benefit. Failure to timely correct the excess benefit will result in a 200% excise tax. The second tax, 10% of the excess benefit, is imposed on organization managers who knowingly and willfully participate in the excess benefit transaction.

Do nonprofits have any safe harbors from intermediate sanctions? Yes. The proposed regulations create a presumption in a nonprofit's favor that a transaction is not an excess benefit. Three requirements must be met:

- ✓ Disinterested board review
- ✓ Appropriate data
- ✓ Adequate documentation

Do the new rules apply to churches? Yes, but there is good news.

When investigating churches for possible excess benefit transactions, the IRS is limited by the same highly restrictive procedures that control their actions for church audits.

When do the new rules become effective? They are imposed for transactions occurring after September 14, 1995, but they do not apply to contracts that were binding before that date.

New Unified Registration Statements (URS) supports 32 jurisdictions

The URS is an alternative to the respective registration forms produced by the cooperating states. In those states, a registering nonprofit organization may use either the state form or the URS. It follows that the URS will prove most useful to those nonprofit organizations that are soliciting regionally or nationally and which are therefore subject to the registration laws of multiple states. However, the URS may be used by any nonprofit organization that is registering as a charitable solicitor in a state which accepts it.

The most recent version of the URS, which was released on December 14, 1998, supports 32 jurisdictions (31 states and the District of Columbia). The states that do not yet accept the URS are Alaska, Arizona, Florida, North Carolina, Utah, West Virginia, and Wisconsin. You can find the URS at: http://www.nonprofits.org/library/gov/urs.

Split-dollar life insurance arrangements under attack

In the typical split-dollar life insurance plan, donors make tax-deductible gifts to charities, which invest the money in cash-value life insurance policies on the donors. The donors often get access to policy loans during their lifetimes, and the charities share in the policy death benefits with the donors' families. Aggressive insurance agents have peddled more than $2 billion of life insurance this way.

Now a bipartisan effort is underway to crack down on split-dollar arrangements. H.R. 630 would clarify current law by specifically denying a charitable contribution deduction for a contribution made to an organization that pays—or reaches an understanding that it will pay—for any personal benefit contract for the donor. The bill would also impose an excise tax on the charity equal to the amount of the premiums paid by the charity. The deduction denial provision would apply to transfer after February 8, 1999.

InsMark, a company that is among the nation's most aggressive marketers of split-dollar plans, will require new policy holders to pay charities a lump sum of cash if an insurance agreement is terminated prematurely. The company denies that its changes are a reaction to government scrutiny.

In 1998, the National Committee on Planned Giving said the split-dollar strategy raises "unacceptable risks" for donors and "may endanger the tax-exempt status of charities." Several nonprofit groups report they already have turned down a number of such "donation" requests because the donations can't be spent for other needs. The Washington-based Council on Foundations supports passage of H.R. 630.

Liberalization of home-office rules

Until 1999, most individuals have not been able to qualify for home-office treatment. That's because of the tough "principal place of business" rule. Under the old rules, a home office must meet the relative importance (the taxpayer's home must serve as a base for the most important functions) and the time test (over half of the taxpayer's time must be spend working in the home office).

But starting in 1999, you are much more likely to qualify for a home office deduction because two additional criteria have been added to the former rules. The new provisions do not eliminate the old tests, but you can now either meet the old tests or the new criteria.

Under the new rules, a home office will be deemed a taxpayer's principal place of business if the taxpayer uses it exclusively and on a regular basis for administrative or management activities of any trade or business and there is no other fixed location where the taxpayer conducts a substantive portion of these activities.

Requirements that still must be met from the old law include:

- ✓ The taxpayer must use an area in the home office exclusively and on a regular basis for business activity.
- ✓ The home office must be a used for the convenience of the employer if the taxpayer is an employee.

IRS revises definition of "temporary" workplace

The IRS has revised its definition of "temporary" workplace for purposes of determining whether transportation between home and a work location outside the home is deductible. A temporary workplace is no longer one where services are performed on an irregular or short-term basis, but, rather, one where employment is expected to last one year or less.

The revised definition will help some taxpayers who might have lost deductions under the prior definition (Adv. Rev. Rul. 99-7).

Indianapolis Baptist Temple (IBT) owes $5.3 million in unpaid withholding taxes

The IRS made a $3.5 million assessment against IBT in 1994, for unpaid social security taxes and income tax withholdings, plus interest and penalties. IBT didn't pay, and the government filed suit in 1998. By mid-1998, the $3.5 million assessment had grown to $5,319,750.27, with additional penalties and interest.

IBT argued that the First Amendment bars any application of the federal tax laws to the church. A U.S. District Court has rejected the position of IBT and found that the federal tax system has a secular purpose, neither advances nor inhibits religion, and does not foster an excessive entanglement with religion (U.S. v. Indianapolis Baptist Temple, U.S. District Court, Southern District of Indiana, 1/19/99).

Christian ministry leaders indicted in Florida

Seven leaders of the Tampa-based Greater Ministries International were arrested on a variety of fraud, conspiracy, and money-laundering charges.

The 20-count indictment charges Gerald Payne, his wife, Betty, and five other ministry leaders with running a scheme that claimed donors could get back double their gifts. The six-year-long scheme paid early investors with donations made by later contributors. Greater Ministries officials took a percentage of each transaction as undisclosed "commission payments."

The double-your-money program fueled growth of a Grand Cayman incorporated empire that included an herbal medicine center, a Kentucky hotel, a line of gold jewelry, thrift stores, a homeless ministry, and a network of foreign missionaries.

A nephew of one Greater Ministries official pleaded guilty to theft and securities fraud charges in 1998 after law enforcement officials determined he had collected up to $14 million with a similar scheme, called Sovereign Ministries International.

Church at Pierce Creek unable to regain its tax-exempt status

A federal district judge has upheld the revocation of tax-exempt status for a New York church that paid for full-page ads in both *USA Today* and *The Washington Times* the week before the 1992 election urging people not to vote for then-candidate Bill Clinton.

The church had also inserted a statement at the bottom of the ad saying, "Tax-deductible donations for this advertisement gladly accepted."

Court reinstates tax exemption of the United Cancer Council

A federal court of appeals has overturned the Tax Court's denial of the tax exemption of the United Cancer Council (UCC). The Tax Court had ruled that the nonprofit was under the "control" of an outside fund-raising firm and, therefore, was in violation of the rule against private inurement. But the court of appeals said that while the nonprofit may have made a bad deal with the fund-raising firm, it was not under its control (United Cancer Council v. Commissioner, No. 98-2181, 2/10/99).

The UCC was in financial trouble in 1984 and entered into a five-year fund-raising contract with Watson & Hughey Co. (W&H), a professional fund-raiser. Although the UCC could review direct mail materials before they were distributed, the materials remained the sole property of W&H. Any contributor lists developed under the contract became the joint property of the UCC and W&H. Nearly 80 million appeals were mailed, raising more than $28 million while incurring $26 million in expenses. This left a $2 million profit for the UCC before paying management fees.

Sierra Club wins in Tax Court

Income from the Sierra Club's affinity credit card arrangement constituted nontaxable royalties, according to the Tax Court. The IRS has tried various theories to tax nonprofits on royalties, but the Tax Court has consistently rejected these attempts.

The IRS has numerous other royalty cases underway involving affinity credit cards and mailing lists. It is not clear if they are yet ready to "throw in the towel" on these issues (Sierra Club Inc. v. Commissioner, T.C. Memo. 1999-86).

Church loan dispute dismissed

A complaint by church members alleging a breach of fiduciary duty in a loan to the church pastor has been dismissed by the District of Columbia Court of Appeals (Kelsey v. Ray, No. 97-CV-1133, 11/12/98).

A pastor received a $260,000 no-interest loan to purchase a new home. A disgruntled church member sued the pastor and current and former deacons and trustees of the church, alleging breach of duty and demanding financial information.

The Court of Appeals dismissed the case because interpretation of the church bylaws would involve impermissible doctrinal interpretation.

Church membership list protected

The Greek Orthodox Archdiocese of North and South America attempted to stop the Greek Orthodox American Leaders (GOAL) from using the Archdiocese mailing list it said was misappropriated (Greek Orthodox Archdiocese of North and South America v. Greek Orthodox American Leaders, No. 98 Civ. 6435, 11/25/98).

GOAL was founded by members of the Archdiocese who were concerned about Archdiocese governance and financial practices. GOAL used the Archdiocese mailing list to distribute a newsletter to 122,000 members of the Archdiocese. It did not deny that the list was used without permission. The Court refused a preliminary injunction for failing to demonstrate a threat of irreparable injury, demonstrating that membership lists may be accorded only limited protection in litigation with those who have an interest in the organization.

Discovery of contributor lists blocked

The Supreme Court of Texas has overturned a trial court order to disclose the contribution lists of the Bay Area Citizens Against Lawsuit Abuse (BACALA) (Bay Area Citizens Against Lawsuit Abuse, No. 97-0812, 12/10/98).

BACALA occupied space in a Chamber of Commerce building, which had been given to the Chamber of the City. Several taxpayers sued to prevent the use on the grounds that the use was "for private special interest." The taxpayers also sought the contributor lists of BACALA.

The case underscores the general right of nonprofits to protect the names of their members and donors unless the disclosure is necessary for a compelling state interest.

CHAPTER ONE

Financial Accountability

We need to practice what we preach about accountability.

In This Chapter

- Organizations promoting accountability
- Accountability to an independent board
- Accountability to donors
- Accountability to government

The public has high expectations of religious organizations. Day after day, thousands in the nonprofit community work tirelessly and selflessly to address physical and spiritual needs worldwide, only to find the public casting a wary eye on them due to the highly publicized misdeeds of a few. Donors recognize that enormous needs exist and they want to respond generously to those needs. But they also want to be sure that optimum use of their sacrificial gifts is employed by the charities they support. There is no acceptable alternative to accountability.

For large nonprofit organizations, accountability issues often relate to complex issues of private inurement or conflicts of interest. In churches and small-to-medium-nonprofits, the issues may be as basic as whether to accept a gift that appears to be a pass-through contribution for the personal benefit of a designated individual.

Financial accountability is based on the principle of stewardship. A steward-manager exercises responsible care over entrusted funds. Good stewardship rarely occurs outside a system of accountability.

Financial accountability is the natural outgrowth of proper organizational leadership. Providing clear, basic explanations of financial activity starts with the daily record of transactions and evolves to the adequate reporting to donors and boards.

U.S. laws provide special tax treatment of religious and charitable institutions. The nonprofit organization that refuses to disclose its finances is shortchanging the public from which it derives its support. It also causes suspicions about how it is using the financial resources at its disposal.

Organizations Promoting Accountability

Being a member of organizations that promote stewardship principles often enhances accountability. Several organizations provide leadership in the area of financial accountability. These organizations include the Evangelical Council for Financial Accountability (ECFA), the National Charities Information Bureau (NCIB), and the Council of Better Business Bureaus, Inc. (CBBB).

The National Committee on Planned Giving and the Committee on Gift Annuities (NCPG/CGA) have adopted model standards for those involved in planned giving. The National Society of Fund Raising Executives (NSFRE) has also prepared fund-raising guidelines.

For missionary organizations, the Interdenominational Foreign Mission Association (IFMA) and the Evangelical Fellowship of Mission Agencies (EFMA) are groups which provide accountability for members.

The strong tenets of these organizations are proper accounting, an independent and responsible volunteer board of directors, full disclosure of finances, and fair treatment for donors.

Accountability to an Independent Board

Board governance

Strong leadership often shuns accountability. Some boards do not live up to their responsibility to hold themselves accountable and to demand accountability of the organizational leadership.

Can your organization's leadership be challenged and voted down? Are the board members permissive and passive or involved and active? Are your values and policies clearly articulated? Are they operative in the organization daily? Are annual evaluations, based on predetermined goals, made of the pastor(s) or the nonprofit chief executive officer (CEO)?

KEY ISSUE

A board should generally meet at least semi-annually. Some boards meet monthly. Meetings should be more than listening to the CEO's report and rubber-stamping a series of resolutions prepared by the CEO.

ECFA members must have a board of not less than five individuals. A majority of the board must be other than employees or staff, or those related by blood or marriage, to meet ECFA standards.

Even when employee membership on the board is slightly less than a majority, the independence of the board may be jeopardized. Employees often lack independence and objectivity in dealing with many board-level matters. The CEO is often a member of an organization's board of directors. Department heads are generally not members of the board.

Recording board actions

The actions of an organization's board and its committees should be recorded by written minutes, including the signature of the group's secretary, prepared within a few days after the meeting concludes. The minute books of some charities are almost nonexistent. Minutes of the most recent board meeting often appear to be placed in proper written form on the eve of the succeeding board meeting. Such lack of organization can be indicative of weak board governance and may leave a poor paper trail to document the board's actions.

The actions of an organization's board typically include the approval and revision of policies that should be organized and printed as the body of board policies. These policies, extracted from the board minutes, should be revised after each board meeting if new policies are adopted or previously existing policies are revised.

Financial reporting

ECFA members must have an independent annual audit according to generally accepted auditing standards (GAAS). Financial statements must be prepared following generally accepted accounting principles (GAAP).

Here is what to look for from your audit firm:

- ✓ A firm thoroughly knowledgeable about current accounting standards and one that understands your segment of Christian nonprofits.
- ✓ A firm that routinely prepares value-added management letters for their audit clients.
- ✓ A firm that helps you reduce your audit fee.
- ✓ A firm that understands your accounting system.

A subcommittee of the board, often called an audit review committee, should recommend the independent accountants to perform the audit (this appointment to be made by the board) and review the audit report (and management letter, if one is prepared) prior to its submission to the board. This committee should not be controlled by employees or staff members.

The board should also receive staff-prepared monthly or quarterly financial statements.

Compensation review

An annual review of the local church minister's or nonprofit organization executive's compensation package is vital. The review should focus on all elements of pay, taxable and nontaxable.

Pay and fringe benefit packages should be determined by an objective evaluation of responsibilities, goals reached, and available resources. A comparison with positions in other organizations may be helpful. National salary surveys may provide meaningful data such as National Association of Church Business Administrators Church Staff Compensation Survey, and Christian Management Association Salary Survey.

REMEMBER

The approved compensation package should be documented in board and/or subcommittee minutes. This action should include guidelines for disbursement of compensation-related funds by the organization's treasurer.

With increased scrutiny on nonprofit salaries (see chapter 3), it is important that compensation amounts be accurately stated. Gross pay may include the following elements (some taxable and some tax-free or tax-deferred):

- ✓ Cash salary
- ✓ Fair rental value of a house, including utilities, provided by the organization
- ✓ Cash housing or furnishings allowance
- ✓ Tax-deferred payments
- ✓ Expense advances that exceed documented business expenses
- ✓ Value of the personal use of organization-owned aircraft or vehicle
- ✓ Value of noncash goods and services
- ✓ Cash bonuses

Budget process

The organization should prepare a detailed annual budget consistent with the major classifications in the financial statements and approved by the board. The budget should allow meaningful comparison with the previous year's financial statements; recast if necessary.

Responsibility for budgetary performance should be clearly assigned to management as appropriate (for example, department heads, field directors, and so on). The controller or treasurer of an organization is normally responsible for budgetary enforcement and reporting. For more information on the budgeting process, see page 131.

Conflicts of interest and related party transactions

Conducting activities

Fairness in decision-making is more likely to occur in an impartial environment. Conflicts of interest and related-party transactions are often confused. However, the distinction between the two concepts is useful.

The potential for a conflict of interest arises in situations in which a person has a responsibility to promote one interest, but has a competing interest at the same time. If the competing interest is exercised over a fiduciary interest, the conflict is realized. Conflicts of interest should be avoided.

Related-party transactions are transactions that occur between two or more parties that have interlinking relationships. These transactions should be disclosed to the governing board. Transactions should be evaluated to ensure they are made on a sound economic basis. Some related-party transactions are clearly to the advantage of the organization and should be pursued. Other related-party transactions are conflicts of interest and should be avoided.

Under ECFA guidelines, transactions with related parties may be undertaken only in the following situations:

- ✓ The audited financial statements of the organization fully disclose material related-party transactions.
- ✓ Related parties are excluded from the discussion and approval of related-party transactions.
- ✓ Competitive bids or comparable valuations exist.
- ✓ The organization's board approves the transaction as being in the best interest of the organization.

Example 1: An organization purchases insurance coverage through a firm owned by a board member. This would constitute a conflict of interest unless the cost of the insurance is disclosed, the purchase is subject to proper approvals, the price is below the competition, and the purchase is in the best interests of the organization. If the purchase passes these tests, it is still a related-party transaction.

Example 2: The CEO and several employees are members of the board. When the resolution on salary and fringe-benefit adjustments comes to the board, should those affected by the resolution discuss and vote on the matter? No. To avoid the appearance of a conflict of interest, the employees should absent themselves from the meeting.

Example 3: A nonprofit board considers a significant loan to a company in which a board member has a material ownership interest. Should this loan even be considered? Only if it is in the best interest of the nonprofit and allowable under state laws and the organization's by-laws.

Example 4: A church receives a significant endowment gift. The church board establishes investment policy guidelines and appoints a subcommittee of the board to carry out the routine investing of the funds.

The Investment Committee is chaired by an investment broker who

Sample Conflict or Duality of Interest Policy Statement

All trustees, officers, agents, and employees of this organization shall disclose all real or apparent conflict or dualities of interest which they discover or which have been brought to their attention in connection with this organization's activities. "Disclosure" shall mean providing properly, to the appropriate person, a written description of the facts comprising the real or apparent conflict or duality of interest. An annual disclosure statement shall be circulated to trustees, officers, and certain identified agents and employees to assist them in considering such disclosures, but disclosure is appropriate and required whenever conflicts or dualities of interest may occur. The written notices of disclosures shall be filed with the Chief Executive Officer or such other person designated by the Chief Executive Officer to receive such notifications. All disclosures of real or apparent conflict or duality of interests shall be noted for the record in the minutes of the meeting of the top governing body.

An individual trustee, officer, agent, or employee who believes that he or she or an immediate member of his or her immediate family might have a real or apparent conflict of interest, in addition to filing a notice of disclosure, must abstain from (1) participating in discussions or deliberations with respect to the subject of the conflict (other than to present factual information or answer questions), (2) using their personal influence to affect deliberations, (3) making motions, (4) voting, (5) executing agreements, or (6) taking similar actions on behalf of the organizations where the conflict or duality of interest might pertain by law, agreement or otherwise. At the discretion of the top governing body or a committee thereof, a person with a real or apparent conflict or duality of interest may be excused from all or any portion of discussion or deliberations with respect to the subject of the conflict.

A member of the top governing body or a committee thereof, who, having disclosed a conflict or duality of interest, nevertheless shall be counted in determining the existence of a quorum at any meeting where the subject of the conflict is discussed. The minutes of the meeting shall reflect the disclosure made, the vote thereon, the abstention from participation and voting by the individual making disclosure.

There shall be no business transactions, whether the nature of employment, contract, purchase, or sale, between the organization and a trustee during his or her term in office, except in the case of employment, for a period of one year thereafter. For purposes of this section, the payment of any benefit to which the trustee might otherwise be entitled, shall not be deemed a business transaction.

The Chief Executive Officer shall ensure that all trustees, officers, agents, employees, and independent contractors of the organization are made aware of the organization's policy with respect to conflicts or duality of interest.

Sample Conflict or Duality of Interest Disclosure Annual Reporting Statement

Certification

I have read and understand Conflict or Duality of Interest Policy. I hereby declare and certify the following real or apparent conflict or dualities of interest:

Disclosure Statement

____

____

____

____

____

____

____

____

____

____

____

____

(If necessary, attach additional documentation.)

Date ________________ ____________________________________

Signature

____

Title

sells mutual funds for which his firm receives commissions. He receives commissions on the sales from his firm. The broker recommends that the purchases of certain mutual funds be made from his firm.

This is a blatant conflict of interest even if the broker fully discloses the fees that would be paid to his firm and commissions that, in turn, would be paid to him and even if the fees are comparable to what other brokers would charge. This biased environment makes it nearly impossible to achieve fairness in decision-making.

Selecting board members

PLANNING IDEA

Information concerning prospective and current board members may reveal potential conflicts that will disqualify the individual. If a conflict is sufficiently limited, the director may simply need to abstain from voting on certain issues. If the conflict of interest is material, the election or re-election of the individual may be inappropriate.

Board compensation

Most nonprofit board members serve without compensation. This practice reinforces an important distinction of nonprofits: the assets of a nonprofit should not be used for the private enrichment of directors, members, or employees.

Board members often have travel-related expenses reimbursed. Mileage may be reimbursed up to the standard IRS business rate (31 cents per mile effective April 1, 1999) without reporting any taxable income to the board member. Travel expenses reimbursed for the spouse of a board member represent taxable income to the board member unless the spouse qualifies for employee treatment and provides services to the nonprofit in conjunction with the trip.

Accountability to Donors

Donors are showing greater concern about the solicitation and use of their contributions. The primary areas of concern are:

Donor communication

ECFA requires that all statements made by an organization in its fund-raising appeals about the use of a gift must be honored by the organization. The donor's intent may be shaped by both the organization's communication of the appeal and by any donor instructions with the gift.

If a donor responds to a specific appeal, the assumption may be made that the donor's intent is that the funds be used as outlined in the appeal. There is a need for clear communication in the appeal to insure that the donor understands precisely how the funds will be used. Any note or correspondence accompanying the gift or conversations between the donor and donee representatives indicate donor intent.

All aspects of a proposed charitable gift should be explained fully, fairly, and accurately to the donor. Any limitations on the use of the gift should be clear and complete both in the response device and the appeal letter. These items should be included in the explanation:

- ✓ **The charity's proposed use of the gift.** Realistic expectations should be communicated regarding what the donor's gift will do within the programs of the donee organization.
- ✓ **Representations of fact.** Any description of the financial condition of the organization, or narrative about events must be current, complete, and accurate. References to past activities or events should be appropriately dated. There should be no material omissions or exaggerations of fact or use of misleading photographs or any other communication tending to create a false impression or misunderstanding.
- ✓ **Valuation issues and procedures.** If an appraisal is required, the donor should fully understand the procedures and who is responsible to pay for the appraisal.
- ✓ **Tax consequences and reporting requirements.** While tax considerations should not be the primary focus of a gift, the donor should clearly understand the current and future income, estate and gift tax consequences, and reporting requirements of the proposed gift. A charitable gift should never be represented as a tax shelter.
- ✓ **Alternative arrangements for making the gift.** The donor should understand the current and deferred gift options that are available.
- ✓ **Financial and family implications.** In addition to the tax consequences, the overall financial implications of the proposed gift and the potential impact on family members should be carefully explained.
- ✓ **Possible conflicts of interest.** Disclose to the donor all relationships which might constitute, or appear to constitute, conflicts of interest. The disclosure should include how and by whom each party is compensated and any cost of managing the gift.

Fund raising appeals must not create unrealistic donor expectations of what a donor's gift will actually accomplish within the limits of the organization's ministry. The following are examples of the application of donor communication principles:

Example 1: **Bible distribution:** An organization distributes Bibles and related literature as its primary purpose. Fund-raising letters appeal for funds to distribute Bibles in a particular country. The organization includes the funds raised in general income. The accounting records do not account for the costs associated with distributing Bibles in that location to determine whether or not the funds donated for that location have been used for the stipulated purpose or whether the project has been overfunded or underfunded.

The organization's handling of the gift funds is inappropriate. It should account for gifts by country with appropriate allocation of costs associated with the distribution. Any overfunding or underfunding should be identified for the particular country.

Example 2: **Child sponsorship:** A child sponsorship organization appeals to donors to support specific children and creates the impression that specific sponsorships directly benefit specific children. Instead, sponsorship funds are pooled and spent on a project basis under the philosophy of child-focused community development programs. Although there is shared benefit to the entire community by worthwhile development, only a small amount of the project budget is exclusively for the sponsored children in the community.

The fund-raising practices of this organization are inappropriate unless:

- ✓ It discloses to donors that child sponsorship gifts are pooled to support child-focused community development projects and that many of the benefits are shared by all the children in the community.
- ✓ The organization insures that sponsored children are receiving direct benefit from the development activities in the community. Community development activities must create specific improvements in the lives of the sponsored children within the community. Periodic reports should be provided to the donor which clearly explain the project activities, how they benefit the sponsored child, as well as the specific progress of the sponsored child.
- ✓ Donor receipts and related accounting records indicate that financial support has been provided in fulfillment of a pledge of support for the pooled sponsorship funds with a preference for an individual child.

Example 3: **Feeding the hungry:** An organization appeals for gifts to feed the hungry and indicates that a certain number of dollars will provide a certain number of meals. The organization does not separately account for the donations and costs of the meal program. The meal costs quoted are based on national rather than local factors. Much of the food and labor is donated and the gifts are primarily used for the general support of the organization rather than being limited to use in the feeding program.

The organization's fund-raising practices are inappropriate. It should account for such gifts as donor-restricted and limited to use only in the feeding program. To avoid a separate accounting for the program, the organization would need to modify appeals to not give the impression that a specific amount will provide a certain number of meals. The following wording might be used for an unrestricted appeal: "This gift is to help feed, clothe, shelter, and minister to the needy at the Christmas season and throughout the year."

Accounting for restricted gifts

Donors often place temporary or permanent restrictions on gifts that limit their use to certain purposes. These stipulations may specify a use for a contributed asset that is more specific than broad limits relating to the nature of the organization, the environment in which it operates, and the purposes specified in its articles of incorporation or bylaws or comparable documents for unincorporated entities. A restricted gift generally results whenever a donor selects a giving option on a response device other than "unrestricted" or "where needed most."

Some organizations lack the proper accounting structure to account for restricted gift income and to track the funds through to the point of expenditure. This may lead to the following problems:

✓ **Inadequate accounting.** All funds given for specific purposes, projects, or programs should be accounted for separately. Charges against the gifts should be allocated based only on disclosed policies (e.g., administrative assessments or indirect costs) or for costs that are directly attributable to the purpose, project, or program.

✓ **Donations received for one project but spent on another.** Separate revenue and expense accounts must be maintained for each project to ensure the integrity of the funds.

✓ **Overfunding or underfunding of projects.** This may require communicating additional information to donors about the use of the funds. In some cases, donor approval may be needed to re-direct the use of funds. If the purpose of a designated gift cannot be fulfilled and the donor is unwilling to remove or change the designation, it may be necessary to make a refund to the donor (see page 170).

A possible disclosure for response devices and receipts is: "Contributions to (name of charity) are administered and disbursed under the supervision of the Board of Trustees/Directors. In the unlikely event that a ministry is overfunded, gifts may be used in another ministry activity as closely in keeping with your interests as possible." The use of a statement of this type

- is only appropriate when events of overfunding are unusual and infrequent

Evangelical Council for Financial Accountability

1-800-3BE-WISE

STANDARDS OF RESPONSIBLE STEWARDSHIP

The ECFA Standards of Responsible Stewardship required for membership:

- **STANDARD #1 – DOCTRINAL STATEMENT**: Every member organization shall subscribe to a written statement of faith clearly affirming its commitment to the evangelical Christian faith and shall conduct its financial and other operations in a manner which reflects those generally accepted Biblical truths and practices.
- **STANDARD #2 – BOARD OF DIRECTORS AND AUDIT REVIEW COMMITTEE**: Every member organization shall be governed by a responsible board of not less than five individuals, a majority of whom shall be other than employees/staff and/or those related by blood or marriage, which shall meet at least semi-annually to establish policy and review its accomplishments. The board shall appoint a functioning audit review committee, a majority of whom shall be other than employees/staff and/or those related by blood or marriage, for the purpose of reviewing the annual audit and reporting its findings to the board.
- **STANDARD #3 – AUDITED FINANCIAL STATEMENTS**: Every member organization shall obtain an annual audit performed by an independent certified public accounting firm in accordance with generally accepted auditing standards (GAAS) with financial statements prepared in accordance with generally accepted accounting principles (GAAP).
- **STANDARD #4 – USE OF RESOURCES**: Every member organization shall exercise management and financial controls necessary to provide reasonable assurance that all resources are used (nationally and internationally) to accomplish the exempt purposes for which they are intended.
- **STANDARD #5 - FINANCIAL DISCLOSURE**: Every member organization shall provide a copy of its current audited financial statements upon written request.
- **STANDARD #6 - CONFLICTS OF INTEREST**: Every member organization shall avoid conflicts of interest. Transactions with related parties may be undertaken only if all of the following are observed; 1) a material transaction is fully disclosed in the audited financial statements of the organization; 2) the related party is excluded from the discussion and approval of such transaction; 3) a competitive bid or comparable valuation exists; and 4) the organization's board has acted upon and demonstrated that the transaction is in the best interest of the member organization.
- **STANDARD #7 - FUND RAISING**: Every member organization shall comply with each of the ECFA Standards for Fund-Raising:
- **7.1: TRUTHFULNESS IN COMMUNICATION**: All representations of fact, description of financial condition of the organization, or narrative about the events must be current, complete and accurate. References to past activities or events must be appropriately dated. There must be no material omissions or exaggerations of fact or use of misleading photographs or any other communication which would tend to create a false impression or misunderstanding.
- **7.2: COMMUNICATION AND DONOR EXPECTATIONS**: Fund-raising

appeals must not create unrealistic donor expectations of what a donor's gift will actually accomplish within the limits of the organization's ministry.

- **7.3: COMMUNICATION AND DONOR INTENT**: All statements made by the organization in its fund-raising appeals about the use of the gift must be honored by the organization. The donor's intent is related to both what was communicated in the appeal and to any donor instructions accompanying the gift. The organization should be aware that communications made in fund-raising appeals may create a legally binding restriction.
- **7.4: PROJECTS UNRELATED TO A MINISTRY'S PRIMARY PURPOSE**: An organization raising or receiving funds for programs that are not part of its present or prospective ministry, but are proper in accordance with its exempt purpose, must either treat them as restricted funds and channel them through an organization that can carry out the donor's intent, or return the funds to the donor.
- **7.5: INCENTIVES AND PREMIUMS**: Organizations making fund-raising appeals which, in exchange for a contribution, offer premiums or incentives (the value of which is not insubstantial, but which is significant in relation to the amount of the donation) must advise the donor of the fair market value of the premium or incentive and that the value is not deductible for tax purposes.
- **7.6: REPORTING**: On request, an organization must provide a report, including financial information, on the project for which it is soliciting gifts.
- **7.7: PERCENTAGE COMPENSATION FOR FUND-RAISERS**: Compensation of outside fund-raising consultants or an organization's own employees based directly or indirectly on a percentage of charitable contributions raised is not allowed.
- **7.8: TAX DEDUCTIBLE GIFTS FOR A NAMED RECIPIENT'S PERSONAL BENEFIT**: Tax deductible gifts may not be used to pass money or benefits to any named individual for personal use.
- **7.9: CONFLICT OF INTEREST ON ROYALTIES**: An officer, director, or other principal of the organization must not receive royalties for any product that is used for fund-raising or promotional purposes by his/her own organization.
- **7.10: ACKNOWLEDGEMENT OF GIFTS IN KIND**: Property or gifts in kind received by an organization should be acknowledged describing the property or gift accurately *without* a statement of the gift's market value. It is the responsibility of the donor to determine the fair market value of the property for tax purposes. The organization should inform the donor of IRS reporting requirements for all gifts in excess of $5,000.
- **7.11: ACTING IN THE INTEREST OF THE DONOR**: An organization must make every effort to avoid accepting a gift from or entering into a contract with a prospective donor which would knowingly place a hardship on the donor, or place the donor's future well-being in jeopardy.
- **7.12: FINANCIAL ADVICE**: The representative of the organization, when dealing with persons regarding commitments on major estate assets, must seek to guide and advise donors so they have adequately considered the broad interests of the family and the various ministries they are currently supporting before they make a final decision. Donors should be encouraged to use the services of their attorneys, accountants, or other professional advisors.

- does not make a restricted gift unrestricted until a future event occurs, and
- does not diminish the organization's moral, social, and perhaps legal obligation to use the funds for the specified purpose, except when such an unanticipated event occurs.

✓ **Inadequate reporting to donors on projects.** ECFA requires members, on request, to provide a report, including financial information, on the project for which it is soliciting gifts. Without a proper accounting system, an accurate and timely report on specific projects may be impossible to prepare.

Use of funds

Most contributors believe that their contributions are being applied to the current program needs identified by the organization, unless there is other specific representation. It is prudent management for organizations to accumulate adequate unrestricted operating funds. The needs of the constituency served should be the most important factor in determining the adequacy of reserve funds.

Example: An organization has $250,000 in savings at the time a direct mail appeal asks for donations to cover operating expenses. A donor questions the ethics of the appeal. Was the appeal improper?

The size of the organization would have a significant bearing on the appropriateness of the appeal. The appeal may be inappropriate if the annual budget of the organization is $50,000 (in other words, the savings account would be five times the annual budget). Yet, an organization with an annual budget of $2M may justify a savings account of $250,000 for contingencies.

Projects unrelated to an organization's primary purpose

Nonprofits sometimes receive funds for programs that are not part of its present or prospective ministry, but are proper according to its exempt purpose (i.e., one of the exempt purposes under the Internal Revenue Code). In these instances the organization must treat them either as restricted funds and channel them through an organization that can carry out the donor's intent, or return the funds to the donor.

Reporting for incentives and premiums

Fund-raising appeals may offer premiums or incentives in exchange for a contribution. If the value of the premiums or incentives is not insubstantial, but significant in relation to the amount of the donation, the donee organization must advise the donor of the fair market value of the premium or incentive and that the value is not deductible for tax purposes (see page 155). ECFA members must comply with the IRS rules on incentives and premiums.

Reporting to donors and the public

ECFA requires an organization to provide a copy of its current financial statements upon written request. Many nonprofit organizations are subject to the public disclosure rules effective June 8, 1999, requiring charities to provide copies of annual information returns (Form 990) and certain other documents when requested to do so (see pages 45-46).

Compensation of gift planners

Payment of finders' fees, commissions, or other fees on a percentage basis by a donee organization to an outside gift planner as a condition for delivery of a gift is never appropriate under ECFA standards. Commission or contingency-based compensation to an organization's own employees is also considered inappropriate by ECFA.

Every effort must be made to keep donor trust. Donor attitudes can be unalterably damaged in reaction to undue pressure and the awareness that a direct commission will be paid to a fund-raiser from his or her gift, thus compromising the trust on which charity relies.

Tax-deductible gifts for a named recipient's personal benefit

According to the Internal Revenue Code and other laws and regulations governing tax-exempt organizations, tax-deductible gifts may not be used to pass money or benefits to any named individual for personal use. Individuals often want to use charitable organizations as a conduit for funds to change the character of personal, nondeductible gifts to deductible charitable contributions. Gifts for the support of specific staff individuals may be deductible as charitable contributions if the donee organization exercises adequate discretion and control over the contributed funds. Chapter 7 covers this topic in more detail.

Conflict of interest on royalties

ECFA requires that an officer, director, or other principal of the organization must not receive royalties for any product used for fund-raising or promotional purposes by his or her organization. The payment of reasonable royalties for items offered for sale is permissible.

Acknowledgment of gifts-in-kind

Property or gifts-in-kind received by an organization should be acknowledged, describing the property or gift accurately *without* an estimate of the gift's market value. It is the responsibility of the donor to determine the fair market value of the property for tax purposes.

Acting in the interest of the donor

Every effort should be made to avoid accepting a gift from or entering into a contract with a prospective donor that would knowingly place a hardship on the donor, or place the donor's future well-being in jeopardy.

Financial advice

Fund-raisers should recognize that it is almost impossible to properly represent the full interests of the donor and the charitable organization simultaneously.

When dealing with persons regarding commitments on major estate assets, gift planners should seek to guide and advise donors so that they may adequately consider the broad interests of the family and the various organizations they are currently supporting before they make a final decision. Donors should be encouraged to discuss the proposed gift with competent and independent attorneys, accountants, or other professional advisors.

Accountability to Government

Almost every church and nonprofit has some reporting requirements to one or more governmental agencies. Many organizations do not fully comply with reporting guidelines.

Churches and nonprofits abhor the thought of increased governmental regulation. Yet failure to self-regulate areas such as executive compensation, unrelated business activities, fund-raising practices, and political lobbying continues to draw the attention of the IRS and Congress.

A few organizations knowingly operate in or at the edge of fraudulent areas. But most organizations have good intentions and any violations are primarily based on ignorance of laws and regulations.

Key Concepts

- Good stewardship rarely occurs outside a system of accountability.
- Adequate board governance is the first step to proper accountability.
- Accountability in donor solicitation and the use of contributions is vital.
- Fulfillment of required reporting to governmental agencies is a must.

CHAPTER TWO

Tax Exemption

Your tax-exempt status is extremely valuable — guard it carefully!

In This Chapter

- Tax exemption for churches
- Advantages and limitations of tax exemption
- Starting a nonprofit
- Unrelated business income
- Private benefit and private inurement
- Filing federal returns
- Postal regulations
- State taxes and fees
- Political activity

Qualifying tax-exempt organizations may have many advantages. One of the most important benefits is the eligibility to attract deductible charitable contributions from individual and corporate donors. Exemption from tax liability, primarily income, sales, and property tax, is also important.

The term "nonprofit organization" covers a broad range of entities such as churches, colleges, universities, health-care providers, business leagues, veterans groups, political parties, country clubs, and united-giving campaigns. Sources of revenue, ownership structure, and activities distinguish nonprofit from for-profit organizations. The most common type of nonprofits is the charitable organization.

The nonprofit organization concept is basically a state law creation. But tax-exempt organizations are based primarily on federal law. The Internal Revenue Code does not use the word "nonprofit." The Code refers to nonprofits as exempt organizations. Certain state statutes use the term "not-for-profit." A not-for-profit organization under state law may or may not be tax-exempt under federal law.

In this book, the term "nonprofit" refers to nonprofit organizations that are exempt from federal income tax. This is key because not all nonprofit organizations are necessarily tax-exempt.

Tax Exemption for Churches

Tax law and IRS regulations do not define "religious." But the courts have defined "religious" broadly. In part, because of these constitutional concerns, some religious organizations are subject to more lenient reporting and auditing requirements under federal tax law.

The "religious" category includes churches, conventions of churches, associations of churches, church-run organizations (such as schools, hospitals, orphanages, nursing homes, publishing entities, broadcasting entities, and cemeteries), religious orders, apostolic groups, integrated auxiliaries of churches, missionary organizations, and Bible and tract societies. IRS regulations define religious worship as: "What constitutes conduct of religious worship or the ministration of sacerdotal functions depends on the interests and practices of a particular religious body constituting a church."

Although not stated in the regulations, the IRS applies the following 14 criteria to decide whether a religious organization can qualify as a "church":

- ✓ Distinct legal existence
- ✓ Recognized creed and form of worship
- ✓ Definite and distinct ecclesiastical government
- ✓ Formal code of doctrine and discipline
- ✓ Distinct religious history
- ✓ Membership not associated with any other church or denomination
- ✓ Organization of ordained ministers
- ✓ Ordained ministers selected after completing prescribed courses of studies
- ✓ Literature of its own
- ✓ Established places of worship
- ✓ Regular congregations
- ✓ Regular religious services
- ✓ Sunday schools for religious instruction of the young
- ✓ Schools for preparation of its ministers

Churches receive favored status in that they are not required to file either an application for exemption (Form 1023) or annual report (Form 990) with the IRS. A church is still subject to filing an annual report on unrelated business income (Form 990-T) and Form 5578 for private schools as well as payroll tax, sales tax, and other forms, if applicable.

Advantages and Limitations of Tax Exemption

Upon approval by the IRS, tax exemption is available to organizations that meet the requirements of the tax code. This exemption provides relief from federal income tax. This income tax exemption may or may not extend to local and state income taxes. Even if an organization receives tax-exempt status, certain federal taxes may still be imposed. Possible taxes are the unrelated business income tax, tax on certain "political" activities, and tax on excessive legislative activities.

Tax exemption advantages

Besides the basic exemption from federal income and excise tax, an organization that is recognized as a charitable organization under the Internal Revenue Code enjoys several advantages:

- ✓ Its donors can be offered the benefit of a deduction for contributions.
- ✓ It can benefit from lower postal rates on third-class bulk mailings.
- ✓ It is in a favored position to seek funding from foundations and other philanthropic entities, many of which will not support organizations other than those recognized under 501(c)(3).
- ✓ It is eligible for government grants available only to entities exempt under 501(c)(3).
- ✓ It often qualifies for exemption not only from state and local income tax but from property taxes (for property used directly for its exempt function) and certain sales and use taxes as well.
- ✓ It may qualify for exemption from the Federal Unemployment Tax Act in certain situations.
- ✓ Its employees may participate in 403(b) tax-sheltered annuities and 401(k) plans.

- ✓ It is an exclusive beneficiary of free radio and television public service announcements (PSAs) provided by local media outlets.
- ✓ If it is a church or a qualified church-controlled organization, it may exclude compensation to employees from the FICA social security base. The organization must be opposed on religious grounds to the payment of FICA social security taxes. The social security liability shifts to the employees of the electing organizations in the form of SECA social security tax.

Tax exemption limitations

Offsetting the advantages of tax-exempt status are some strict requirements:

- ✓ An organization must be engaged "primarily" in qualified charitable or educational endeavors.
- ✓ There are limitations to the extent to which it can engage in substantial legislative activities or other political activities.
- ✓ An organization may not engage in unrelated business activities or commercial activities to an impermissible extent.
- ✓ There is a prohibition against private inurement or private benefit.
- ✓ Upon dissolution, the organization's assets must be distributed for one or more exempt purposes.

Starting a Nonprofit

The choice of a nonprofit organizational form is a basic decision. Most churches are unincorporated. However, an increasing number of churches are incorporating for the purpose of limiting legal liability. Most other nonprofit organizations are corporations. While incorporation may usually be desirable, it is generally not mandatory.

Organizations using the corporate form will need articles of incorporation and bylaws. An unincorporated organization will typically have the same instruments although the articles may be in the form of a constitution.

Several planning questions should be asked. If the organization is formed for charitable purposes, is public status desired or is a private foundation acceptable? Are any business activities contemplated and to what degree will the organization be incorporated? Is an attorney competent in nonprofit matters available to help with the preparation of the legal documents? What provisions will the bylaws contain? Who will serve on the board of directors? What name will be used for the organization?

The following materials may be needed or useful when starting a church or other nonprofit organization:

Package 1023	Application for Recognition of Exemption with Instructions
Publication 557	Tax-Exempt Status for Your Organization

Obtaining an employer identification number

All entities, whether exempt from tax or not, must obtain an Employer Identification Number (EIN) by filing IRS Form SS-4. An EIN is required for each church even though churches are not required to file with the IRS for tax-exempt status. This number is not a "tax-exempt number," but is simply the organization's unique identifier in the IRS's records, similar to an individual's social security number.

When the IRS approves an organization for exemption from federal income tax (not required for churches), it will receive a "determination letter." This letter does not assign the organization a "tax-exempt number."

If an organization is a "central organization" that holds a "group exemption letter," the IRS will assign that group a four-digit number, known as its Group Exemption Number (GEN). This number must be supplied with the central organization's annual report to the IRS (updating its list of included subordinate organizations). The number also is inserted on Form 990 (if required) of the central organization and the subordinate organizations included in the group exemption.

When an organization applies for exemption from state or local income, sales, or property taxes, the state or local jurisdiction may provide a certificate or letter of exemption, which, in some jurisdictions, includes a serial number. This number is often called a "tax-exempt number." This number should not be confused with an EIN.

Application for recognition of tax-exempt status

Although churches are not required to apply to the IRS for tax-exempt status under Section 501(c)(3) of the Internal Revenue Code and are exempt from filing Form 990, it may be appropriate to apply for recognition in some situations:

TIP

- ✓ Independent local churches that are not a part of a national denominational body often file for tax-exempt status to provide evidence of their status. The local congregation may wish to file for group exemption if it is a parent church of other local congregations or separately organized ministries.

  National denominations typically file for group exemption to cover all local congregations. A copy of the national body's IRS determination letter may be used by the local group to provide evidence of tax-exempt status.

- ✓ Some donors, or their professional advisors, may ask if a local church is

Form **SS-4**
(Rev. February 1998)
Department of the Treasury
Internal Revenue Service

Application for Employer Identification Number

(For use by employers, corporations, partnerships, trusts, estates, churches, government agencies, certain individuals, and others. See instructions.)

▶ **Keep a copy for your records.**

EIN

OMB No. 1545-0003

Please type or print clearly.

1 Name of applicant (legal name) (see instructions)
Lynn Haven Church

2 Trade name of business (if different from name on line 1)

3 Executor, trustee, "care of" name

4a Mailing address (street address) (room, apt., or suite no.)
P.O. Box 4382

5a Business address (if different from address on lines 4a and 4b)
3801 North Florida Avenue

4b City, state, and ZIP code
Miami, FL 33168

5b City, state, and ZIP code
Miami, FL 33168

6 County and state where principal business is located
Dade County, Florida

7 Name of principal officer, general partner, grantor, owner, or trustor—SSN or ITIN may be required (see instructions) ▶

8a Type of entity (Check only one box.) (see instructions)
Caution: *If applicant is a limited liability company, see the instructions for line 8a.*

- ☐ Sole proprietor (SSN)
- ☐ Partnership
- ☐ REMIC
- ☐ State/local government
- ☑ Church or church-controlled organization
- ☐ Other nonprofit organization (specify) ▶ ______ (enter GEN if applicable)
- ☐ Other (specify) ▶
- ☐ Personal service corp.
- ☐ National Guard
- ☐ Farmers' cooperative
- ☐ Estate (SSN of decedent)
- ☐ Plan administrator (SSN)
- ☐ Other corporation (specify) ▶
- ☐ Trust
- ☐ Federal government/military

8b If a corporation, name the state or foreign country (if applicable) where incorporated — State: **Florida** — Foreign country:

9 Reason for applying (Check only one box.) (see instructions)

- ☑ Started new business (specify type) ▶ **Church**
- ☐ Hired employees (Check the box and see line 12.)
- ☐ Created a pension plan (specify type) ▶
- ☐ Banking purpose (specify purpose) ▶
- ☐ Changed type of organization (specify new type) ▶
- ☐ Purchased going business
- ☐ Created a trust (specify type) ▶
- ☐ Other (specify) ▶

10 Date business started or acquired (month, day, year) (see instructions)
2/1/99

11 Closing month of accounting year (see instructions)
June

12 First date wages or annuities were paid or will be paid (month, day, year). **Note:** *If applicant is a withholding agent, enter date income will first be paid to nonresident alien. (month, day, year)* . . . ▶ **2/01/2000**

13 Highest number of employees expected in the next 12 months. **Note:** *If the applicant does not expect to have any employees during the period, enter -0-. (see instructions)* . . . ▶

Nonagricultural	Agricultural	Household
3		

14 Principal activity (see instructions) ▶

15 Is the principal business activity manufacturing? . . . ☐ Yes ☑ No
If "Yes," principal product and raw material used ▶

16 To whom are most of the products or services sold? Please check one box. ☐ Business (wholesale)
☐ Public (retail) ☐ Other (specify) ▶ ☐ N/A

17a Has the applicant ever applied for an employer identification number for this or any other business? . . . ☐ Yes ☑ No
Note: *If "Yes," please complete lines 17b and 17c.*

17b If you checked "Yes" on line 17a, give applicant's legal name and trade name shown on prior application, if different from line 1 or 2 above.
Legal name ▶ Trade name ▶

17c Approximate date when and city and state where the application was filed. Enter previous employer identification number if known.

Approximate date when filed (mo., day, year)	City and state where filed	Previous EIN

Under penalties of perjury, I declare that I have examined this application, and to the best of my knowledge and belief, it is true, correct, and complete.

Business telephone number (include area code) **305-688-7432**

Fax telephone number (include area code)

Name and title (Please type or print clearly.) ▶ **Mike R. Thomas, Treasurer**

Signature ▶ Mike R. Thomas   Date ▶ 1/31/00

Note: *Do not write below this line. For official use only.*

Please leave blank ▶	Geo.	Ind.	Class	Size	Reason for applying

For Paperwork Reduction Act Notice, see page 4.   Cat. No. 16055N   Form **SS-4** (Rev. 2-98)

Note: Nearly every church or other nonprofit organization needs an Employer Identification Number (EIN) obtained by filing this form.

listed in IRS Publication 78, the Cumulative List of Organizations identifying entities to which tax deductible contributions may be made. Only churches that have applied and been approved for tax-exempt status are listed in Publication 78.

There is no requirement for churches to be listed in Publication 78. However, a listing in the publication generally eliminates any question about the deductibility of contributions to the church as charitable contributions.

✓ If a local congregation ordains ministers, it may be helpful to apply for tax-exempt status. Ministers that are ordained by a local church may be required to provide evidence that the church is tax-exempt. This could be particularly true if the minister files Form 4361 applying for exemption for self-employment tax.

Churches or other charitable organizations desiring recognition of tax-exempt status should submit Form 1023. If approved, the IRS will issue a determination letter describing the category of exemption granted.

The IRS must be notified that the organization is applying for recognition of exemption within 15 months from the end of the month in which it was organized. Applications made after this deadline will not be effective before the date on which the application for recognition of exemption is filed.

Large and small organizations often find that obtaining an exemption letter from the IRS is an intimidating process. Organizations faced with the process are typically new, with a general mission in mind. The mission is often not fully developed and therefore it may not be clearly articulated. It may be helpful to have your application reviewed by a CPA or attorney before it is filed.

Determination letter request

A user fee of $465 (with Form 8718) must accompany applications for recognition of tax-exempt status where the applicant has gross receipts that annually exceed $10,000. For an organization that has had annual gross receipts of $10,000 or less during the past four years, the fee is $150. Start-ups may qualify for the reduced fee. Group exemption letter fees are $500.

Granting tax exemption

Upon approval of the application for exemption, the IRS will provide a determination letter. This letter may be an advance determination or a definitive (or final) determination. The exempt status is usually effective as of the date of formation of the organization, if filing deadlines are met.

An advance determination letter provides tentative guidance regarding status but is a final determination relating to operations and structure of the organization. An advance determination is effective for five years. Before the end of the advance determination period, the organization must show that it qualifies for nonprivate foundation status. During the advance determination period, contributors may make tax-deductible donations to the organization.

A newly created organization seeking status as a publicly supported organization is entitled to receive, if it so elects, a definitive ruling if it has completed a tax year consisting of eight full months as of the time of filing the application.

A definitive (or final) determination letter represents a determination by the IRS position that the organizational and operational plans of the nonprofit entitle it to be classified as exempt.

Group exemption

An affiliated group of organizations under the common control of a central organization can obtain a group exemption letter. Churches that are part of a denomination are not required to file a separate application for exemption if they are covered by the group letter.

The central organization is required to report annually its exempt subordinate organizations to the IRS (the IRS does not provide a particular form for this reporting). The central organization is responsible to evaluate the tax status of its subordinate groups.

Unrelated Business Income

All income of tax-exempt organizations is presumed to be tax-exempt from federal income tax unless the income is generated by an activity that is

- ✓ not substantially related to the organization's exempt purpose or function,
- ✓ a trade or business, and
- ✓ regularly carried on.

Unrelated business income (UBI) is permitted for tax-exempt organizations. However, churches and other nonprofits may have to pay tax on income derived from activities unrelated to their exempt purpose. UBI must not comprise a substantial part of the organization's operation. There is no specific percentage limitation on how much UBI is "substantial." However, organizations with 50% to 80% of their activities classified as unrelated have faced revocation of their tax-exempt status.

CAUTION

Form 990-T must be completed to report the source(s) of UBI and related expenses and to compute any tax. UBI amounts are also reportable on Form 990 (if the filing of Form 990 is required).

Although exempt from filing Form 990, churches must file Form 990-T if they have $1,000 or more of gross UBI in a year. There is a specific deduction of $1,000 in computing unrelated business taxable income. This specific deduction applies to a diocese, province of a religious order, or a convention or association of churches with respect to each parish, individual church, district, or other local unit.

Unrelated business income consequences

Some church and nonprofit executives are paranoid about UBI to the point that they feel it must be avoided altogether. Some people equate UBI with the automatic loss of exempt status. A more balanced view is to understand the purpose of the UBI and minimize the UBI tax through proper planning.

The most common adverse result of having UBI is that all or part of it may be taxed. A less frequent, but still possible, result is that the organization will lose its tax exemption. It is possible that the IRS will deny or revoke the tax-exempt status of an organization when it regularly derives over one-half of its annual revenue from unrelated activities.

Congress recognized that some nonprofits may need to engage in unrelated business activities to survive. For example, a nonprofit with unused office space might rent the space to another organization. Also, nonprofits are expected to invest surplus funds to supplement the primary sources of the organization's income.

A trade or business regularly carried on

A trade or business means any activity regularly carried on which produces income from the sale of goods and services and where there is a reasonable expectation of a profit. To decide whether a trade or business is regularly carried on, the IRS considers whether taxable organizations would carry on a business with the same frequency and continuity. Intermittent activities may escape the "regularly carried on" definition.

Example 1: If a church sells sandwiches at an area bazaar for only two weeks, the IRS would not treat this as the regular conduct of a trade or business.

Example 2: A one-time sale of property is not an activity that is regularly carried on and therefore does not generate unrelated business income unless the property was used in an unrelated business activity.

Example 3: A church is located in the downtown section of a city. Each Saturday, the church parking lot is operated commercially to accommodate shoppers. Even though the business activity is carried on for only one day each week on a year-round basis, this constitutes the conduct of a trade or business. It is subject to the unrelated business income tax.

Substantially related

According to the IRS regulations, a trade or business must "contribute importantly to the accomplishment of the exempt purposes of an organization" if it is to

Form **990** — **Return of Organization Exempt From Income Tax**

Under section 501(c) of the Internal Revenue Code (except black lung benefit trust or private foundation) or section 4947(a)(1) nonexempt charitable trust

Department of the Treasury Internal Revenue Service

Note: *The organization may have to use a copy of this return to satisfy state reporting requirements.*

OMB No. 1545-0047 — **1999** — This Form is Open to Public Inspection

A For the 1999 calendar year, OR tax year period beginning , 1999, and ending ,

B Check if: ☐ Change of address ☐ Initial return ☐ Final return ☐ Amended return (required also for state reporting)

Please use IRS label or print or type. See Specific Instructions.

C Name of organization: Athens Children's home

Number and street (or P.O. box if mail is not delivered to street address) / Room/suite: 1212 South Palo Verde

City or town, state or country, and ZIP+4: Phoenix, AZ 85035

D Employer identification number: 35 ⋮ 7438041

E Telephone number

F Check ▶ ☐ if exemption application is pending

G Type of organization—▶☐ Exempt under section 501(c)(3) ◀ (insert number) OR ▶ ☐ section 4947(a)(1) nonexempt charitable trust

Note: *Section 501(c)(3) exempt organizations and 4947(a)(1) nonexempt charitable trusts MUST attach a completed Schedule A (Form 990).*

H(a) Is this a group return filed for affiliates? ☐ Yes ☒ No

(b) If "Yes," enter the number of affiliates for which this return is filed: ▶

(c) Is this a separate return filed by an organization covered by a group ruling? ☐ Yes ☒ No

I If either box in H is checked "Yes," enter four-digit group exemption number (GEN) ▶

J Accounting method: ☐ Cash ☒ Accrual ☐ Other (specify) ▶

K Check here ▶ ☐ if the organization's gross receipts are normally not more than $25,000. The organization need not file a return with the IRS; but if it received a Form 990 Package in the mail, it should file a return without financial data. **Some states require a complete return.**

Note: *Form 990-EZ may be used by organizations with gross receipts less than $100,000 and total assets less than $250,000 at end of year.*

Part I — Revenue, Expenses, and Changes in Net Assets or Fund Balances (See Specific Instructions on page 13.)

Section	Line	Description	Inner line	Inner amount	Line	Amount
Revenue	1	Contributions, gifts, grants, and similar amounts received:				
	a	Direct public support	1a	314,812		
	b	Indirect public support	1b	41,042		
	c	Government contributions (grants)	1c			
	d	**Total** (add lines 1a through 1c) (attach schedule of contributors) (cash $ noncash $)			1d	355,854
	2	Program service revenue including government fees and contracts (from Part VII, line 93)			2	
	3	Membership dues and assessments			3	
	4	Interest on savings and temporary cash investments			4	10,483
	5	Dividends and interest from securities			5	
	6a	Gross rents	6a			
	b	Less: rental expenses	6b			
	c	Net rental income or (loss) (subtract line 6b from line 6a)			6c	
	7	Other investment income (describe ▶)			7	
	8a	Gross amount from sale of assets other than inventory — (A) Securities / (B) Other	8a			
	b	Less: cost or other basis and sales expenses	8b			
	c	Gain or (loss) (attach schedule)	8c			
	d	Net gain or (loss) (combine line 8c, columns (A) and (B))			8d	
	9	Special events and activities (attach schedule)				
	a	Gross revenue (not including $ 51,842 of contributions reported on line 1a)	9a	74,712		
	b	Less: direct expenses other than fundraising expenses	9b	29,003		
	c	Net income or (loss) from special events (subtract line 9b from line 9a)			9c	45,709
	10a	Gross sales of inventory, less returns and allowances	10a			
	b	Less: cost of goods sold	10b			
	c	Gross profit or (loss) from sales of inventory (attach schedule) (subtract line 10b from line 10a)			10c	
	11	Other revenue (from Part VII, line 103)			11	
	12	**Total revenue** (add lines 1d, 2, 3, 4, 5, 6c, 7, 8d, 9c, 10c, and 11)			12	412,046
Expenses	13	Program services (from line 44, column (B))			13	259,028
	14	Management and general (from line 44, column (C))			14	84,933
	15	Fundraising (from line 44, column (D))			15	59,012
	16	Payments to affiliates (attach schedule)			16	
	17	**Total expenses** (add lines 16 and 44, column (A))			17	402,973
Net Assets	18	Excess or (deficit) for the year (subtract line 17 from line 12)			18	9,073
	19	Net assets or fund balances at beginning of year (from line 73, column (A))			19	144,098
	20	Other changes in net assets or fund balances (attach explanation)			20	
	21	Net assets or fund balances at end of year (combine lines 18, 19, and 20)			21	153,171

For Paperwork Reduction Act Notice, see page 1 of the separate instructions. Cat. No. 11282Y Form **990** (1999)

Note: Form 990 has a total of five pages. Only one page is shown here.

be considered "substantially related." Even if all the profits from a business go to support the work of the nonprofit, the profits may still be taxed.

KEY ISSUE

Example: If a church operates a restaurant and devotes all the proceeds to mission work, the church will not escape taxation on the restaurant's income.

Types of income that may be "related" are

- ✓ the sale of products made by handicapped individuals as a part of their rehabilitation;
- ✓ the sale of homes constructed by students enrolled in a vocational training course; and
- ✓ a retail grocery store operated to provide emotional therapy for disturbed adolescents.

Tours conducted by nonprofits usually create UBI. Tours may be exempt from UBI only if they are strongly educationally oriented, with reports, daily lectures, and so on. Tours with substantial recreational or social purposes are not exempt.

The definition of "unrelated trade or business" *does not* include

- ✓ activities in which unpaid volunteers do most of the work for an organization;
- ✓ activities provided primarily for the convenience of the organization's members; or
- ✓ activities involving the sale of merchandise mostly donated to the organization.

Rental income

Nonprofits often rent facilities, equipment, and other assets for a fee. Rental income usually represents UBI with the following exceptions:

KEY ISSUE

- ✓ Renting to another nonprofit may be termed "related" if the rental expressly serves the landlord's exempt purposes.
- ✓ Mailing lists produce UBI, with specific exceptions.
- ✓ Rental of real estate is excluded from UBI unless the excludable property is acquired or improved with indebtedness. Rental income from the property becomes UBI to the extent of the ratio of the "average acquisition indebtedness" during the year to the total purchase price. The nonprofit may deduct the same portion of the expenses directly connected with the production of the rental income. Depreciation is allowable using only the straight-line method.

Form **990-T**
Department of the Treasury
Internal Revenue Service

Exempt Organization Business Income Tax Return
(and proxy tax under section 6033(e))

For calendar year 1999 or other tax year beginning ...., and ending ....
▶ See separate instructions.

OMB No. 1545-0687
1999

A ☐ Check box if address changed

B Exempt under section
☒ 501(C)(3)
☐ 408(e) ☐ 220(e)
☐ 408A ☐ 530(a)
☐ 529(a)

C Book value of all assets at end of year
$4,384,975

Please Print or Type

Name of organization: Family Bible Crusades
Number, street, and room or suite no. (If a P.O. box, see page 6 of instructions.): 400 North Sunset Avenue
City or town, state, and ZIP code: Lemon Grove, CA 92045

D Employer identification number (Employees' trust, see instructions for Block D on page 6.): 35 4427081

E NEW unrelated bus. activity codes (See instructions for Block E on page 6.): 6512

F Group exemption number (see instructions for Block F on page 6) ▶

G Check organization type ▶ ☒ 501(c) corporation ☐ 501(c) trust ☐ 401(a) trust ☐ Other trust

H Describe the organization's primary unrelated business activity. ▶ Apartment Rental

I During the tax year, was the corporation a subsidiary in an affiliated group or a parent-subsidiary controlled group? ▶ ☐ Yes ☒ No
If "Yes," enter the name and identifying number of the parent corporation. ▶

J The books are in care of ▶ Family Bible Crusades Telephone number ▶ ( )

Part I Unrelated Trade or Business Income

			(A) Income	(B) Expenses	(C) Net
1a	Gross receipts or sales				
b	Less returns and allowances ______ c Balance ▶	1c			
2	Cost of goods sold (Schedule A, line 7)	2			
3	Gross profit (subtract line 2 from line 1c)	3			
4a	Capital gain net income (attach Schedule D)	4a			
b	Net gain (loss) (Form 4797, Part II, line 18) (attach Form 4797)	4b			
c	Capital loss deduction for trusts	4c			
5	Income (loss) from partnerships and S corporations (attach statement)	5			
6	Rent income (Schedule C)	6			
7	Unrelated debt-financed income (Schedule E)	7	79,410	52,301	27,109
8	Interest, annuities, royalties, and rents from controlled organizations (see page 7 of instructions)	8			
9	Investment income of a section 501(c)(7), (9), or (17) organization (Schedule G)	9			
10	Exploited exempt activity income (Schedule I)	10			
11	Advertising income (Schedule J)	11			
12	Other income (see page 8 of the instructions—attach schedule)	12			
13	**TOTAL** (combine lines 3 through 12)	13	79,410	52,301	27,109

Part II Deductions Not Taken Elsewhere (See page 8 of the instructions for limitations on deductions.) (Except for contributions, deductions must be directly connected with the unrelated business income.)

14	Compensation of officers, directors, and trustees (Schedule K)	14	
15	Salaries and wages	15	
16	Repairs and maintenance	16	
17	Bad debts	17	
18	Interest (attach schedule)	18	
19	Taxes and licenses	19	
20	Charitable contributions (see page 10 of the instructions for limitation rules)	20	
21	Depreciation (attach Form 4562) 21		
22	Less depreciation claimed on Schedule A and elsewhere on return 22a	22b	
23	Depletion	23	
24	Contributions to deferred compensation plans	24	
25	Employee benefit programs	25	
26	Excess exempt expenses (Schedule I)	26	
27	Excess readership costs (Schedule J)	27	
28	Other deductions (attach schedule)	28	
29	**Total deductions** (add lines 14 through 28)	29	
30	Unrelated business taxable income before net operating loss deduction (subtract line 29 from line 13)	30	27,109
31	Net operating loss deduction	31	
32	Unrelated business taxable income before specific deduction (subtract line 31 from line 30)	32	27,109
33	Specific deduction (Generally $1,000, but see line 33 instructions for exceptions)	33	1,000
34	**Unrelated business taxable income** (subtract line 33 from line 32). If line 33 is greater than line 32, enter the smaller of zero or line 32	34	26,109

For Paperwork Reduction Act Notice, see instructions. Cat. No. 11291J Form **990-T** (1999)

Note: Form 990-T has a total of four pages. Only page one is shown here.
Caution: Professional assistance may be needed to complete this form.

Debt-financed income

To discourage exempt organizations from borrowing money to purchase passive income items, Congress imposed a tax on debt-financed income. An organization may have debt-financed income if

✓ it incurs debt to purchase or improve an income-producing asset; and

✓ some of that debt remains within the 12 months prior to when income is received from the asset.

An organization also may have debt-financed income if it accepts gifts or bequests of mortgaged property in some circumstances.

There are exceptions to the debt-financed income rules, including

✓ substantially all (85% or more) of any property is used for an organization's exempt purposes;

✓ use of property by a related exempt organization to further its exempt purposes;

✓ life income contracts, if the remainder interest is payable to an exempt charitable organization;

✓ neighborhood land rule, if an organization acquires real property in its "neighborhood" (the neighborhood restriction does not apply to churches) mainly to use it for exempt purposes within ten years (15 years for churches).

Activities that are not taxed

Income from the following sources is generally not considered as UBI:

✓ **Passive income.** Income earned from most passive investment activities is not UBI unless the underlying property is subject to debt. Types of passive income include

- dividends, interest, and annuities
- capital gains or losses from the sale, exchange, or other disposition of property
- rents from real property (some rent is UBI if the rental property was purchased or improved subject to a mortgage)
- royalties (oil and gas working interest income generally constitute UBI)

✓ **Volunteers.** Any business where volunteers perform most of the work without compensation does not qualify as UBI. To the IRS, "substantially" means at least 85% of total work performed.

Example: A used-clothing store operated by a nonprofit orphanage where volunteers do all the work in the store would likely be exempt.

✓ **Convenience.** A cafeteria, bookstore, or residence operated for the convenience of patients, visitors, employees, or students is not a business. Stores, parking lots, and other facilities may be dually used (part related and part unrelated).

✓ **Donated goods.** The sale of merchandise, mostly received as gifts or contributions, does not qualify as UBI. A justification for this exemption is that contributions of property are merely being converted into cash.

✓ **Low-cost items.** Items (costing no more than $7.20—1999 adjusted amount) distributed incidental to the solicitation of charitable contributions are not subject to UBI. The amounts received are not considered as an exchange for the low-cost articles and therefore they do not create UBI.

✓ **Mailing lists.** Mailing lists exchanged with or rented to another exempt organization are excluded from UBI, although the commercial sale of the lists will generally create UBI. The structuring of the agreement as a royalty arrangement may make the income exempt from UBI treatment.

Calculating the unrelated business income tax

Income tax rules applicable to businesses, such as depreciation method limitations and rates, apply to the UBI computation. Direct and indirect costs may be used to offset income. The first $1,000 of annual net unrelated income is exempt from taxation.

For 1999, the corporate tax rates are

Taxable Income			Tax Rate
$ 0	to	$50,000	15% plus
$ 50,001	to	$75,000	25% plus
$ 75,001	to	$100,000	34% plus
$100,001	to	$335,000	39% plus
$335,001	to	$10,000,000	34%

Unrelated business income summary

Be aware of the type of activities that may create UBI in your organization.

- ✓ Maintain careful records of income and related expenses (both direct and indirect, including depreciation) for any activities that might be considered unrelated to the exempt purpose of your organization. These records should include allocations of salaries and fringe benefits based on time records or, at a minimum, time estimates.

  It may be wise to keep a separate set of records on potential unrelated activities. This separate set of records would need to be submitted to the IRS only upon audit.

- ✓ Be sure that board minutes, contracts, and other documents reflect the organization's view of relatedness of various activities to the exempt purpose of the entity.

- ✓ If the organization has over $1,000 of gross UBI in a given fiscal (tax) year, file Form 990-T.

Private Benefit and Private Inurement

Tax laws and regulations impose prohibitions on nonprofit organizations concerning private benefit and private inurement.

Private benefit

Nonprofit organizations must serve public, and not private, interests. The private benefit prohibition applies to anyone outside the intended charitable class. The law does allow some private benefit if it is incidental to the public benefits involved. It is acceptable if the benefit to the public cannot be achieved without necessarily benefiting private individuals.

Example: The IRS revoked exemption of a charity where it served the commercial purposes and private interests of a professional fund-raiser where the fund-raiser distributed only 3% of the amount collected to the nonprofit organization.

Private inurement

Private inurement is a subset of private benefit. This is an absolute prohibition that generally applies to a distinct class of private interests. These "insiders" may be founders, trustees or directors, officers, managers, or significant donors. Transactions involving these individuals are not necessarily prohibited, but they must be subject to reasonableness, documentation, and applicable reporting to the IRS.

Inurement arises whenever a financial benefit represents a transfer of resources to an individual solely by virtue of the individual's relationship with the organization, without regard to accomplishing its exempt purposes. When an individual receives something for nothing or less than it is worth, private inurement may have occurred. Excessive, and therefore unreasonable, compensation can also result in prohibited inurement. The IRS may ask the following questions to determine if private inurement exists:

- ✓ Did the expenditure further an exempt purpose, and, if so, how?
- ✓ Was the payment at fair market value or did it represent reasonable compensation for goods and services?
- ✓ Does a low- or no-interest loan to an employee or director fall within a reasonable compensation package?
- ✓ On an overseas trip for the nonprofit, did the employee (and perhaps a spouse) stay an additional week for a personal vacation and charge the expenses to the organization?

Example 1: An organization lost its exemption when it engaged in numerous transactions with an insider, including the purchase of a 42-foot boat for the personal use of the insider. The insider also benefitted from several real estate transactions, including donations and sales of real property to the organization which were never reflected on its books.

Example 2: A church lost its tax-exemption after it operated commercial businesses and paid substantial private expenses of its founders, including expenses for jewelry and clothing in excess of $30,000 per year. The church also purchased five luxury cars for the founders' personal use. None of these benefits were reported as personal income to the founders.

Example 3: A tax-exempt organization transfers an auto to an employee for $100. The transfer was not approved by the board and does not constitute a portion of a reasonable pay package. The fair market value of the auto is $2,000. The net difference of $1,900 is not reported to the IRS as compensation. Private inurement has occurred.

Example 4: Same facts as Example 3, except the transfer was approved by the board and properly constituted a portion of the reasonable pay package, and the $1,900 was added to the employee's Form W-2 as compensation. There is no private inurement.

A two-tiered scheme of penalty taxes is imposed on insiders who improperly benefit from excess benefit transactions and on organization managers who are involved in illegal transactions. Sanctions cannot be imposed on the organizations themselves.

A first-tier penalty tax equal to 25% of the amount of the excess benefit is followed by a tax of 200% if there is no correction of the excess benefit within a certain time period.

Filing Federal Returns

Nearly all nonprofit organizations must file an annual return with the IRS (churches are exempt from filing Form 990 or 990-EZ). The basic filing requirements are

FORM TO BE FILED	CONDITIONS
No form filed	Gross annual receipts normally under $25,000
Form 990-EZ	Gross annual receipts between $25,000 and $100,000 with total assets of less than $250,000
Form 990	Gross annual receipts over $100,000 or assets over $250,000 with gross annual receipts between $25,000 and $100,000
Form 990-T	Any organization exempt under Sec. 501(a) with $1,000 or more gross income from an unrelated trade or business
Form 1120	Any nonprofit corporation that is not tax-exempt
Form 5500	Pension, profit-sharing, medical benefit, cafeteria, and certain other plans must annually file one of several series 5500 Forms

Public inspection of information returns

The IRS issued final regulations, effective June 8, 1999, on the exempt organization disclosure rules. Here are the key provisions of the regulations:

✓ **Materials made available for public inspection.** Nonprofits, other than private foundations, must provide access to application for tax exemption (Form 1023) and any supporting documents filed by the organization in support of its application. It also includes any letter or other documents issued by the IRS in connection with the application.

Nonprofits must also provide access to their three most recent information returns. This generally includes Forms 990, 990-EZ, and schedules and attachments filed with the IRS. There is not a requirement to disclose parts of the information returns that identify names and address of contributors to the organization. Neither does the organization have to disclose Form 990-T.

✓ **Places and times for public inspection.** Specified documents must be made available at the nonprofit's principal, regional, and district offices during normal business hours. An office is considered a regional or district office only if (1) it has three or more paid, full-time employees or (2) the aggregate hours per week worked by its paid employees (either full-time or part-time) is 120 or more.

✓ **Responding to requests.** If a person requests copies in person, the request generally must be fulfilled on the day of the request. In unusual circumstances, an organization will be permitted to furnish the copies on the next business day. When the request is made in writing, the organization must provide the requested copies within 30 days. If the organization requires advance payment for reasonable copying and mailing fees, it can provide copies within 30 days of the date it is paid, instead of the date of the request.

✓ **Fees for providing copies.** Reasonable fees may be charged by nonprofits for copying and mailing documents. The fees cannot exceed the amounts charged by the IRS—currently, $1 for the first page and 15 cents for each subsequent page—plus actual mailing costs. An organization can require payment in advance. To protect requesters from unexpected fees, when an organization receives a request in writing without advance payment, it must obtain consent before providing copies that will result in fees of more than $20.

✓ **Documents widely available.** A nonprofit organization does not have to comply with requests for copies if it has made the appropriate materials widely available. This requirement is satisfied if the document is posted on the organization's World Wide Web page on the Internet or in another database of similar materials.

Reporting substantial organizational changes

An organization's tax-exempt status remains in effect if there are no material changes in the organization's character, purposes, or methods of operation. Significant changes should be reported by letter to the IRS soon after the changes occur.

Example: An organization received tax-exempt status for the operation of a religious radio ministry. Several years later, the organization decided to add a facility for homeless children. This change would likely be considered to be material and should be reported to the IRS.

Change in accounting methods

A nonprofit organization may adopt any reasonable method of accounting to keep its financial records that clearly reflects income. These methods include the cash receipts and disbursements method; the accrual method; or any other method (including a combination of methods) that clearly reflects income.

An organization that wishes to change from one method of accounting to another generally must secure the consent of the IRS to make that change. Consent must be obtained both for a general change of method, and for any change of method with respect to one or more particular items. Thus, a nonprofit organization that generally uses the cash method, but uses the accrual method with respect to publications for which it maintains inventories, may change its method of accounting by adopting the accrual method for all purposes. But the organization must secure the IRS's consent to do so.

To obtain the consent of the IRS to change an accounting method, the organization should file IRS Form 3115, Application for Change in Accounting Method. The form must be filed within 180 days after the beginning of the tax year in which the change is made. There is a more expeditious consent for a change from the cash to accrual method filed under Revenue Procedure 85-37.

Change of fiscal years

Generally, an exempt organization may change its fiscal year simply by timely filing Form 990 with the appropriate Internal Revenue Service Center for the "short year." The return for the short year should indicate at the top of page 1 that a change of accounting period is being made. It should be filed not later than the 15th day of the fifth month following the close of the short year.

If neither Form 990 nor Form 990-T must be filed, the ministry is not required to notify the IRS of a change in the fiscal year, with one exception. The exception applies to exempt organizations that have changed their fiscal years within the previous ten calendar years. For this exception, Form 1128 must be filed with the IRS.

Other

- ✓ **Form 5578.** Form 5578 may be completed and furnished to the IRS to provide information regarding nondiscrimination policies of private schools instead of completing the information at item 31 of Form 990, Schedule A. If Form 990 is not required to be filed, Form 5578 should be submitted, if applicable. Form 5578 must be filed for schools operated by a church, including preschools.

- ✓ **Form 8717 and 8718.** Nonprofits wishing IRS private letter rulings on exempt organization information or on employee plans must include new forms 8717 or 8718, respectively, with the appropriate fees.

- ✓ **Form 8282.** If a nonprofit donee sells or otherwise disposes of gift property for which an appraisal summary is required on Form 8283 within two years after receipt of the property, it generally must file Form 8282 with the IRS. See Chapter 7 for more information on these reporting rules.

✓ **Employee and nonemployee payments.** As an employer, a nonprofit organization must file federal and state forms concerning payment of compensation and the withholding of payroll taxes. Payments to nonemployees may require the filing of information returns. See Chapters 4 and 5 for more coverage on these requirements.

Postal Regulations

Churches and other nonprofits may qualify to mail at special standard nonprofit mail rates (formerly called bulk third-class). The application (Form 3624) is available at the post office where you wish to deposit the mail (see page 47 for a sample of Form 3624). The following information must be provided (some apply only if the organization is incorporated):

✓ description of the organization's primary purpose which might be found in the articles of incorporation or bylaws;

✓ evidence that the organization is nonprofit such as a federal (and state) tax exemption determination letter; and

✓ materials showing how the organization actually operated in the previous 6 to 12 months such as program literature, newsletters, bulletins, and any other promotional materials.

The U.S. Postal Service offers rate incentives to nonprofit mailers that provide automation-compatible mail. Automated mail must be readable by an Optical Character Reader (OCR). Contact your local post office for more information.

State Taxes and Fees

Separate filings are often necessary to obtain exemption from state income tax. The requirements vary from state to state. In some states it is also possible to obtain exemption from licensing fees, sales, use, franchise, and property taxes.

TIP

A nonprofit organization may be required to report to one or more states in relation to its exemption from or compliance with state income, sales, use, or property taxation. Many states accept a copy of Form 990 as adequate annual reporting for tax-exempt status purposes. Annual reporting to the state in which the organization is incorporated is normally required even if there is no requirement to file Form 990 with the IRS. Check with the offices of the secretary of state and attorney general to determine required filings.

UNITED STATES POSTAL SERVICE.

Application to Mail at Special Bulk Third-Class Rates

Section A—Application *(Please read section B on page 2 before completion.)*

Part 1 *(For completion by applicant)*

- All information entered below must be legible so that our records will show the correct information about your organization.
- The complete name of the organization must be shown in item 1. The name shown must agree with the name that appears on all documents submitted to support this application.
- A complete address representing a physical location for the organization must be shown in item 2. If you receive mail through a post office box, show your street address first and then the box number.
- The applicant named in item 5 must be the individual submitting the application for the organization and must be an officer of the organization. Printers and mailing agents may not sign for the organization.
- No additional organization categories may be added in item 6. To be eligible for the special rates, the organization must qualify as one of the types listed.
- The applicant must sign the application in item 12.
- The date shown in item 14 must be the date that the application is submitted to the post office.

No application fee is required. All information must be complete and typewritten or printed legibly.

1. Complete Name of Organization *(If voting registration official, include title)*
Chapel Hill Charity

2. Street Address of Organization *(Include apartment or suite number)*
300 South Hillcrest Avenue

3. City, State, ZIP+4 Code
Athens, OH 45701

4. Telephone *(Include area code)*
614-832-9061

5. Name of Applicant *(Must represent applying organization)*
Lewis E. Foster

6. Type of Organization *(Check only one)*

☒ (01) Religious ☐ (03) Scientific ☐ (05) Agricultural ☐ (07) Veterans' ☐ (09) Qualified political committee *(Go to item 9)*
☐ (02) Educational ☐ (04) Philanthropic ☐ (06) Labor ☐ (08) Fraternal ☐ (10) Voting registration official *(Go to item 9)*

7. Is this a for-profit organization or does any of the net income inure to the benefit of any private stockholder or individual? ☐ Yes ☒ No

8. Is this organization exempt from federal income tax? *(If 'Yes,' you must attach a copy of the exemption issued by the Internal Revenue Service that shows the section of the IRS code under which the organization is exempt. If an application for exempt status is pending with the IRS, you must check 'No.')* ☒ Yes ☐ No

9. Has this organization previously mailed at the special bulk rates? If 'Yes,' list the post offices where mailings were most recently deposited at these rates. ☐ Yes ☒ No

10. Has your organization had special bulk third-class rate mailing privileges denied or revoked? If 'Yes,' please list the post office (city and state) where the application was denied or authorization was revoked. ☐ Yes ☒ No

11. Post office (not a station or branch) where authorization requested and bulk mailings will be made *(City, state, ZIP Code)*

I certify that the statements made by me are true and complete. I understand that anyone who furnishes false or misleading information on this form or who omits material information requested on the form may be subject to criminal sanctions (including fines and imprisonment) and/or civil sanctions (including multiple damages and civil penalties).

I further understand that, if this application is approved, a postage refund for the difference between the regular and special bulk rates may be made for only those regular bulk third-class mailings entered at the post office identified above while this application is pending, provided that the conditions set forth in Domestic Mail Manual E370.5.0 and E370.9.0 are met.

12. Signature of Applicant
Lewis E. Foster

13. Title
Manager

14. Date
1/20/99

Part 2 *(For completion by postmaster at originating office when application filed)*

1. Signature of Postmaster *(Or designated representative)*

2. Date Application Filed With Post Office *(Round stamp)*

PS Form **3624,** January 1995 *(Page 1 of 3)*

Note: This form may be obtained at the post office where you wish to mail at special third-class bulk rates.

Do not send a list of major contributors to the state unless it is specifically required. While this list is not open to public inspection with respect to the federal filing, it may not be confidential for state purposes.

Property taxes

Church property is generally exempt from property tax. Whether real estate of a nonprofit organization is exempt from property tax usually depends on its use and ownership. Many states restrict the exemption of church property to property used for worship. It is also important to note that not all religious organizations are churches. Contact the office of the county tax assessor or collector to determine what property tax exemptions are available.

Parsonages are usually exempt from real estate tax. This is true though there may be several ministers on the staff of one church and therefore multiple parsonages. If the pastor owns the parsonage instead of the church, the parsonage is usually subject to property tax.

Church parking lots are usually exempt if properly recorded. It may be possible to obtain an exemption for vacant land. Property tax exemption of church camps and recreation facilities often comes under attack because of income that may be generated through their use. Property partially used for church use and partially leased to a third-party for-profit entity generally results in the proration of the tax exemption.

An initial (and perhaps annual) registration of the property with the proper state authorities is generally necessary to record exempt property. The initial purchase of real estate with notification of state authorities is usually not sufficient to exempt property from tax.

Sales taxes

There are presently four states with no sales tax law. In most states a nonprofit organization is exempt from sales tax as a purchaser of goods used in ministry. It is generally necessary to obtain recognition of sales tax exemption from the state revenue department. Some states will accept a federal tax-exemption as sufficient for a state sales tax exemption.

Even if an organization is exempt from paying sales tax, purchases used for the private benefit of the organization's members or employees are not eligible for exemption.

When a nonprofit organization sells goods to others, a sales tax may or may not be applicable. There are some indications that states may begin a stricter enforcement of laws on the books allowing them to impose sales tax on sales by nonprofit organizations. Occasional dinners and sales of goods at bazaars are typically exempt from sales tax.

Sales by a nonprofit within the state where the nonprofit is located are sometimes taxable. Sales to customers located outside of the state, or interstate sales, may not be subject to sales tax. A 1992 Supreme Court case cleared the way for

Congress to decide whether states can require organizations to collect state sales taxes on out-of-state mail order purchases. Until Congress acts, nonprofits may continue to ship publications and other taxable materials into states where they have no employees or other significant contacts without having to collect taxes.

When a nonprofit organization operates a conference or convention outside of its home state, it is often possible to obtain sales tax exemption for purchases made within the state where the meeting is held. Sales of products at the convention would generally be covered under sales tax laws without an approved exemption.

Use taxes

Besides sales taxes, many states also have use taxes. A use tax is imposed on the purchaser of a product or service. The use tax is designed to prevent avoidance of a local sales tax by buying property through the mail or in person in another state.

Churches and nonprofit organizations should determine whether they are subject to a use tax on various types of transactions.

Municipal service fees

Several states have recently proposed legislation to permit municipalities to impose "service fees" on property owned by tax-exempt organizations. Cities and counties would be authorized to collect a fee from tax-exempt property to pay for certain municipal services, typically fire and police protection, road construction and maintenance, and snow removal.

While the proposed legislation refers to the amounts to be collected as municipal service charges or fees, the assessments have the characteristics of property taxes. The fees are based on the value of property, not the services consumed. Property owners other than tax-exempt organizations would not be subject to the fees, yet would receive the same services.

Political Activity

Churches and other organizations exempt from federal income tax under section 501(c)(3) of the Internal Revenue Code are prohibited from participating or intervening, directly or indirectly, in any political campaign on behalf of or in opposition to any candidate for public office.

To avoid violating the political campaign provisions of the law:

- ✓ Do not use a rating program to evaluate candidates.
- ✓ Do not endorse a candidate directly or indirectly through a sermon, speech, newsletter, or sample ballot.
- ✓ Do not publish a candidate's statement.

ACTION STEPS 123

- ✓ Do not publish the names of candidates who agree to adhere to certain practices.
- ✓ Do not publish candidate responses to a questionnaire that evidences a bias on certain issues.
- ✓ Do not publish responses to an unbiased questionnaire focused on a narrow range of issues.
- ✓ Do not raise funds for a candidate.
- ✓ Do not provide volunteers, mailing lists, publicity, or free use of facilities unless all parties and candidates in the community receive the same services.
- ✓ Do not pay campaign expenses for a candidate.
- ✓ Do not distribute statements about candidates or display campaign literature on organization's premises.

If the IRS finds that an organization has engaged in these activities, it could result in a loss of exempt status. Also, the IRS may assess an excise tax on the amount of the funds spent on the activity.

Are there any political campaign activities that may legally be engaged in by a church or nonprofit? Forums or debates may be conducted to educate voters at which all candidates are treated equally, or a mailing list may be rented to candidates on the same basis as it is made available to others. Organizations may engage in voter registration or get-out-the-vote activities. However, it is wise to avoid defining a target group by political or ideological criteria (e.g., encouraging individuals to vote who are "registered Republicans").

Key Concepts

- Tax exemption is a privilege—not to be taken lightly.
- Churches are generally tax-exempt from federal income taxes without applying for this status.
- Most nonchurch organizations must apply for federal tax-exempt status.
- Churches and other nonprofits may be subject to the unrelated business income tax.
- Tax-exempt funds must not be diverted for personal use. This is called private inurement or benefit.
- Exemption from federal income tax does not automatically provide exemption from state taxes such as property, sales, and use tax.

CHAPTER THREE

Compensation Planning

In This Chapter

- Reasonable compensation
- Organization-provided housing
- Maximizing fringe benefits
- Nondiscrimination rules
- Paying employee expenses

Compensation plans should provide tax-effective benefits. A dollar of benefit costs to the organization may be multiplied when received by the employee as tax-free or tax-deferred.

Reasonable Compensation

Employees of churches and nonprofit organizations may receive reasonable compensation for their efforts. Excessive compensation can result in private inurement and may jeopardize the tax-exempt status of the organization. Reasonable compensation is based on what would ordinarily be paid for like services by a like organization under similar circumstances.

The intermediate sanction regulations impose penalties when a nonprofit organization provides excessive compensation or benefits to certain key employees and other individuals (see pages 7-8).

A review of the changes in the Consumers Price Index from one year to the next may be helpful when projecting salary increases:

1985	3.8%	1990	6.1%	1995	2.5%
1986	1.1%	1991	3.1%	1996	3.3%
1987	4.4%	1992	2.9%	1997	1.7%
1988	4.4%	1993	2.7%	1998	1.6%
1989	4.6%	1994	2.7%	1999	2.0% (est.)

Organization-Provided Housing

Nonminister employees

Housing provided to nonminister employees by a church or nonprofit organization for its convenience, as a condition of employment, and on its business premises is

- ✓ exempt from income tax and FICA tax withholding by the church; and
- ✓ excluded from wages reporting by the church and employee.

If these criteria are not met, the fair rental value should be reported as compensation on Form W-2 and is subject to withholding and FICA taxation.

Minister's housing allowance

Qualified ministers receive preferred treatment for their housing. If a minister has a home provided as part of compensation, the minister pays no income tax on the rental value of the home. If a home is not provided but the minister receives a rental or housing allowance, the minister pays no tax on the allowance if it is used for housing expenses subject to certain limitations.

Every minister should have a portion of salary designated as a housing allowance. For a minister living in organization-owned housing, the housing allowance may be only a modest amount to cover incidental expenses such as maintenance, furnishings, and utilities. But a properly designated housing allowance may be worth thousands of dollars in tax savings for ministers living in their own homes or rented quarters.

Ministers may exclude the housing allowance under the following rules:

- ✓ The allowance must be officially designated before payment by the organization. The designation should be evidenced in writing, preferably by resolution of the top governing body, in an employment contract, or, at a minimum, in the church budget and payroll records.

  If the only reference to the housing allowance is in the organization's budget, the budget should be formally approved by the top governing body.

- ✓ Only actual expenses can be excluded from income. The expenses must be paid from ministerial income earned in the current year.

For extensive coverage of the minister's housing allowance, see the 2000 edition of *The Zondervan Minister's Tax and Financial Guide.*

Sample Housing Allowance Resolutions

PARSONAGE OWNED BY OR RENTED BY A CHURCH

Whereas, The Internal Revenue Code permits a minister of the gospel to exclude from gross income "the rental value of a home furnished as part of compensation" or a church-designated allowance paid as a part of compensation to the extent that actual expenses are paid from the allowance to maintain a parsonage owned or rented by the church;

Whereas, Nelson Street Church compensates the senior minister for services in the exercise of ministry; and

Whereas, Nelson Street Church provides the senior minister with the rent-free use of a parsonage owned by (rented by) the church as a portion of the compensation for services rendered to the church in the exercise of ministry;

Resolved, That the compensation of the senior minister is $2,500 per month of which $200 per month is a designated housing allowance; and

Resolved, That the designation of $200 per month as a housing allowance shall apply until otherwise provided.

HOME OWNED OR RENTED BY MINISTER

Whereas, The Internal Revenue Code permits a minister of the gospel to exclude from gross income a church-designated allowance paid as part of compensation to the extent used for actual expenses in owning or renting a home; and

Whereas, Nelson Street Church compensates the senior minister for services in the exercise of ministry;

Resolved, That the compensation of the senior minister is $3,500 per month of which $1,250 per month is a designated housing allowance; and

Resolved, That the designation of $1,250 per month as a housing allowance shall apply until otherwise provided.

EVANGELISTS

Whereas, The Internal Revenue Code permits a minister of the gospel to exclude from gross income a church-designated allowance paid as part of compensation to the extent used in owning or renting a permanent home; and

Whereas, Nelson Street Church compensates Rev. John Doe for services in the exercise of ministry as an evangelist;

Resolved, That the honorarium paid to Rev. Doe shall be $1,512 consisting of $312 travel expenses (with documentation provided to the church), $500 housing allowance, and a $700 honorarium.

Maximizing Fringe Benefits

Personal use of employer-provided vehicles

Vehicles provided by organizations to employees for business use are often used for personal purposes. The IRS (see IRS Publication 535) treats most types of personal use of an employer-provided vehicle as a noncash fringe benefit, and generally requires the fair market value of such use to be included in the employee's gross income (to the extent that the value is not reimbursed to the employer).

If the employee reimburses the employer in a chargeback system for the full dollar value of the personal use, it will cost the employee more than if the employer includes the personal use value in the income of the employee.

Example: The personal use value of an automobile provided to a lay employee is determined to be $100; a chargeback system would require the employee to pay $100 to the employer. If, on the other hand, the employer includes the $100 in the employee's income, the employee will be subject to payroll taxes on $100 of income. Assuming a federal income tax rate of 28% and an FICA rate of 7.65% (based on annual gross pay of $72,600 or less for 1999), the total would be $35.65 compared with the $100 cash out-of-pocket chargeback.

Valuation of personal vehicle use

There are three special valuation rules, in addition to a set of general valuation principles, which may be used under specific circumstances for valuing the personal use of an employer-provided vehicle. This value must be included in the employee's compensation if it is not reimbursed by the employee.

Under the general valuation rule, the value is based on what the cost would be to a person leasing from a third party the same or comparable vehicle on the same or comparable terms in the same geographic area.

The special valuation rules, which are used by most employers, are:

✓ **Cents-per-mile valuation rule.** Generally, this rule may be used if the employer reasonably expects that the vehicle will be regularly used in the employer's trade or business, and if the vehicle is driven at least 10,000 miles a year and the vehicle is primarily used by employees. This valuation rule is available only if the fair market value of the vehicle, as of the date the vehicle was first made available for personal use by employees, does not exceed a specified value set by the IRS. For 1999, this value is $15,600.

The value of the personal use of the vehicle is computed by multiplying the number of miles driven for personal purposes by the current IRS standard mileage rate (31 cents per mile effective April 1, 1999). For this valuation rule, personal use is "any use of the vehicle other than use in the employee's trade or business of being an employee of the employer."

✓ **Commuting valuation rule.** This rule may be used to determine the value of personal use only where the following conditions are met:

- The vehicle is owned or leased by the employer and is provided to one or more employees for use in connection with the employer's trade or business and is used as such.
- The employer requires the employee to commute to and/or from work in the vehicle for bona fide noncompensatory business reasons. One example of a bona fide noncompensatory business reason is the availability of the vehicle to an employee who is on-call and must have access to the vehicle when at home.
- The employer has a written policy that prohibits employees from using the vehicle for personal purposes other than for commuting or de minimis personal use such as a stop for a personal errand on the way home from work.
- The employee required to use the vehicle for commuting is not a "control" employee of the employer. A control employee is generally defined as any employee who is an officer of the employer whose compensation equals or exceeds $50,000 or is a director of the employer whose compensation equals or exceeds $100,000.

The personal use of an employer-provided vehicle that meets the above conditions is valued at $1.50 per one-way commute.

✓ **Annual lease valuation rule.** Under this rule, the fair market value of a vehicle is determined and that value is used to determine the annual lease value amount by referring to an annual lease value table published by the IRS (see page 54). The annual lease value corresponding to this fair market value, multiplied by the personal use percentage, is the amount to be added to the employee's gross income. If the organization provides the fuel, 5.5 cents per mile must be added to the annual lease value. Amounts reimbursed by the employee are offset.

The fair market value of a vehicle owned by an employer is generally the employer's cost of purchasing the vehicle (including taxes and fees). The fair market value of a vehicle leased by an employer generally is either the manufacturer's suggested retail price less 8%, or the retail value as reported in a nationally recognized publication that regularly reports automobile retail values.

If the three special valuation rules described above do not apply, the value of the personal use must be determined by using a set of general valuation principles. Under these principles, the value must be generally equal to the amount that the employee would have to pay in a normal business transaction to obtain the same or comparable vehicle in the geographic area in which that vehicle is available for use.

ANNUAL LEASE VALUE TABLE

Fair Market Value of Car	Annual Lease Value	Fair Market Value of Car	Annual Lease Value
$0 - $999	$600	$19,000 - $19,999	$5,350
1,000 - 1,999	850	20,000 - 20,999	5,600
2,000 - 2,999	1,100	21,000 - 21,999	5,850
3,000 - 3,999	1,350	22,000 - 22,999	6,100
4,000 - 4,999	1,600	23,000 - 23,999	6,350
5,000 - 5,999	1,850	24,000 - 24,999	6,600
6,000 - 6,999	2,100	25,000 - 25,999	6,850
7,000 - 7,999	2,350	26,000 - 27,999	7,250
8,000 - 8,999	2,600	28,000 - 29,999	7,750
9,000 - 9,999	2,850	30,000 - 31,999	8,250
10,000 - 10,999	3,100	32,000 - 33,999	8,750
11,000 - 11,999	3,350	34,000 - 35,999	9,250
12,000 - 12,999	3,600	36,000 - 37,999	9,750
13,000 - 13,999	3,850	38,000 - 39,999	10,250
14,000 - 14,999	4,100	40,000 - 41,999	10,750
15,000 - 15,999	4,350	42,000 - 43,999	11,250
16,000 - 16,999	4,600	44,000 - 45,999	11,750
17,000 - 17,999	4,850	46,000 - 47,999	12,250
18,000 - 18,999	5,100	48,000 - 49,999	12,750

Federal income tax withholding on auto benefits

Withholding of federal income tax is required on auto benefits for lay employees unless the employee is notified that the employer elects not to withhold by January 31 of the calendar year to which the election applies or, if later, within 30 days after the employee is given the automobile. The notification must be provided in writing and the employer must still withhold social security taxes if required to normally do so. If withholding is provided, the employer can treat the compensation as regular wages subject to the regular withholding rates or as supplemental wages subject to a flat 20% rate.

Tax-sheltered annuities and 401(k) plans

Tax-sheltered annuities

Employees of churches and other nonprofit organizations may have a Section 403(b) salary reduction arrangement based on a written plan. These plans are also called tax-sheltered annuities (TSAs).

Both nonelective and elective employer contributions for a minister to a TSA are excludable for income and social security tax (SECA) purposes. Elective contributions for nonministers are subject to FICA. While permissible, after-tax employee contributions are the exception in TSAs.

There are three separate, yet interrelated, limitations on the amount of contributions to a TSA that are excludable from gross income. See the 2000 edition of *The Zondervan Minister's Tax & Financial Guide* for additional information on TSA contribution limitations.

Tax-Sheltered Annuity Agreement

In order to provide benefits for retirement, the Employee desires to have contributions made on his or her behalf to purchase a non-forfeited annuity contract from ________________ .

The Employer and Employee hereby agree that, with respect to the Employee's compensation for services rendered to the Employer commencing on the annual period ending ____________, 200__ such compensation shall be reduced by $_______ or ______% per ________________(period).

Each Employee shall ensure that the reduction in compensation shall in no event exceed the Employee's "exclusion allowance" as defined in Section 403(b)(2), or the limitation set forth in Section 415 and 402(g) of the Internal Revenue Code.

The Employee may, from time to time, by written instruction to the Employer, change from one division to another under the annuity contract.

This agreement must be amended by an instrument in writing signed by the Employer and the Employee and may be terminated by either the Employer or the Employee upon not less than 30 days' notice to the other. No designation or redesignation of investments or withdrawal shall be construed as an amendment or termination of this Agreement.

This Agreement is not a contract of employment between the parties hereto, and no provision hereof shall restrict the right of the Employer to discharge the Employee or the right of the Employee to terminate his or her employment.

Note: The above plan includes wording related to the stringent nondiscrimination rules. However, if your organization is a church or elementary or secondary school that is controlled, operated, or principally supported by a church or convention of association of churches, the nondiscrimination rules do not apply.

401(k) plans

A church or nonprofit organization may offer a 401(k) plan to its employees. Under a 401(k) plan, an employee can elect to have the church make tax-deferred contributions (up to $10,000 for 1999) to the plan.

401(k) and 403(b) Plans Compared

Provision	401(k)	403(b)
Federal taxation of employee salary reductions	Exempt from income tax Subject to FICA Exempt from SECA	Exempt from income tax Subject to FICA Exempt from SECA
State taxation of employee salary reductions	All states exempt employee salary reductions.	A few states tax employee salary reductions.
Roll-over available to 403(b) plan	No	Yes
Roll-over available to a pension plan or 401(k) plan, including plans of businesses	Yes	No
Roll-over available to IRA	Yes	Yes
Loans	Allowable, within certain limits	Allowable, within same limits as 401(k)
Calendar year maximum on elective deferral contributions	Lesser of percentage specified in plan document or statutory limit ($10,000 in 1999).	Generally, 20% of includable compensation, not to exceed statutory limit ($10,000 in 1999). NOTE: Catch-up elections allowing up to $12,500 annually are available to employees with over 15 years of service.
Per participant maximum on annual additions, including elective deferrals and employer matching contributions	Lesser of 25% of includable compensation or $30,000	Lesser of 25% of includable compensation or $30,000. Certain modifications can be made to this limitation.
Subject to exclusion allowance limit	No	Yes
Anti-discrimination testing	Two tests are required: One is for the employee's 401(k) portion of the plan and the other is for the employer's matching 401(m) portion of the plan. These tests can limit 401(k) contributions and matching contributions made on behalf of highly compensated employees. Churches are not exempt.	Only the employer's matching 401(m) portion of the plan is subject to an anti-discrimination test. Therefore, if no employer contributions are made, anti-discrimination testing is not required. Churches are exempt.
Subject to ERISA with its Form 5500 filing and other requirements	Yes, for most employers. Churches are exempt.	Any employer can avoid coverage by stringent non-involvement in plan. Churches are exempt.

Employer-provided dependent care assistance plan

A church or nonprofit organization can provide employees with child care or disabled dependent care services to allow employees to work. The amount excludable from tax is limited to the smaller of the employee's earned income, the spouse's earned income, or $5,000 ($2,500 if married filing separately).

The dependent care assistance must be provided under a separate written plan that does not favor highly compensated employees and that meets other qualifications (see sample plan below).

Dependent care assistance payments are excluded from income if the payments cover expenses that would be deductible by the employee as child and dependent care expenses on Form 2441 if the expenses were not reimbursed. If the employee is married, both spouses must be employed. There are special rules if one spouse is a student or incapable of self-care.

Sample Dependent Care Assistance Plan

Whereas, Willowbrook Church desires to establish a dependent care assistance plan under Section 129 of the Internal Revenue Code,

Resolved, That a dependent care assistance plan shall be established as follows:

1. The plan will not discriminate in favor of highly compensated employees.
2. Notification of the availability of the plan will be provided to all eligible employees.
3. Each year, on or before January 31, the plan will furnish to each employee a written statement showing the amounts paid or expenses incurred by the employer in providing dependent care assistance to such employee during the previous calendar year.
4. Dependent care assistance will be reported in Box 10 of Form W-2.
5. If dependent care assistance is provided to highly compensated employees, only those employees must include benefits provided under the plan in gross income.
6. Payments from the plan must be for expenses that would be deductible by the employee as child and dependent care expenses incurred to enable the employee to work.
7. The plan will only cover dependents of common-law employees of the church.
8. The exclusion for dependent care assistance payments is limited to $5,000 a year ($2,500 in the case of a married individual filing separately).
9. If child care services are provided on the premises of the church, the value of the services made available to the employee is excludable from income.

Resolved, That this dependent care assistance plan shall become effective on ____________, 200__.

Medical expense reimbursement plan

Organizations often provide benefit plans covering an employee's major medical expenses. Some plans even cover some dental and optometry expenses.

With even the best employee benefit plans, there are usually after-tax expenses that the employee must pay out-of-pocket. These expenses may relate to the plan deductible, co-insurance, or simply noncovered items.

A medical expense reimbursement plan (MERP) is an excellent way to pay expenses not covered under another employee benefit plan—tax-free! With a MERP, the employee merely submits the otherwise out-of-pocket medical bills to the organization and receives a reimbursement. Since the nondiscrimination rules apply to these plans, it is often wise to make the benefit available to all full-time employees. MERP payments to individuals that are self-employed for income tax purposes represent taxable income.

Here's how a medical reimbursement plan could work for your organization:

✓ **Determine the relation of the MERP to the compensation package and set any limits.** Determine if the medical reimbursement benefit will be handled as:

- strictly a salary reduction (for example, an employee chooses to have $50 withheld each month under the medical reimbursement plan and may submit documentation for medical expenses up to $600 per year for reimbursement), or
- funded by the employer in addition to present gross pay and fringe benefits (for example, the organization elects to pay up to $500 per year without any salary reduction), or
- salary reduction plus employer funding (for example, the employer agrees to pay $500 plus the employee has a salary reduction of $600 per year).

✓ **Formally adopt the plan.** The plan should be approved by the organization's top governing body annually based on the structure and amounts determined. This action would generally occur in December for the following year.

✓ **Reimburse expenses under the plan.** Employees submit documentation after the primary carrier has considered the claims. If a particular expense is noncovered under the primary plan, it could be submitted under the medical reimbursement plan without being denied by the carrier.

A MERP established with employee-provided funds is a "use it or lose it" concept. If the employee does not submit sufficient expenses in the course of a year to use up the amount set aside under the plan, the amount remaining in the plan cannot be paid over to the employee without causing all benefits paid under the plan to become taxable. Therefore, it is important that the employee estimate expenses conservatively.

Form 5500 (or 5500-C or 5500-R) must be filed for employee-funded MERPs. There is no filing requirement for employer-funded MERPs.

A medical reimbursement plan does require administrative effort to establish it, annually review it, and process claim payments. However, the benefit can easily save several hundreds of dollars per year for each employee.

Sample Medical Expense Reimbursement Plan

Whereas, Valley View Church desires to provide medical care benefits relating to expenses not covered under the medical policy of the Church;

Resolved, That Valley View Church establishes a Medical Expense Reimbursement Plan effective _______________, 200__ for the benefit of all full-time employees (working at least 30 hours or more per week) and their dependents (employee's spouse and minor children) under Section 105(b), (e) of the Internal Revenue Code;

Resolved, That medical reimbursement accounts shall be maintained for each full-time employee from which covered expenses (as defined in Section 213 of the Internal Revenue Code) for the employee or their dependents shall be reimbursed. Reimbursements to an employee shall not exceed $______ during one calendar year, plus any additional amount contributed by the employee under a written salary reduction agreement to the Plan for that year;

Resolved, That there shall be only one salary reduction election by each employee each year. This election may be changed during the year only in the following situations: (1) change in family status, e.g., marriage or divorce; birth, adoption, or death of a family member; (2) change of spousal employment status and/or health plan coverage; or (3) change in coverage under the employer's own health insurance policy;

Resolved, That the submission of medical expenses must be in a form and in sufficient detail to meet the requirements of the Church. Expenses may be submitted until March 31 for the previous calendar year. At that time, any balance remaining in an employee's account as of the end of the calendar year, shall be forfeited by the employee; and

Resolved, That the plan shall be administered in a nondiscriminatory manner and shall remain in effect until modified or terminated by a later resolution.

Note: The above plan is a combined employer-funded and employee salary reduction plan.

Compensation-related loans

Some churches and nonprofit organizations make loans to employees. The loans are often restricted to the purchase of land or a residence or the construction of a residence.

Before a loan is made, the organization should determine if the transaction is legal under state law. Such loans are prohibited in many states.

If an organization receives interest of $600 or more in a year relating to a loan secured by real estate, a Form 1098 (see page 91) must be provided to the payor. For the interest to be deductible as an itemized deduction, an employee loan must be secured by the residence and properly recorded.

If an organization makes loans to employees at below-market rates, the organization may be required to report additional compensation to the employee. If the loan is below $10,000, there is no additional compensation to the borrower. For loans over $10,000, additional compensation is calculated equal to the foregone interest that would have been charged if the loan had been made at a market rate of interest. The market rate of interest is the "applicable federal rate" for loans of similar duration. The IRS publishes these rates monthly. The additional compensation must be reported on Form W-2, Box 1.

There are certain exceptions to the general rules on below-market loans. These exceptions relate to loans secured by a mortgage and employee relocation loans.

Social security tax reimbursement

Churches and nonprofit organizations often reimburse ministers for a portion or all their self-employment tax (SECA) liability. Reimbursement also may be made to lay employees for all or a portion of the FICA tax that has been withheld from their pay. Any social security reimbursement must be reported as taxable income for both income and social security tax purposes. The FICA reimbursement to a lay employee is subject to income tax and FICA withholding.

Because of the deductibility of the self-employment tax in both the income tax and self-employment tax computations, a full reimbursement is effectively less than the gross 15.3% rate:

Marginal Tax Rate	Effective SECA Rate
0%	14.13%
15	13.07
28	12.15
31	11.94

For missionaries who are not eligible for the income tax deduction of one-half of the self-employment tax due to the foreign earned-income exclusion, the full reimbursement rate is effectively 14.13%.

It is usually best to reimburse an employee for self-employment tax on a monthly or quarterly basis. An annual reimbursement may leave room for misunderstanding between the organization and the employee if the employee is no longer employed at the time the reimbursement is due.

Property transfers

✓ **Unrestricted.** If an employer transfers property (for example, a car, residence, equipment, or other property) to an employee at no charge, this constitutes taxable income to the employee. The amount of income is generally the fair market value of the property transferred.

✓ **Restricted.** To recognize and reward good work, some churches or nonprofits transfer property to an employee subject to certain restrictions. The ultimate transfer will occur only if the employee lives up to the terms of the agreement. Once the terms are met, the property is transferred free and clear. Property that is subject to substantial risk of forfeiture and is nontransferable is substantially not vested. No tax liability will occur until title to the property is vested with the employee.

The exclusion is not an exemption from tax but is a deferral of tax. When restricted property becomes substantially vested, the employee must report the transfer as taxable income. The amount reported must be equal to the excess of the fair market value of the property at the time it becomes substantially vested, over the amount the employee pays for the property.

Example: A church transfers a house to the pastor subject to the completion of 20 years of service for the church. The pastor does not report any taxable income from the transfer until the 20th year.

✓ **Property purchased from employer.** If the employer allows an employee to buy property at a price below its fair market value, the employer must include in income as extra wages the difference between the property's fair market value and the amount paid and liabilities assumed by the employee.

Moving expenses

Moving expenses reimbursed by an employer, based on substantiation, are excludable from an employee's gross income. To qualify for this exclusion, the expenses must be deductible as moving expenses if they are not reimbursed.

The definition of deductible moving expenses is quite restrictive. Amounts are excludable only to the extent they would be deductible as moving expenses, i.e., only the cost of moving household goods and travel, other than meals, from the old residence to the new residence. Distance and timing tests must also be met.

Reimbursements to nonminister employees that do not exceed deductible moving expenses are not subject to withholding. However, excess payments are subject to FICA and federal income tax withholding. Nondeductible reimbursements to minister-employees are only subject to income tax withholding if a voluntary withholding agreement is in force.

Nondeductible payments to minister or nonminister employees must be included as taxable compensation, for income tax purposes, on Form W-2.

Reimbursements to a self-employed individual (for income tax purposes) are reportable on Form 1099-MISC and are not deductible for purposes of the social security calculation on Schedule SE.

Example: A church paid a moving company $2,200 in 1999 for an employee's move. The employer also reimbursed the employee $350. All of the expenses qualify as deductible moving expenses. The employer should report $350 on Form W-2, only in Box 13, using Code P. The $2,200 of expenses paid directly to the moving company are not reportable.

Allowances and other nonaccountable expense reimbursements

REMEMBER

Many organizations pay periodic allowances to employees for car expenses, library, entertainment, and so on. Other organizations reimburse employees for professional expenses with no requirement to account adequately for the expenses. This is a nonaccountable plan. Allowances or reimbursements under a nonaccountable plan must be included in the taxable income of the employee and are subject to income tax and FICA withholding for nonminister employees.

Gifts

All cash gifts to employees must be included in taxable compensation. Noncash gifts of nominal value to employees are tax-free. Gifts to certain non-employees up to $25 may be tax-free.

Nondiscrimination Rules

WARNING!

To qualify for exclusion from income, many fringe benefits must be nondiscriminatory. This is particularly true for many types of benefits for certain key employees. Failure to comply with the nondiscrimination rules does not disqualify a fringe benefit plan entirely. The benefit simply is fully taxable for the highly compensated or key employees.

The nondiscrimination rules apply to the following types of fringe benefit plans:

- ✓ qualified tuition and fee discounts,
- ✓ eating facilities on or near the employer's premises,

- ✓ educational assistance benefits,
- ✓ dependent care plans,
- ✓ tax-sheltered annuities (TSAs), 401(k) plans, and other deferred compensation plans,
- ✓ group-term life insurance benefits,
- ✓ self-insured medical plans, and
- ✓ cafeteria plans (including medical reimbursement plans).

Fringe benefit plans that limit benefits only to officers or highly compensated employees are clearly discriminatory. An officer is an employee who is appointed, confirmed, or elected by the board of the employer. A highly compensated employee for 1999 is

- ✓ paid more than $80,000, or
- ✓ if the employer elects, was in the top 20% of paid employees for compensation for the previous year.

Paying Employee Expenses

An accountable plan is a reimbursement or expense allowance arrangement that requires (1) a business purpose for the expenses, (2) employees to substantiate the expenses, and (3) the return of any excess reimbursements.

PLANNING IDEA

The substantiation of expenses and return of excess reimbursements must be handled within a reasonable time. The following methods meet the "reasonable time" definition:

- ✓ The fixed date method applies if
  - an advance is made within 30 days of when an expense is paid or incurred;
  - an expense is substantiated to the employer within 60 days after the expense is paid or incurred; and
  - any excess amount is returned to the employer within 120 days after the expense is paid or incurred.
- ✓ The periodic statement method applies if

Sample Accountable Expense Reimbursement Plan

Whereas, Income tax regulations provide that an arrangement between an employee and employer must meet the requirements of business connection, substantiation, and return of excess payments in order to be considered a reimbursement;

Whereas, Plans that meet the three requirements listed above are considered to be accountable plans, and the reimbursed expenses are generally excludable from an employee's gross compensation;

Whereas, Plans that do not meet all the requirements listed above are considered nonaccountable plans, and payments made under such plans are includable in gross employee compensation; and

Whereas, Poplar Grove Church desires to establish an accountable expense reimbursement policy in compliance with the income tax regulations;

Resolved, That Poplar Grove Church establish an expense reimbursement policy effective ________, 200__ whereby employees serving the church may receive advances for or reimbursement of expenses if

A. There is a stated business purpose of the expense related to the ministry of the church and the expenses would qualify for deductions for federal income tax purposes if the expenses were not reimbursed,

B. The employee provides adequate substantiation to the church for all expenses, and

C. The employee returns all excess reimbursements within a reasonable time.

and,

Resolved, That the following methods will meet the "reasonable time" definition:

A. An advance is made within 30 days of when an expense is paid or incurred;

B. An expense is substantiated to the church within 60 days after the expense is paid or incurred; or

C. An excess amount is returned to the church within 120 days after the expense is paid or incurred.

and,

Resolved, That substantiation of business expenses will include business purpose, business relationship (including names of persons present), cost (itemized accounting), time, and place of any individual nonlodging expense of $75 or more and for all lodging expenses. Auto mileage reimbursed must be substantiated by a daily mileage log separating business and personal miles. The church will retain the original copies related to the expenses substantiated.

Note: The above resolution includes the basic guidelines for an accountable expense reimbursement plan. If the employer desires to place a dollar limit on reimbursements to be made under the plan employee-by-employee, a separate resolution may be adopted for this purpose.

- the employer provides employees with a periodic statement that sets forth the amount paid under the arrangement in excess of substantiated expenses;
- statements are provided at least quarterly; and
- the employer requests that the employee provide substantiation for any additional expenses that have not yet been substantiated and/or return any amounts remaining unsubstantiated within 120 days of the statement.

If employees substantiate expenses and return any unused excess payments to the church or nonprofit organization, payments to the employee for business expenses have no impact on tax reporting. They are not included on Form W-2 for the employee or Form 1099-MISC for the self-employed. Although Section 179 expense deductions can be claimed by an employee on their Form 1040, Section 179 amounts are not eligible for reimbursement under an accountable expense reimbursement plan.

Nonaccountable expense reimbursement plans

If business expenses are not substantiated by the employee to the church or nonprofit organization, or if the amount of the reimbursement to the employee exceeds the actual expenses and the excess is not returned within a reasonable period of time, reporting is required.

Nonaccountable reimbursements and excess reimbursements over IRS limits must be reported as wages on Form W-2. They are generally subject to federal income tax and FICA withholding for employees other than ministers.

Accountable plans and the self-employed

Nonaccountable reimbursements and excess reimbursements over IRS limits paid to self-employed workers must be reported as compensation on Form 1099-MISC. No reporting to the IRS is required for accountable expense reimbursements to self-employed workers.

Reimbursement of an organization's operating expenses

The reimbursement of operating expenses of an organization should be distinguished from reimbursements of employee business expenses. Accountable expense reimbursement plans generally relate to payments for employee business expenses.

TIP

Many organizations set a limit on overall accountable expense plan reimbursements. If organization operating expenses are mixed with employee business expenses, the employee may be penalized.

Example: A minister uses personal funds to pay for the printing of the weekly church bulletin. This printing is a church operating expense, not an employee business expense. If the church has imposed an overall expense reimbursement limit on the minister, the inclusion of the bulletin printing in the employee reimbursement plan would improperly count these dollars against the plan limit.

Per diem allowance

The federal per diem rate, which is the sum of the federal lodging rate and meals and incidental expenses rate, is $185 for 1999 for the 52 high-cost areas and $115 per day for all other areas. The federal meals and incidental expense rate is $42 for the high-cost areas and $34 for any other locality. The federal lodging rate is $143 for the high-cost areas and $81 for other localities. Allowances that do not exceed these rates need not be reported to the IRS. Although no receipts are required, employees must document the date, place, and business purpose. The high-cost areas are identified in IRS Publications 463 and 1542.

Key Concepts

- Your organization will benefit from compensation planning as you try to stretch ministry dollars to cover personnel costs.
- Maximizing tax-free fringe benefits by adequate planning is vital for your employees.
- Proper use of the housing allowance for ministers who work for your organization is crucial.
- Do not ignore the nondiscrimination rules that apply to certain fringe benefits.
- The use of an accountable expense reimbursement plan for all employees of your organization is vital.

CHAPTER FOUR

Employer Reporting

In This Chapter

- The classification of workers
- Reporting compensation
- Payroll tax withholding
- Depositing withheld payroll taxes
- Filing the quarterly payroll tax forms
- Filing the annual payroll tax forms
- Refunds and abatements

The withholding and reporting requirements with which employers must comply are complicated. The special tax treatment of qualified ministers simply adds another level of complexity.

Churches and nonprofit organizations are generally required to withhold federal (and state and local, as applicable) income taxes and social security taxes, and pay employer social security tax on all wages paid to all full-time or part-time employees (except qualified ministers) who earn at least $100 during the year.

The Classification of Workers

KEY ISSUE

Whether an individual is classified as an employee or independent contractor has far-reaching consequences. This decision determines an organization's responsibility under the Federal Insurance Contributions Act (FICA), income tax withholding responsibilities, potential coverage under the Fair Labor Standards Act (see pages 185-86), and coverage under an employer's benefit plans. Misclassification can lead to significant penalties.

Questions frequently arise about the classification of certain nonprofit workers. Seasonal workers and those working less than full-time such as secretaries, custodians, and musicians require special attention for classification purposes. If a worker receives pay at an hourly rate, it will be difficult to justify independent contractor status. This conclusion would be true even if the workers are part-time.

Since 1935, the IRS has relied on 20 common law factors (see bottom of this page) to determine whether workers are employees or independent contractors. Pressure continues to build on Congress and the IRS to provide clearer guidance on who can be an independent contractor and when.

Employees

If a worker is a nonministerial employee, the employer must withhold federal income tax (and state income tax, if applicable) and Federal Insurance Contributions Act (FICA) taxes; match the employee's share of FICA taxes; and, unless exempted, pay unemployment taxes on employee's wages. In addition, the employer may incur obligations for employee benefit plans such as vacation, sick pay, health insurance, and pension plan contributions.

Among other criteria, employees comply with instructions, have a continuous relationship, perform work personally, work full- or part-time, are subject to dismissal, can quit without incurring liability, are often reimbursed for expenses, and must submit reports.

Independent contractors

If the worker is classified as an independent contractor, quarterly estimated income taxes and social security taxes under the Self-Employment Contributions Act (SECA) are paid by the worker. There is no unemployment tax liability or income or social security tax withholding requirement for independent contractors.

Independent contractors normally set the order and sequence of work, set their hours of work, work for others at the same time, are paid by the job, offer their services to the public, have an opportunity for profit or loss, furnish their tools, and may do work on another's premises, and there is often substantial investment by the worker.

Common law rules

The IRS generally applies the common law rules to decide if an individual is an employee or self-employed (independent contractor) for income tax purposes. Generally the individual is an employee if the employer has the legal right to control both what and how it is done, even if the individual has considerable discretion and freedom of action.

Workers are generally considered employees if they

- ✓ Must follow the organization's work instructions;
- ✓ Receive on-the-job training;

Independent Contractor Status Myths

- *Myth*: A written contract will characterize a person as an independent contractor.

  Fact: It is the substance of the relationship that governs.

- *Myth*: Casual labor or seasonal workers are independent contractors or their classification is a matter of choice.

  Fact: There is never a choice. The classification is determined by the facts and circumstances.

- *Myth*: If a person qualifies as an independent contractor for federal payroll tax purposes, he or she is automatically exempt for Workers' Compensation and state unemployment tax purposes.

  Fact: State Workers' Compensation and unemployment tax laws are often broader and an individual may actually be covered under these laws even though qualifying as an independent contractor for federal payroll tax purposes.

✓ Provide services that must be rendered personally;

✓ Provide services that are integral to the organization;

✓ Hire, supervise, and pay assistants for the organization;

✓ Have an ongoing work relationship with the organization;

✓ Must follow set hours of work;

✓ Work full-time for the organization;

✓ Work on the organization's premises;

✓ Must do their work in an organization-determined sequence;

✓ Receive business expense reimbursements;

✓ Receive routing payments of regular amounts;

✓ Need the organization to furnish tools and materials;

- ✓ Do not have a major investment in job facilities;
- ✓ Cannot suffer a loss from their services;
- ✓ Work for one organization at a time;
- ✓ Do not offer their services to the general public;
- ✓ Can be fired by the organization;
- ✓ May quit work at any time without penalty.

KEY ISSUE

Key issue: The amount of control and direction the church has over a worker's services is the most important overall issue. So some of the above factors may be given greater weight than others.

The classification of ministers

It is important that the organization decide if the services of ministers employed by the organization qualify for special tax treatment as ministerial services.

Special Tax Provisions for Ministers

- Exclusion for income tax purposes of the housing allowance and the fair rental value of a church-owned parsonage provided rent-free to clergy.
- Exemption of clergy from self-employment tax under very limited circumstances.
- Treatment of clergy (who do not elect social security exemption) as self-employed for social security tax purposes for income from ministerial services.
- Exemption of clergy compensation from mandatory income tax withholding.
- Eligibility for a voluntary income tax withholding arrangement between the minister-employee and the church.
- Potential double deduction of mortgage interest and real estate taxes as itemized deductions and as housing expenses for housing allowance purposes.

Most ordained, commissioned, or licensed ministers serving local churches will qualify for the above six special tax provisions with respect to services performed in the exercise of ministry. The IRS and courts apply certain tests to ministers serving local churches including whether the minister administers the sacraments, conducts worship services, is considered a spiritual leader by the church, and if the minister performs management services in the "control, conduct, or maintenance of a religious organization." It may not be necessary for a minister to meet all of these tests to qualify for the special tax treatment. For a complete discussion of this topic, see the 2000 edition of *The Zondervan Minister's Tax & Financial Guide.*

CROSS REFERENCE

Ordained, commissioned, or licensed ministers not serving local churches may qualify as ministers for federal tax purposes without meeting additional tests if their duties include the following:

- ✓ Administration of church denominations and their integral agencies, including teaching or administration in parochial schools, colleges, or universities that are under the authority of a church or denomination.
- ✓ Performing services for an institution that is not an integral agency of a church pursuant to an assignment or designation by ecclesiastical superiors, but only if the services relate to church purposes.

If a church does not assign or designate the minister's services, they will be qualified services only if they involve performing sacerdotal functions or conducting religious worship.

Sample Board Resolution for Ministerial Assignment

Whereas, ____Name of assigning church____ recognizes the calling of ____Name of minister assigned____ as a minister and is (ordained, licensed, or commissioned) and

Whereas, We believe that the assignment of ____Name of minister assigned____ will further the efforts and mission of our church and we desire to provide support and encouragement;

Resolved, That ____Name of minister assigned____ is hereby assigned to ____Name of ministry to which assigned____ effective ________, 200__ to serve as ____Position Title____ and

Resolved, That this assignment is made for a period of one year upon which time it will be reviewed and may be renewed, and

Resolved, That this assignment is contingent upon the quarterly submission of activity and financial reports by ____Name of minister assigned____ to our church.

Reporting Compensation

Minister-employees

Form W-2s are annually provided to minister-employees. There is no requirement to withhold income taxes, but they may be withheld under a voluntary agreement. Social security taxes are not withheld.

Nonminister-employees

If an employee does not qualify for tax treatment as a minister, the organization is liable to withhold and pay FICA and income taxes. Certain FICA tax exceptions are discussed later.

Nonemployees

A self-employed minister and other self-employed recipients of compensation should receive Form 1099-MISC instead of Form W-2 (if the person has received compensation of at least $600 for the year).

Payroll Tax Withholding

FICA social security

Most churches and nonprofit organizations must withhold FICA taxes from their employees' wages and pay it to the IRS along with the employer's share of the tax. Minister-employees are an exception to this rule. In 1999 both the employer and the employee pay a 6.2% tax rate on the social security wage base of up to $72,600. Similarly, both the employer and the employee pay a 1.45% medicare tax rate on all pay above $72,600. The rates remain the same for 2000. The 2000 social security wage base is estimated to be $76,800.

There are a few exceptions to the imposition of FICA. Generally wages of less than $100 paid to an employee in a calendar year are not subject to FICA. Services excluded from FICA include

- ✓ services performed by a minister of a church in the exercise of ministry or by a member of a religious order in the exercise of duties required by such order;
- ✓ services performed in the employ of a church or church-controlled organization that opposes for religious reasons the payment of social security taxes (see later discussion of filing Form 8274);

✓ services performed by a student in the employ of a school, college, or university.

Churches and church-controlled organizations opposed to social security taxes

In 1984 the law was changed to allow qualifying churches and church-controlled organizations to claim exemption from payment of FICA taxes. An organization must certify opposition "for religious reasons to the payment of employer social security taxes." Very few organizations qualify to file Form 8274.

Organizations in existence on September 30, 1984, were required to file Form 8274 by October 30, 1984. Any organization created after September 30, 1984, must file before the first date on which a quarterly employment tax return is due from the organization.

Organizations desiring to revoke their exemption made earlier by filing Form 8274 should file Form 941 with full payment of social security taxes for that quarter.

Federal income tax

Most nonprofit organizations are exempt from the payment of federal income tax on the organization's income (see page 36 for the tax on unrelated business income). But they must withhold and pay federal, state, and local income taxes on the wages paid to each employee. Minister-employees are an exception to this rule.

An employee-minister may have a voluntary withholding agreement with a church or nonprofit employer relating to the minister's income taxes. An agreement to withhold income taxes from wages must be in writing. There is no required form for the agreement. A minister may request voluntary withholding by submitting Form W-4 (Employee Withholding Allowance Certificate) to the employer indicating the additional amount to be withheld in excess of the tax table or the written request may be in another form.

TIP

The self-employed minister for income tax purposes reports and pays income taxes through the estimated tax (Form 1040-ES) procedure. There is no provision for federal income tax withholding from payments made to independent contractors, even on a voluntary basis.

Federal income taxes for all employees (except ministers) are calculated based on the chart and tables shown in IRS Publication 15. State and local income taxes are usually required to be withheld according to state withholding tables.

✓ **Form W-4.** All employees, part- or full-time, must complete a W-4 form. (Ministers are an exception to this requirement unless a voluntary withholding arrangement is used.) The withholding allowance information completed on this form gives the basis to determine the amount of income tax to be withheld.

All Form W-4s on which employees claim exempt status (and the

Form **W-4** — Department of the Treasury, Internal Revenue Service

Employee's Withholding Allowance Certificate

OMB No. 1545-0010 — **1999**

► For Privacy Act and Paperwork Reduction Act Notice, see page 2.

1 Type or print your first name and middle initial: Walter R. — Last name: Knight

2 Your social security number: 511 20 7943

Home address (number and street or rural route): 601 Oakridge Boulevard

3 ☐ Single ☒ Married ☐ Married, but withhold at higher Single rate.
Note: If married, but legally separated, or spouse is a nonresident alien, check the Single box.

City or town, state, and ZIP code: Vinton, VA 24179

4 If your last name differs from that on your social security card, check here. **You** must call 1-800-772-1213 for a new card . . . ► ☐

5 Total number of allowances you are claiming (from line H above or from the worksheets on page 2 if they apply) . . 5 | 4

6 Additional amount, if any, you want withheld from each paycheck . . . . . 6 | $

7 I claim exemption from withholding for 1999, and I certify that I meet **BOTH** of the following conditions for exemption:
- Last year I had a right to a refund of **ALL** Federal income tax withheld because I had **NO** tax liability **AND**
- This year I expect a refund of **ALL** Federal income tax withheld because I expect to have **NO** tax liability.

If you meet both conditions, write "EXEMPT" here . . . . . ► 7

Under penalties of perjury, I certify that I am entitled to the number of withholding allowances claimed on this certificate, or I am entitled to claim exempt status.

Employee's signature (Form is not valid unless you sign it) ► Walter R. Knight — **Date** ► 1/01/2000

8 Employer's name and address (Employer: Complete 8 and 10 only if sending to the IRS) — 9 Office code (optional) — 10 Employer identification number

Cat. No. 10220Q

Note: This form must be completed by all lay employees, full- or part-time by February 18 of each year. If a minister completes this form, it can be the basis to determine income tax withholding under a voluntary agreement.

Form **W-5** — Department of the Treasury, Internal Revenue Service

Earned Income Credit Advance Payment Certificate

OMB No. 1545-1342 — **1999**

► Use the current year's certificate only.
► Give this certificate to your employer.
► This certificate expires on December 31, 1999.

Type or print your full name: Daniel L. Wheeler — **Your social security number**: 304 78 6481

Note: *If you get advance payments of the earned income credit for 1999, you **must** file a 1999 Federal income tax return. To get advance payments, you **must** have a qualifying child and your filing status must be any status **except** married filing a separate return.*

		Yes	No
1	I expect to be able to claim the earned income credit for 1999, I do not have another Form W-5 in effect with any other current employer, and I choose to get advance EIC payments	X	
2	Do you have a qualifying child?	X	
3	Are you married?	X	
4	If you are married, does your spouse have a Form W-5 in effect for 1999 with any employer?		X

Under penalties of perjury, I declare that the information I have furnished above is, to the best of my knowledge, true, correct, and complete.

Signature ► Daniel L. Wheeler — **Date** ► 1/01/2000

Cat. No. 10227P

Note: This form should be completed if an employee elects to receive advance payments of the earned income credit.

employees' wages would normally exceed $200 weekly) or claim more than 10 withholding allowances must be filed with the IRS.

✓ **Form W-5.** An eligible employee uses Form W-5 to elect to receive advance payments of the earned income tax credit (EITC). Employees may be eligible for the EITC if their 1999 taxable and nontaxable earned income was less than $10,200 if there is no qualifying child; less than $26,928 if there is one qualifying child; or less than $30,580 if there are two or more qualifying children.

The portion of your housing allowance excluded from the Form W-2 and the fair rental value of church-provided housing must be included when calculating the EITC. Also includable are 403(b) and 401(k) voluntary tax-sheltered annuity deferrals.

If eligible for the earned income credit, an employee may choose to receive an advance instead of waiting until they file their annual Form 1040.

✓ **Form W-7.** Certain individuals who are not eligible for a social security number (SSN) may obtain an Individual Taxpayer Identification Number. The following individuals may file Form W-7: (1) nonresident aliens who are required to file a U.S. tax return, (2) nonresident aliens who are filing a U.S. tax return only to claim a refund, (3) individuals being claimed as dependents on U.S. tax returns and who are not eligible to obtain a social security number, (4) individuals being claimed as husbands or wives for exemptions on U.S. tax returns and who are not eligible to obtain a SSN, and (5) U.S. residents who must file a U.S. tax return but are not eligible for a SSN.

Self-employment tax

Self-employment taxes (SECA) should never be withheld from the salary of an employee. But under the voluntary withholding agreement for ministers' federal income taxes, additional federal income tax may be withheld sufficient to cover the minister's self-employment tax liability. When these withheld amounts are paid to the IRS, they must be identified as "federal income tax withheld" (and not social security taxes withheld).

Personal liability for payroll taxes

Church and nonprofit officers and employees may be personally liable if payroll taxes are not withheld and paid to the IRS. If the organization has willfully failed to withhold and pay the taxes, the IRS has the authority to assess a 100% penalty of withheld income and social security taxes.

This penalty may be assessed against the individual responsible for withholding and paying the taxes, even if the person is an unpaid volunteer such as a church treasurer.

Depositing Withheld Payroll Taxes

The basic rules for depositing payroll taxes are

✓ If your total accumulated and unpaid employment tax is less than $1,000 in a calendar quarter, taxes can be paid directly to the IRS when the organization files Form 941. These forms are due one month after the end of each calendar quarter.

✓ If payroll taxes are over $1,000 for a quarter, deposits must be made monthly or before the 15th day of each month for the payroll paid during the preceding month. Large organizations with total employment taxes of over $50,000 per year are subject to more frequent deposits. (See page 8 in the Recent Developments section for certain penalty relief provided by the IRS for organizations subject to electronic funds transfer requirements.)

To determine if an organization is a monthly depositor under the new rules, you must determine if the accumulated liabilities in the "look-back period" reached a threshold of $50,000. Those with an accumulated liability of less than $50,000 in the look-back period are generally monthly depositors (except those qualifying for quarterly deposits with liabilities of $1,000 or less).

A new organization (or one filing payroll tax returns for the first time) will be required to file monthly until a "look-back" period is established. A look-back period begins on July 1 and ends on June 30 of the preceding calendar year.

The cost of missing deposit deadlines can be very high. Besides interest, the organization can be hit with penalties at progressively stiffer rates. These range from 2% if you deposit the money within five days of the due date, to 15% if it is not deposited within 10 days of the first delinquency notice or on the day that the IRS demands immediate payment, whichever is earlier.

Deposit coupons

✓ **Form 8109.** Use Form 8109 deposit coupons to make deposits of the taxes covered by the following forms: Form 941, Form 990-T, and Schedule A.

The preprinted name and address of the organization and the Employer's Identification Number (EIN) appear on the coupons. Deliver or mail the completed coupon with the appropriate payment to a qualified depository for federal taxes.

✓ **Form 8109-B.** Use Form 8109-B deposit coupons to make tax deposits only in the following two situations:

- You have reordered preprinted deposit coupons (Form 8109) but have not yet received them.

- You are a new entity and have already been assigned an EIN, but have not yet received your initial supply of preprinted deposit coupons (Form 8109).

Form 8109-B may be obtained only from the IRS.

Filing the Quarterly Payroll Tax Forms

Employers must report covered wages paid to their employees by filing Form 941 with the IRS.

Form 941

Church and other nonprofit employers who withhold income tax and both social security and medicare taxes, must file Form 941 quarterly. There is no requirement to file Form 941 if your organization has not been required to withhold payroll taxes even if you have one or more employee-ministers (but without any voluntary withholding).

Most common errors made on Form 941

The IRS has outlined the most common errors discovered during the processing of Form 941, Employer's Quarterly Federal Tax Return, and the best way to avoid making these mistakes. A checklist for avoiding errors follows:

- ✓ Do not include titles or abbreviations, such as Dr., Mr., or Mrs.
- ✓ Make sure that taxable social security wages and the social security tax on line 6a, the social security tax on line 6b, and the taxable medicare wages and the medicare tax on line 7 are reported separately. Most employers will need to complete both lines 6a and 7.
- ✓ The preprinted form sent by the IRS should be used. If the return is prepared by a third-party preparer, make certain that the preparer uses exactly the name that appears on the preprinted form that was sent.
- ✓ Check the math for lines 5, 10, 13, and 14. Line 14 should always be the sum of lines 5, 10, and 13.
- ✓ Make sure the social security tax on line 6a is calculated correctly (12.4% x social security wages).
- ✓ Make sure the medicare tax on line 7 is calculated correctly (2.9% x medicare wages).
- ✓ Be sure to use the most recent Form 941 that the IRS sends. The IRS enters

Form **941** (Rev. January 1999)
Department of the Treasury
Internal Revenue Service

Employer's Quarterly Federal Tax Return

▶ See separate instructions for information on completing this return.

Please type or print.

Enter state code for state in which deposits were made ONLY if different from state in address to the right ▶ (see page 2 of instructions).

Name (as distinguished from trade name)	Date quarter ended	OMB No. 1545-0029
Barnett Ridge Church		T
Trade name, if any	Employer identification number	FF
		FD
Address (number and street)	City, state, and ZIP code	FP
P.O. Box 517	Selma, AL 36701	I
		T

If address is different from prior return, check here ▶ ☐

IRS Use: 1 1 1 1 1 1 1 1 1 1 2 3 3 3 3 3 3 3 3 4 4 4 5 5 5 / 6 7 8 8 8 8 8 8 8 8 9 9 9 9 9 10 10 10 10 10 10 10 10 10 10

If you do not have to file returns in the future, check here ▶ ☐ and enter date final wages paid ▶

If you are a seasonal employer, see **Seasonal employers** on page 1 of the instructions and check here ▶ ☐

1	Number of employees in the pay period that includes March 12th . ▶ 1		
2	Total wages and tips, plus other compensation	2	24,811
3	Total income tax withheld from wages, tips, and sick pay	3	4,642
4	Adjustment of withheld income tax for preceding quarters of calendar year	4	
5	Adjusted total of income tax withheld (line 3 as adjusted by line 4—see instructions)	5	4,642
6	Taxable social security wages . . . 6a 16,340 × 12.4% (.124) =	6b	2,026
	Taxable social security tips . . . 6c × 12.4% (.124) =	6d	
7	Taxable Medicare wages and tips . . . 7a 16,340 × 2.9% (.029) =	7b	474
8	Total social security and Medicare taxes (add lines 6b, 6d, and 7b). Check here if wages are not subject to social security and/or Medicare tax . . . ▶ ☐	8	2,500
9	Adjustment of social security and Medicare taxes (see instructions for required explanation) Sick Pay $ ____ ± Fractions of Cents $ ____ ± Other $ ____ =	9	
10	Adjusted total of social security and Medicare taxes (line 8 as adjusted by line 9—see instructions)	10	2,500
11	**Total taxes** (add lines 5 and 10)	11	7,142
12	Advance earned income credit (EIC) payments made to employees	12	
13	Net taxes (subtract line 12 from line 11). **If $1,000 or more, this must equal line 17, column (d) below (or line D of Schedule B (Form 941))**	13	7,142
14	Total deposits for quarter, including overpayment applied from a prior quarter	14	7,142
15	**Balance due** (subtract line 14 from line 13). See instructions	15	0
16	**Overpayment.** If line 14 is more than line 13, enter excess here ▶ $ ____ and check if to be: ☐ Applied to next return **OR** ☐ Refunded.		

- **All filers:** If line 13 is less than $1,000, you need not complete line 17 or Schedule B (Form 941).
- **Semiweekly schedule depositors:** Complete Schedule B (Form 941) and check here . . . ▶ ☐
- **Monthly schedule depositors:** Complete line 17, columns (a) through (d), and check here . . . ▶ ☐

17 Monthly Summary of Federal Tax Liability. Do not complete if you were a semiweekly schedule depositor.

(a) First month liability	(b) Second month liability	(c) Third month liability	(d) Total liability for quarter
2,603	2,548	1,991	7,142

Sign Here Under penalties of perjury, I declare that I have examined this return, including accompanying schedules and statements, and to the best of my knowledge and belief, it is true, correct, and complete.

Signature ▶ Alan W. Dunn Print Your Name and Title ▶ Alan W. Dunn, Treas. Date ▶ 4/30/00

For Privacy Act and Paperwork Reduction Act Notice, see back of form. Cat. No. 17001Z Form **941** (Rev. 1-99)

Note: File this form to report social security (FICA) and medicare taxes and federal income tax withheld.

Form **941c** (Rev. October 1996) Department of the Treasury Internal Revenue Service

Supporting Statement To Correct Information

Do Not File Separately

▶ **File with Form 941, 941-M, 941-SS, 943, 945, or 843.**

OMB No. 1545-0256

Page No.

Name: Little Valley Church

Employer identification number: 35-6309294

Telephone number

A This form supports adjustments to: **Check one box.**
[X] Form 941 [ ] Form 941-SS [ ] Form 945
[ ] Form 941-M [ ] Form 943

B This form is filed with the return for the period ending (month, year) ▶ 3/31/00

C Enter the date you discovered the error(s) reported on this form. (If you are making more than one correction and the errors were not discovered at the same time, please explain in Part V.) ▶ 3/1/00

Part I Signature and Certification (You **MUST** complete this part for the IRS to process your adjustments for overpayments.) Skip Part I if all your adjustments are underpayments. (See the instructions for Part I.)

I certify that **Forms W-2c**, Corrected Wage and Tax Statement, have been filed (as necessary) with the Social Security Administration, and that (check appropriate boxes):

[ ] All overcollected income taxes for the current calendar year and all social security and Medicare taxes for the current and prior calendar years have been repaid to employees. For claims of overcollected employee social security and Medicare taxes in earlier years, a written statement has been obtained from each employee stating that the employee has not claimed and will not claim refund or credit of the amount of the overcollection.

[ ] All affected employees have given their written consent to the allowance of this credit or refund. For claims of overcollected employee social security and Medicare taxes in earlier years, a written statement has been obtained from each employee stating that the employee has not claimed and will not claim refund or credit of the amount of the overcollection.

[ ] The social security tax and Medicare tax adjustments represent the employer's share only. An attempt was made to locate the employee(s) affected, but the affected employee(s) could not be located or will not comply with the certification requirements.

[ ] None of this refund or credit was withheld from employee wages.

Sign Here Signature ▶ Curtis R. Lee Title ▶ Treasurer Date ▶ 4/30/00

Part II Income Tax Withholding (Including Backup Withholding) Adjustment

	(a) Period Corrected (For quarterly returns, enter date quarter ended. For annual returns, enter year.)	(b) Withheld Income Tax Previously Reported for Period	(c) Correct Withheld Income Tax for Period	(d) Withheld Income Tax Adjustment
1	12/31/99	400	600	200
2				
3				
4				

5 Net withheld income tax adjustment. If more than one page, enter total of ALL columns (d) on first page only. Enter here and on the **appropriate** line of the return with which you file this form ▶ 5 — 200

Part III Social Security Tax Adjustment (Use the tax rate in effect during the period(s) corrected. You must also complete Part IV.)

	(a) Period Corrected (For quarterly returns, enter date quarter ended. For annual returns, enter year.)	(b) Wages Previously Reported for Period	(c) Correct Wages for Period	(d) Tips Previously Reported for Period	(e) Correct Tips for Period	(f) Social Security Tax Adjustment
1	12/31/99	2000	4500			155
2						
3						
4						
5	Totals. - If more than one page, enter totals on first page only ▶					

6 Net social security tax adjustment. If more than one page, enter total of **ALL** columns (f) on first page only. Enter here and on the appropriate line of the return with which you file this form ▶ 6 — 155

7 Net wage adjustment. If more than one page, enter total of **ALL** lines 7 on first page only. If line 5(c) is smaller than line 5(b), enter difference in parentheses ▶ 7 — 2500

8 Net tip adjustment. If more than one page, enter total of **ALL** lines 8 on first page only. If line 5(e) is smaller than line 5(d), enter difference in parentheses ▶ 8

For Paperwork Reduction Act Notice, see page 3. Form **941c** (Rev. 10-96)

Note: Use this form to correct income, social security (FICA), and medicare tax information reported on Form 941. It may be necessary to issue Form W-2c to employees relating to prior year data.

the date the quarter ended after the employer identification number. If the form is used for a later quarter, the IRS will have to contact the employer.

- ✓ Make sure there is never an entry on both lines 18 and 19. There cannot be a balance due and a refund.

Form 941c

Form 941c may be used to correct income, social security, and medicare tax information reported on Forms 941, 941-M, 941SS, or 943. Attach it to the tax return on which you are claiming the adjustment (Form 941, and so on) or to Form 843, Claim for Refund and Request for Abatement. Also issue the employee(s) a Form W-2c for the prior year, if applicable.

Filing the Annual Payroll Tax Forms

Form W-2

By January 31 each employee must be given a Form W-2. To help you in the completion of the 1999 version of the Form W-2, an explanation of certain boxes is provided. For additional help, call 304–263–8700.

Be sure to reconcile the data reflected on Forms W-2, W-3, and 941 before distributing Form W-2s to employees. If these forms do not reconcile, the IRS generally sends a letter to the employer requesting additional information.

Void—Put an X in this box when an error has been made on this W-2.

Box 1—Wages, tips, other compensation. Items to include in Box 1 before any payroll deductions are

- ✓ total wages paid during the year (including love offerings paid by the church or nonprofit organization to a minister or other employee);
- ✓ the value of noncash payments, including taxable fringe benefits;
- ✓ business expense payments under a nonaccountable plan;
- ✓ payments of per diem or mileage allowance paid for business expense purposes that exceed the IRS specified rates;
- ✓ payments made by a church or nonprofit organization to an employee's Individual Retirement Plan;
- ✓ payments for nonexcludable moving expenses;

Checklist for Completing Box 1 of Form W-2

Data Included for Minister Only	Both	Nonminister Only	
	yes		Salary
no		yes	Housing/furnishings allowance (designated in advance)
no		yes	Parsonage rental value
no		yes	Utilities paid by church or nonprofit
	yes		Social security/medicare "allowance" or reimbursement
	no		Transportation/travel and other business and professional expense reimbursements *only if* paid under a board-adopted accountable reimbursement plan
	yes		"Reimbursements" if not paid under an accountable reimbursement plan
	yes		Love offerings or cash gifts in excess of $25
	no		Contributions to a tax-sheltered annuity plan
	no		Health/dental/long-term care insurance premiums paid directly or reimbursed by the employer
	no		Group term life insurance premiums (for up to $50,000 coverage) paid directly by the employer
	no		Excludable moving expense paid for or reimbursed to an employee
	yes		Nonexcludable moving expenses paid for or reimbursed to an employee
	yes		Value of personal and nonbusiness use of organization's vehicle

- ✓ all other compensation, including taxable fringe benefits. "Other compensation" represents amounts an organization pays to an employee from which federal income tax is not withheld. If you prefer, you may show other compensation on a separate Form W-2; and
- ✓ the cash housing allowance or the fair market rental value of housing and utilities must be reported as taxable income for lay employees unless furnished on the employer's premises and the employee is required to accept the lodging as a condition of employment.

Exclude the following:

- ✓ the fair rental value of a church-provided parsonage or a properly designated housing allowance for ministers;
- ✓ auto or business expense reimbursements paid through an accountable expense plan; and
- ✓ contributions to 403(b) tax-sheltered annuities or 401(k) plans.

a Control number	22222	Void ☐	For Official Use Only ▶ OMB No. 1545-0008

b Employer identification number 35-2946039	1 Wages, tips, other compensation 14586.00	2 Federal income tax withheld 2039.00
c Employer's name, address, and ZIP code ABC Charity 2670 N. Hull Road Traverse City, MI 49615	3 Social security wages 15786.00	4 Social security tax withheld 979.00
	5 Medicare wages and tips 15786.00	6 Medicare tax withheld 229.00
	7 Social security tips	8 Allocated tips
d Employee's social security number 517-28-6451	9 Advance EIC payment	10 Dependent care benefits
e Employee's name (first, middle initial, last) Michael A. Black	11 Nonqualified plans	12 Benefits included in box 1
15550 Cleveland Avenue Traverse City, MI 49615	13 See instrs. for box 13 E 1200.00 P 984.73	14 Other
f Employee's address and ZIP code	15 Statutory employee ☐ Deceased ☐ Pension plan ☐ Legal rep. ☐ Deferred compensation ☐	

16 State	Employer's state I.D. no.	17 State wages, tips, etc.	18 State income tax	19 Locality name	20 Local wages, tips, etc.	21 Local income tax
MI	6309294	15786.00	205.00			

Form **W-2** Wage and Tax Statement **1999**

Department of the Treasury—Internal Revenue Service

For Privacy Act and Paperwork Reduction Act Notice, see separate instructions.

Copy A For Social Security Administration—Send this entire page with Form W-3 to the Social Security Administration; photocopies are **not** acceptable.

Cat. No. 10134D

Box 2—Federal income tax withheld. Enter the total federal income tax withheld according to the chart and tables in IRS Publication 15.

A qualified minister may enter into a voluntary withholding arrangement with the employing organization. Based on Form W-4 or other written withholding request, federal income tax withholding may be calculated from the chart and tables in Publication 15 excluding any housing allowance amount.

The minister may request that an additional amount of income tax be withheld to cover self-employment tax. The additional amount withheld is reported as income tax withheld on the quarterly Form 941 and in Box 2 of Form W-2.

An organization that provides additional compensation to the employee-minister to cover part or all of the self-employment tax liability may:

- ✓ pay the additional compensation directly to the IRS by entering that amount on the organization's Form 941 and in Boxes 1 and 2 of Form W-2, or
- ✓ pay the additional compensation to the minister with the minister being responsible for remitting the amounts to the IRS with a Form 1040-ES. If this procedure is followed, the organization reports this amount only as additional compensation on Form 941 and only in Box 1 of Form W-2.

Box 3—Social security wages. Show the total wages paid (before payroll deductions) subject to employee social security tax (FICA). This amount must not exceed $72,600 in 1999 (the maximum social security tax wage base). Generally all cash and noncash payments reported in Box 1 must also be shown in Box 3. Include non-accountable employee business expenses reported in Box 1. Voluntary salary reduction tax-sheltered annuity contributions for nonminister employees are included in Box 3.

Box 3 should be blank for qualified ministers.

Box 4—Social security tax withheld. Show the total FICA social security tax (not including the organization's share) withheld or paid by you for the employee. The amount shown must equal 6.2% of the amount in Box 3 and must not exceed $4,501.20 for 1999. Do not include the matching employer FICA tax.

Some organizations pay the employee's share of FICA tax for some or all non-minister employees instead of deducting it from the employee's wages. These amounts paid by the organization must be included in Boxes 1, 3, and 5 as wages and proportionately in Boxes 4 and 6 as social security and medicare tax withheld. In these instances, the effective cost to the employer is 8.28% instead of 7.45% for wages up to $72,600 and 1.47% rather than 1.45% for wages above $72,600.

Box 4 should be blank for qualified ministers. Any amount of withholding to meet the minister's SECA tax liability must be reported in Box 2, not in Box 4 or Box 6.

Box 5—Medicare wages. The wages subject to medicare tax are the same as those subject to social security tax (Box 3), except there is no wage limit for the medicare tax.

Example: You paid a nonminister employee $74,000 in wages. The amount shown in Box 3 (social security wages) should be $72,600, but the amount shown in Box 5 (Medicare wages) should be $74,000. If the amount of wages paid was less than $72,600, the amounts entered in Boxes 3 and 5 will be the same.

Box 5 should be blank for qualified ministers.

Box 6—Medicare tax withheld. Enter the total employee medicare tax (not your share) withheld or paid by you for your employee. The amount shown must equal 1.45% of the amount in Box 5. Box 6 should be blank for qualified ministers.

Box 9—Advance EIC payment. Show the total paid to the employee as advance earned income credit payments.

Box 10—Dependent care benefits. Show the total amount of dependent care benefits under Section 129 paid or incurred by you for your employee including any amount over the $5,000 exclusion. Also include in Box 1, Box 3, and Box 5 any amount over the $5,000 exclusion.

Box 11—Nonqualified plans. Enter the total amount of distributions to the employee from a nonqualified deferred compensation plan. Include an amount in Box 11 only if it is also includable in Box 1 or Boxes 3 and 5.

Box 12—Benefits included in Box 1. Show the total value of the taxable fringe benefits included in Box 1 as other compensation.

If the organization owns or leases a vehicle for an employee's use, the value of the personal use of the vehicle is taxable income. The value of the use of the vehicle is established by using one of the methods described on pages 56-58. The amount of the personal use must be included in Boxes 1 and 12 (and in Boxes 3 and 5 if a lay employee). The employee is required to maintain a mileage log or similar records to substantiate business and personal use of the vehicle and submit this to the employer. If not substantiated, the employer must report 100 percent of the use of the vehicle as taxable income.

If the employee fully reimburses the employer for the value of the personal use of the vehicle, then no value would be reported in either Box 1 or in Box 12.

Box 13—Additional entries. The following items are most frequently inserted in Box 13 by churches and other nonprofit organizations:

C—Group-term life insurance. If you provided your employee more than $50,000 of group-term life insurance, show the cost of the coverage over $50,000. Also include the amount in Box 1 (also in Boxes 3 and 5 if a lay employee).

D—Section 401(k) cash or deferred arrangement.

E—Section 403(b) voluntary salary reduction agreement to purchase an annuity contract. This amount would not be included in Box 1 for either ministerial or lay employees. This amount would be included in Boxes 3 and 5 for a lay employee.

F—Section 408(k)(6) salary reduction simplified employee pension (SEP).

L—Generally payments made under an accountable plan are excluded from the employee's gross income and are not required to be reported on Form W-2. But if you pay a per diem or mileage allowance, and the amount paid exceeds the amount substantiated under IRS rules, you must report as wages on Form W-2 the amount in excess of the amount substantiated. Report the amount treated as substantiated (the nontaxable portion) in Box 13. In Box 1, show the portion of the reimbursement that is more than the amount treated as substantiated. For lay employees the excess amount is subject to income tax withholding, social security tax, medicare tax, and possibly federal unemployment tax.

P—Qualified moving expenses paid directly to an employee must be reported on Form W-2, only in Box 13, using Code P. Report nonqualified moving expense reimbursements and payments in Box 1 for either ministerial or lay employees. This amount is included in Boxes 3 and 5 for lay employees.

R—Employer contributions to a medical savings account.

S—Salary reductions to a savings incentive match plan for employees with a SIMPLE retirement account.

T—Employer payments under an adoption assistance plan.

Do not include any per diem or mileage allowance or other reimbursements for employee business expenses in Boxes 1 or 13 if the total reimbursement is less than or equal to the amount substantiated.

Example 1: An employee receives mileage reimbursement at the rate of 31 cents per mile effective April 1, 1999, and substantiates the business miles driven to the organization. The mileage reimbursement is not reported on Form W-2.

Example 2: An employee receives a mileage allowance of $2,000 per year and does not substantiate the business miles driven. The $2,000 allowance is includable in Box 1 as compensation for a minister and Boxes 1, 3, and 5 for a lay employee. The business mileage is deductible as a miscellaneous deduction on the employee's Schedule A, subject to limitations.

Payments made to nonminister employees under a nonaccountable plan are reportable as wages on Form W-2 and are subject to income tax withholding, social security tax, medicare tax, and possibly federal unemployment tax.

Payments made to minister-employees under a nonaccountable plan are reportable as wages on Form W-2 and may be subject to income tax withholding under a voluntary agreement, but are not subject to mandatory withholding or social security (FICA) or medicare tax.

Box 14—Other. You may use this box for any other information you want to give your employee. Label each item and include information such as health insurance premiums deducted or educational assistance payments.

The minister's housing allowance could be included in this box with the words "Housing Allowance." However, some organizations prefer to provide the minister with a separate statement reflecting the housing allowance amount.

Box 15—Check the appropriate boxes. The boxes that apply to employees of churches and nonprofit organizations are:

Pension plan. Check this box if the employee was an active participant (for any part of the calendar year) in a retirement plan (including a 401(k) plan and a simplified employee pension plan) maintained by the organization. An employee is an active participant for purposes of this box if the employee participated in a Section 401(a) qualified plan, Section 403(a) qualified annuity plan (nonvoluntary contributions), Section 403(b) annuity contract or custodial account, Section 408(k) simplified employee pension, or Section 501(c)(18) trust.

Subtotal. Check this box only when submitting 42 or more Forms W-2.

Deferred compensation. Check this box if you made contributions for the employee to a Section 403(b) annuity contract or custodial account (voluntary salary reduction), Section 408(k)(6) salary reduction (SEP), Section 457 deferred compensation plan, or Section 501(c)(18)(D) trust.

DO NOT STAPLE

a Control number	33333	For Official Use Only ▶ OMB No. 1545-0008

b Kind of Payer ▶ 941 [X] Military [ ] 943 [ ] CT-1 [ ] Hshld. emp. [ ] Medicare govt. emp. [ ]

1 Wages, tips, other compensation 243987.00	2 Federal income tax withheld 29142.00
3 Social security wages 236431.00	4 Social security tax withheld 14659.00
5 Medicare wages and tips 243987.00	6 Medicare tax withheld 3538.00
7 Social security tips	8 Allocated tips
9 Advance EIC payments	10 Dependent care benefits
11 Nonqualified plans	12 Deferred compensation
13	
14	
15 Income tax withheld by third-party payer	

c Total number of Forms W-2

d Establishment number

e Employer identification number
35-2946039

f Employer's name
ABC Charity

2760 N. Hull Road
Traverse City, MI 49615

g Employer's address and ZIP code

h Other EIN used this year

i Employer's state I.D. no.

Contact person	Telephone number	Fax number	E-mail address
	( )	( )	

Under penalties of perjury, I declare that I have examined this return and accompanying documents, and, to the best of my knowledge and belief, they are true, correct, and complete.

Signature ▶ Daniel L. Lewis Title ▶ Treasurer Date ▶ 1/31/00

Form **W-3 Transmittal of Wage and Tax Statements** 1999 Department of the Treasury Internal Revenue Service

Send this entire page with the entire Copy A page of Forms W-2 to the Social Security Administration. Photocopies are NOT acceptable.
Do not send any remittance (cash, checks, money orders, etc.) with FORMS W-2 and W-3.

---

a Year/Form corrected 1999 / W-2	Void [ ]	OMB No. 1545-0008

b Employee's name, address, and ZIP code [ ] Corrected Name	c Employer's name, address, and ZIP code
Norman R. Tice 418 Trenton Street Springfield, OH 45504	Little Valley Church 4865 Douglas Road Springfield, OH 45504

d Employee's correct SSN	e Employee's SSA number	f Employer's Federal EIN	g Employer's state I.D. number
304-64-7792	69-	35-6309294	

h Previously reported ▶ Stat. emp. [ ] De-ceased [ ] Pension plan [ ] Legal rep. [ ] Def'd. comp. [ ] Hshld. emp. [ ]
i Corrected ▶ Stat. emp. [ ] De-ceased [ ] Pension plan [ ] Legal rep. [ ] Def'd. comp. [ ] Hshld. emp. [ ]
j Employer's use

Complete k and/or l **only** if **incorrect** on the last form you filed. Show **incorrect** item here. ▶ k Employee's **incorrect** SSN | l Employee's name (as **incorrectly** shown on previous form)

CHANGES

Form W-2 box	(a) As previously reported	(b) Correct information	(c) Increase (decrease)
1 Wages, tips, other comp.	10000.00	12500.00	2500.00
2 Federal income tax withheld	1800.00	2000.00	200.00
3 Social security wages	10000.00	12500.00	2500.00
4 Social security tax withheld	620.00	775.00	155.00
5 Medicare wages and tips	10000.00	12500.00	2500.00
6 Medicare tax withheld	145.00	181.25	36.25
7 Social security tips			
8 Allocated tips			
State wages, tips, etc.			
State income tax			
Local wages, tips, etc.			
Local income tax			

Form **W-2c** (Rev. 1-99) **Corrected Wage and Tax Statement** **Copy 1 For State, City, or Local Tax Department** Department of the Treasury Internal Revenue Service

Form W-3

A Form W-3 is submitted to the IRS as a transmittal form with Form W-2s. Form W-3 and all attached W-2s must be submitted to the Social Security Administration Center by February 28. No money is sent with Form W-3.

Form W-2c

Use Form W-2c to correct errors on a previously filed Form W-2.

Form W-3c

Use Form W-3c to transmit corrected W-2c forms to the Social Security Administration.

Unemployment taxes

The federal and state unemployment systems provide temporary unemployment compensation to workers who have lost their jobs. Employers provide the revenue for this program by paying federal unemployment taxes, under the Federal Unemployment Tax Act (FUTA), and state unemployment taxes. These are strictly employer taxes and no deductions are taken from employees' wages.

The current federal unemployment tax law exempts from coverage

- ✓ services performed in the employ of a church, a convention, or association of churches or an organization that is operated primarily for religious purposes and that is operated, supervised, controlled, or principally supported by a church or convention or association of churches;
- ✓ services performed by a duly ordained, commissioned, or licensed minister of a church in the exercise of ministry or by a member of a religious order in the exercise of duties required by such order.

States may expand their coverage of unemployment taxes beyond the federal minimum. In many states, exemption is also provided for

- ✓ services performed in the employ of a separately incorporated church school if the school is operated primarily for religious purposes and is operated, supervised, controlled, or principally supported by a church or convention or association of churches;
- ✓ services performed in the employ of an unincorporated church-controlled elementary or secondary school.

Recent court cases reflect attempts by states to subject religious organizations, including churches, to state unemployment taxes.

FUTA reporting requirements

Nonprofit organizations that are liable for FUTA taxes are required to file Form 940, or 940-EZ Employer's Annual Federal Unemployment Tax Return. This form covers one calendar year and is due on or before January 31. Tax deposits may be required before filing the annual return. You must use Form 8109, Federal Tax Deposit Coupon, when making each federal unemployment tax deposit.

The taxable wage base under the Federal Unemployment Tax Act is $7,000 for 1999. The gross FUTA tax rate is 6.2% for 1999. The credit against FUTA tax for payments to state unemployment funds remains at a maximum 5.4%. The net rate is 0.8%. There are no states with credit reductions for 1999, so employers in all states pay FUTA taxes at the net rate of 0.8% for 1999. The 0.2% FUTA surtax has been extended through 1999.

Refunds and Abatements

In certain instances, Form 843, Claim for Refund and Request for Abatement, is used to file a claim for refund of overpaid taxes, interest, penalties, and additions to tax.

Example 1: On your employment tax return you reported and paid more federal income tax than you withheld from an employee. Use Form 843 to claim a refund.

Example 2: The IRS assessed penalties or interest relating to your employment tax return. You paid the penalties or interest. You later realized that the penalties or interest had been incorrectly calculated or assessed. Use Form 843 to file a claim for refund.

Key Concepts

- The proper classification of all your workers as employees or self-employed is a crucial matter for both your organization and the workers.
- Understanding the special tax treatments for ministers is very important.
- The failure to timely file and pay payroll taxes will leave your organization open to scrutiny by the IRS.
- Reporting all taxable compensation to the IRS requires considerable understanding of the tax laws and regulations.

CHAPTER FIVE

Information Reporting

In This Chapter

- General filing requirements
- Reporting on the receipt of funds
- Reporting on the payment of funds
- Summary of payment reporting requirements

Information reporting may be required for many noncontribution funds received by your organization. Payments to nonemployees will often require filings with the IRS also.

General Filing Requirements

Information forms (1098 and 1099) must be provided to the payers/recipients on or before January 31 following the calendar year that the funds were paid or received. Copies of the forms (or magnetic media) must be filed with the IRS by February 28, following the year that the funds were paid or received.

An extension of time to file may be requested by filing Form 8809, Request for Extension of Time to File Information Returns, with the IRS by the due date of the returns.

Magnetic media reporting may be required for filing information returns with the IRS. If you are required to file 250 or more information returns, you must file on magnetic media. The 250-or-more requirement applies separately to each type of form. A Form 4419, Application for Filing Information Returns on Magnetic Media, must be filed to apply to use magnetic media.

Payers filing returns on paper forms must use a separate transmittal Form 1096, Annual Summary and Transmittal of U.S. Information Returns, for each different type of information form. For example, if you file Forms 1098, 1099-MISC, and 1099-S, complete one Form 1096 to transmit Forms 1098, another Form 1096 to transmit Forms 1099-MISC, and a third Form 1096 to transmit Forms 1099-S.

DO NOT STAPLE 6969

Form **1096** — Department of the Treasury, Internal Revenue Service

Annual Summary and Transmittal of U.S. Information Returns

OMB No. 1545-0108 — **1999**

ATTACH IRS LABEL HERE

FILER'S name
ABC Charity

Street address (including room or suite number)
2670 N. Hull Road

City, state, and ZIP code
Traverse City, MI 49615

If you are not using a preprinted label, enter in box 1 or 2 below the identification number you used as the filer on the information returns being transmitted. Do not fill in both boxes 1 and 2.

Name of person to contact if the IRS needs more information

Telephone number
( )

For Official Use Only

1 Employer identification number	2 Social security number	3 Total number of forms	4 Federal income tax withheld	5 Total amount reported with this Form 1096
35-7431092		10	$	$ 5842.00

Enter an "X" in only one box below to indicate the type of form being filed. If this is your FINAL return, enter an "X" here . . . ▶ ☐

W-2G 32	1098 81	1098-E 84	1098-T 83	1099-A 80	1099-B 79	1099-C 85	1099-DIV 91	1099-G 86	1099-INT 92	1099-LTC 93	1099-MISC 95	1099-MSA 94	1099-OID 96
☐	☐	☐	☐	☐	☐	☐	☐	☐	☐	☐	X	☐	☐

1099-PATR 97	1099-R 98	1099-S 75	5498 28	5498-MSA 27
☐	☐	☐	☐	☐

Please return this entire page to the Internal Revenue Service. Photocopies are NOT acceptable.

Obtaining correct identification numbers

Organizations required to file information returns with the IRS must obtain the correct taxpayer identification number (TIN) to report income paid, real estate transactions, and mortgage interest paid to or by the organization.

Form **W-9** (Rev. December 1996) — Department of the Treasury, Internal Revenue Service

Request for Taxpayer Identification Number and Certification

Give form to the requester. Do NOT send to the IRS.

Please print or type

Name (If a joint account or you changed your name, see **Specific Instructions** on page 2.)
Richard K. Bennett

Business name, if different from above. (See **Specific Instructions** on page 2.)

Check appropriate box: ☑ Individual/Sole proprietor ☐ Corporation ☐ Partnership ☐ Other ▶ ....

Address (number, street, and apt. or suite no.)
829 Garner Street

Requester's name and address (optional)

City, state, and ZIP code
Thomasville, NC 27360

Part I Taxpayer Identification Number (TIN)

List account number(s) here (optional)

Enter your TIN in the appropriate box. For individuals, this is your social security number (SSN). However, if you are a resident alien OR a sole proprietor, see the instructions on page 2. For other entities, it is your employer identification number (EIN). If you do not have a number, see **How To Get a TIN** on page 2.

Note: *If the account is in more than one name, see the chart on page 2 for guidelines on whose number to enter.*

Social security number: 403-98-1297

OR

Employer identification number:

Part II For Payees Exempt From Backup Withholding (See the instructions on page 2.) ▶

Part III Certification

Under penalties of perjury, I certify that:

1. The number shown on this form is my correct taxpayer identification number (or I am waiting for a number to be issued to me), **and**
2. I am not subject to backup withholding because: **(a)** I am exempt from backup withholding, or **(b)** I have not been notified by the Internal Revenue Service (IRS) that I am subject to backup withholding as a result of a failure to report all interest or dividends, or **(c)** the IRS has notified me that I am no longer subject to backup withholding.

Certification Instructions.—You must cross out item **2** above if you have been notified by the IRS that you are currently subject to backup withholding because you have failed to report all interest and dividends on your tax return. For real estate transactions, item **2** does not apply. For mortgage interest paid, acquisition or abandonment of secured property, cancellation of debt, contributions to an individual retirement arrangement (IRA), and generally, payments other than interest and dividends, you are not required to sign the Certification, but you must provide your correct TIN. (See the instructions on page 2.)

Sign Here Signature ▶ Richard K. Bennett Date ▶ 1/1/2000

Form W-9, Request for Taxpayer Identification Number and Certification, is used to furnish the correct TIN to the organization and in certain other situations to:

- ✓ certify that the TIN furnished is correct;
- ✓ certify that the recipient of the income is not subject to backup withholding; or
- ✓ certify exemption from backup withholding.

If the recipient does not furnish a completed Form W-9, the church or nonprofit organization is required to withhold 31% of the payment, deposit the withholding with Form 8109 or 8109-B, and report amounts withheld on Form 1099-INT, 1099-MISC, or 1099-R, as applicable.

Reporting on the Receipt of Funds

Receipt of interest on mortgages

Use Form 1098, Mortgage Interest Statement, to report mortgage interest of $500 or more received by your organization during the year from an individual, including a sole proprietor. You need not file Form 1098 for interest received from a corporation, partnership, trust, estate, or association. A transmittal Form 1096 must accompany one or more Form 1098s.

8181 ☐ VOID ☐ CORRECTED

RECIPIENT'S/LENDER'S name, address, and telephone number			OMB No. 1545-0901 1999 Form 1098	Mortgage Interest Statement
Debra Heights Church 1517 Cedar Street Rochester, MN 55902				
RECIPIENT'S Federal identification no. 35-8814073	PAYER'S social security number 441-09-7843	1 Mortgage interest received from payer(s)/borrower(s) $ 1819.00		Copy A For Internal Revenue Service Center
PAYER'S/BORROWER'S name Julie M. Chapman		2 Points paid on purchase of principal residence $		File with Form 1096.
Street address (including apt. no.) 125 Orchard Drive		3 Refund of overpaid interest $		For Privacy Act and Paperwork Reduction Act Notice and instructions for completing this form, see the 1999 Instructions for Forms 1099, 1098, 5498, and W-2G.
City, state, and ZIP code Cedar Falls, IA 50613		4		
Account number (optional)				

Form 1098 Cat. No. 14402K Department of the Treasury - Internal Revenue Service

Do NOT Cut or Separate Forms on This Page — Do NOT Cut or Separate Forms on This Page

Reporting on the Payment of Funds

Payments of interest

File Form 1099-INT, Statement for Recipients of Interest Income, for each person to whom you paid interest reportable in Box 1 of at least $10 in any calendar year. This form is also required if you withheld any federal income tax under the backup withholding rules (31% rate), regardless of the amount of the payment. In certain instances, the $10 limit increases to $600.

The $10 limit applies if the interest is on "evidences of indebtedness" (bonds and promissory notes) issued by a corporation in "registered form." A note or bond is in "registered form" if its transfer must be effected by the surrender of the old instrument and either the reissuance by the corporation of the old instrument to the new holder or the issuance by the corporation of a new instrument to the new holder.

There is no requirement to file Form 1099-INT for payments made to a corporation or another tax-exempt organization.

9292 ☐ VOID ☐ CORRECTED

PAYER'S name, street address, city, state, ZIP code, and telephone no.		Payer's RTN (optional)	OMB No. 1545-0112	
Lancaster Community Church 1425 Spencer Avenue Logansport, IN 46947			1999 Form 1099-INT	Interest Income
PAYER'S Federal identification number 35-7921873	RECIPIENT'S identification number 438-42-9973	1 Interest income not included in box 3 $ 913.00		Copy A For Internal Revenue Service Center File with Form 1096.
RECIPIENT'S name James R. Moore		2 Early withdrawal penalty $	3 Interest on U.S. Savings Bonds and Treas. obligations $	For Privacy Act and Paperwork Reduction Act Notice and instructions for completing this form, see the 1999 Instructions for Forms 1099, 1098, 5498, and W-2G.
Street address (including apt. no.) 604 Linden Avenue		4 Federal income tax withheld $	5 Investment expenses $	
City, state, and ZIP code Wabash, IN 46992		6 Foreign tax paid $	7 Foreign country or U.S. possession	
Account number (optional)	2nd TIN Not. ☐			

Form 1099-INT Cat. No. 14410K Department of the Treasury - Internal Revenue Service

Do NOT Cut or Separate Forms on This Page — Do NOT Cut or Separate Forms on This Page

Example 1: Sleepy Hollow Church financed a new church by issuing registered bonds. 1099-INT forms must be provided to each bond investor receiving $10 or more in interest during any calendar year.

If Sleepy Hollow engaged a bond broker to handle the issuance of the bonds, the broker would issue 1099-INT forms. If Sleepy Hollow issued the bonds without using a bond broker, the church would issue the 1099-INT forms.

Example 2: Sleepy Hollow Church borrows funds from church members. The notes are transferrable. There is no requirement to return the bonds to the church for reissuance. The $600 limit applies for the issuance of 1099-INT forms for the payment of interest on these notes.

Payments to annuitants

File Form 1099-R for each person to whom you have made a designated distribution that is a total distribution from a retirement plan or a payment to an annuitant of $1 of more. If part of the distribution is taxable and part is nontaxable, Form 1099-R should reflect the entire distribution.

Example: ABC Charity makes payments of $1,000 during the year to one of their annuitants, Mary Hughes. (Several years earlier, Mary entered into the charitable gift annuity agreement by giving a check to ABC.)

A portion of each annuity payment is a tax-free return of principal and the remainder is annuity income for Mary. ABC will generally report the entire $1,000 in Box 1 on Form 1099-R and check Box 2b unless ABC determines the taxable amount for the year.

9898 ☐ VOID ☐ CORRECTED

PAYER'S name, street address, city, state, and ZIP code ABC Charity 8049 Riverside Blvd. Sacramento, CA 95831		1 Gross distribution $ 1000.00 2a Taxable amount $	OMB No. 1545-0119 1999 Form 1099-R	**Distributions From Pensions, Annuities, Retirement or Profit-Sharing Plans, IRAs, Insurance Contracts, etc.**
		2b Taxable amount not determined ☐	Total distribution ☐	**Copy A For Internal Revenue Service Center**
PAYER'S Federal identification number 35-0479214	RECIPIENT'S identification number 703-41-3669	3 Capital gain (included in box 2a) $	4 Federal income tax withheld $	**File with Form 1096.**
RECIPIENT'S name Mary D. Hughes		5 Employee contributions or insurance premiums $	6 Net unrealized appreciation in employer's securities $	For Privacy Act and Paperwork Reduction Act Notice and instructions for completing this form, see the **1999 Instructions for Forms 1099, 1098, 5498, and W-2G.**
Street address (including apt. no.) P.O. Box 9042		7 Distribution code / IRA/SEP/SIMPLE ☐	8 Other $ %	
City, state, and ZIP code El Toro, CA 92630		9a Your percentage of total distribution %	9b Total employee contributions $	
Account number (optional)		10 State tax withheld $ $	11 State/Payer's state no.	12 State distribution $ $
		13 Local tax withheld $ $	14 Name of locality	15 Local distribution $ $

Form **1099-R** Cat. No. 14436Q Department of the Treasury - Internal Revenue Service

Do NOT Cut or Separate Forms on This Page — Do NOT Cut or Separate Forms on This Page

Form W-4P, Withholding Certificate for Pension or Annuity Payments, should be completed by recipients of income from annuity, pension, and certain other deferred compensation plans to inform payers whether income tax is to be withheld and on what basis.

Form **W-4P**
Department of the Treasury
Internal Revenue Service

Withholding Certificate for Pension or Annuity Payments

▶ For Privacy Act and Paperwork Reduction Act Notice, see page 4.

OMB No. 1545-0415

1999

Type or print your full name: Arnold B. Luther

Your social security number: 501 : 19 : 4129

Home address (number and street or rural route): P.O. Box 185

Claim or identification number (if any) of your pension or annuity contract

City or town, state, and ZIP code: Asheboro, NC 27203

Complete the following applicable lines:

1 Check here if you **do not want** any Federal income tax withheld from your pension or annuity. (Do not complete lines 2 or 3.) ▶ ☐

2 Total number of allowances and marital status you are claiming for withholding from each **periodic** pension or annuity payment. (You may also designate an additional dollar amount on line 3.) . . . . ▶ ____ (Enter number of allowances.)

Marital status: ☐ Single ☐ Married ☐ Married, but withhold at higher Single rate

3 Additional amount, if any, you want withheld from each pension or annuity payment. **Note:** *For periodic payments, you cannot enter an amount here without entering the number (including zero) of allowances on line 2* . . . ▶ $

Your signature ▶ Arnold B. Luther **Date ▶** 1-5-00

Cat. No. 10225T

Payments to nonresident aliens

Payments for personal services made to non-citizens (nonresident aliens) who are temporarily in this country are often subject to federal income tax withholding at a 30% rate. A nonresident alien is a person who is neither a U.S. citizen nor a resident of the United States. Some payments may be exempt from income tax withholding if the person is from a country with which the United States maintains a tax treaty. Salary payments to nonresident aliens employed in the United States are subject to income tax withholding based on the regular withholding tables.

Single, nonrecurring fixed or determinable payments to nonresident aliens are generally subject to withholding. Honoraria paid to visiting speakers usually fit this definition. It is not clear if love offerings are subject to withholding.

All payments to nonresident aliens, other than expense reimbursements and amounts reported on Form W-2, must be reported on Form 1042 and 1042-S. These forms are filed with the IRS Service Center in Philadelphia by March 15 for the previous calendar year, and a copy of Form 1042-S must be sent to the nonresident alien.

Payments of royalties and for other services

File Form 1099-MISC for each recipient (other than corporations) to whom you have paid

- ✓ at least $10 in royalties, or
- ✓ at least $600 in rents (for example, office rent or equipment rent), payments for services (nonemployee compensation), or medical health care payments.

Note: You must include payments of attorneys' fees, generally in Box 7, even if the firm providing the legal services is incorporated.

9595 ☐ VOID ☐ CORRECTED

PAYER'S name, street address, city, state, ZIP code, and telephone no. ABC Charity 110 Harding Avenue Cincinnati, OH 45963		1 Rents $ 2 Royalties $ 3 Other income $	OMB No. 1545-0115 1999 Form 1099-MISC	Miscellaneous Income
PAYER'S Federal identification number 35-1148942	RECIPIENT'S identification number 389-41-8067	4 Federal income tax withheld $	5 Fishing boat proceeds $	Copy A For Internal Revenue Service Center
RECIPIENT'S name Mark A. Mitchell		6 Medical and health care payments $	7 Nonemployee compensation $ 2400.00	File with Form 1096. For Privacy Act and Paperwork Reduction Act Notice and instructions for completing this form, see the 1999 Instructions for Forms 1099, 1098, 5498, and W-2G.
Street address (including apt. no.) 1512 Warren Avenue		8 Substitute payments in lieu of dividends or interest $	9 Payer made direct sales of $5,000 or more of consumer products to a buyer (recipient) for resale ▶ ☐	
City, state, and ZIP code Norwood, OH 45212		10 Crop insurance proceeds $	11 State income tax withheld $	
Account number (optional)	2nd TIN Not. ☐	12 State/Payer's state number	13 $	

Form 1099-MISC Cat. No. 14425J Department of the Treasury - Internal Revenue Service

Do NOT Cut or Separate Forms on This Page — Do NOT Cut or Separate Forms on This Page

Example: A charity has established a written, nondiscriminatory employee medical expense reimbursement plan under which the charity pays the medical expenses of the employee, spouse, and dependents.

If $600 or more is paid in the calendar year to a doctor or other provider of health care services, a Form 1099-MISC must be filed.

Benevolence payments to nonemployees are not reportable on Form 1099-MISC (or any other information form). Benevolence payments to employees are reportable on Form W-2.

Do not include the payment of a housing allowance to a minister on Form 1099-MISC. Advances, reimbursements, or expenses for traveling and other business expenses of an employee are not reportable on Form 1099-MISC. These payments may be reportable on Form W-2 if they do not comply with the accountable expense plan rules.

Advances, reimbursements, or expenses for traveling and other business expenses of a self-employed person are not reportable on Form 1099-MISC if made under an accountable expense reimbursement plan. Under this type of plan, expenses are reimbursed only if they are substantiated as to amount, date, and business nature, and any excess reimbursements must be returned to the organization.

Advances, reimbursements, or expenses for traveling and other business expenses of a self-employed person that are not substantiated to the paying organization are reportable on Form 1099-MISC.

Example 1: ABC Ministry organizes a seminar and engages a speaker. The speaker is paid a $750 honorarium, and ABC reimbursed the travel expenses of $200 upon presentation of proper substantiation by the speaker. Form 1099-MISC should be issued to the speaker for $750.

Example 2: Same facts as Example 1, except of the $750 payment, $250 is designated for travel expenses and the speaker accounted to ABC for the travel. Since the honorarium of $500, after excluding the substantiated payments, is less than the $600 limit, there is no requirement to issue a Form 1099-MISC to the speaker.

The answer to this example would be different if ABC paid an honorarium to the same speaker during the same calendar year of $100 or more, bringing the total for the year to the $600 level.

Example 3: ABC Ministry contracts for janitorial services with an unincorporated janitorial service and pays $2,000 during the year for this service. ABC should issue a Form 1099-MISC for these payments.

Payments to volunteers

Payments to volunteers that represent a reimbursement under an accountable business expense reimbursement plan for expenses directly connected with the volunteer services are not reportable by the charity.

Payments for auto mileage up to the maximum IRS rate for business miles (31 cents effective April 1, 1999) are generally considered to be tax-free for volunteers. When an organization provides liability insurance for its volunteers, the value of the coverage can be excluded from the volunteer's income as a working condition fringe benefit.

TIP

Payments to or on behalf of volunteers that are not business expenses are reported on Form W-2 or Form 1099-MISC, depending on whether or not a common law employee relationship exists. When the relationship between an organization takes the form of an employer-employee relationship, payments other than expense reimbursement are reported on Form W-2. Payments to nonemployee volunteers for medical, education, or personal living expenses must be reported as nonemployee compensation on Form 1099-MISC. Payments to volunteers for lodging, meals, and incidental expenses may be made under the per diem rules if the duration of the travel is under one year.

Moving expenses

REMEMBER

Employers are no longer required to provide Form 4782, Employee Moving Expense Information, to employees. Qualified employee moving expenses paid directly to an employee are reportable on Form W-2, only in Box 13, using Code P. The payments do not constitute compensation if the expenses would be otherwise deductible by the employee as moving expenses.

Qualified moving expenses an employer pays to a third party on behalf of the employee (for example, to a moving company) and services that an employer furnishes in kind to an employee are not reported on Form W-2.

A minister must move at least 50 miles to qualify to deduct moving expenses or receive a tax-free reimbursement. Many ministers move less than 50 miles which makes the expenses nondeductible and reimbursements by the church fully taxable for both income and social security tax purposes.

Summary of Payment Reporting Requirements

Below is an alphabetical list of some payments and the forms necessary to report them. It is not a complete list of payments, and the absence of a payment from the list does not suggest that the payment is exempt from reporting.

Types of Payment	Report on Form
Advance earned income credit	W-2
Annuities, periodic payments	1099-R
* Attorneys' fees	1099-MISC
Auto reimbursements (nonaccountable plan):	
Employee	W-2
Nonemployee	1099-MISC
Awards:	
Employee	W-2
Nonemployee	1099-MISC
Bonuses:	
Employee	W-2
Nonemployee	1099-MISC
Cafeteria/flexible benefit plan	5500, 5500-C, or 5500-R
Car expense (nonaccountable plan):	
Employee	W-2
Nonemployee	1099-MISC
Christmas bonuses:	
Employee	W-2
Nonemployee	1099-MISC
Commissions:	
Employee	W-2
Nonemployee	1099-MISC
Compensation:	
Employee	W-2
Nonemployee	1099-MISC
Dependent care payments	W-2
Director's fees	1099-MISC
Education expense reimbursement (nonaccountable plan):	
Employee	W-2
Nonemployee	1099-MISC
Employee business expense reimbursement (nonaccountable plan)	W-2
Fees:	
Employee	W-2
Nonemployee	1099-MISC
Group-term life insurance (PS 58 costs)	W-2 or 1099-R

Interest, mortgage	1098
Interest, other than mortgage	1099-INT
Long-term care benefits	1099-LTC
Medical expense reimbursement plan (employee-funded)	5500, 5500-C, or 5500-R
Mileage (nonaccountable plan):	
Employee	W-2
Nonemployee	1099-MISC
Mortgage interest	1098
Moving expense:	
**Employee	W-2
Nonemployee	1099-MISC
Prizes:	
Employee	W-2
Nonemployee	1099-MISC
Real estate proceeds	1099-S
Rents	1099-MISC
Royalties	1099-MISC
Severance pay	W-2
Sick pay	W-2
Supplemental unemployment	W-2
Vacation allowance:	
Employee	W-2
Nonemployee	1099-MISC
Wages	W-2

* The exemption from reporting payments made to corporations no longer applies to payments for legal services.

** Qualified moving expenses paid directly to an employee must be reported on Form W-2, only in Box 13, using Code P.

Key Concepts

- The receipt of certain funds, such as mortgage interest, by your organization may trigger information reporting to the IRS.
- Payments for rent, various services, and other items will often require the preparation of annual information returns.
- Securing correct taxpayer identification numbers should routinely occur in connection with the filing of information returns.

CHAPTER SIX

Your Financial Records

In This Chapter

- The money comes in
- The money goes out
- Accounting records
- Financial reports
- Audit guidelines
- Budgeting

It takes a practical set of accounting records and financial reports to communicate the financial condition of your organization.

Controlling and managing the organization's money is also very important. It is essential that the procedures for the handling of finances be reduced to writing. The governing board should establish and maintain the basic financial procedures for the organization. Too often, a new treasurer is handed a file box of accounting records with no written guidelines to follow. It is little wonder that the accounting system functions effectively one year and is in shambles the next.

Sound procedures should be developed, installed, and maintained year after year. These procedures will be different for every organization depending on the size of the organization, capability, and availability of personnel.

The Money Comes In

Church offerings are one of the most fundamental elements of church finance. Without them, a church would soon close it doors. The same is true for donations received by nonprofit organizations.

Church offerings come in various forms. Most commonly, the offering plates are passed during the service. In other churches, offerings are placed in containers located outside the sanctuary.

Most offerings received by churches are unrestricted. But nearly every church receives some donor-restricted funds. These donor-restricted funds require special treatment in the process of counting and recording offerings.

Why do money-handling problems so often arise in churches? It's primarily because cash is so easily misappropriated. It is small, lacks owner identification, and has immediate transferability. If offerings are not counted before they go from two-person control to one-person control, some or all of the cash can easily disappear.

Handling offerings with care will generate credibility. Few happenings can cause more consternation in a church than just the possibility that the offerings have been mishandled. And yet many churches leave the door wide open or at least ajar for problems with the handling of offerings. Often overlooked is the fact that sound controls over the offering protect church leaders in the event of false accusations regarding mishandling of funds.

So, how does a church avoid having problems with the handling of offerings? It is impossible to totally eliminate all problems. But following the guidelines on pages 106-8 will certainly reduce your risk.

All funds received should be recorded in detail. The bulk of the income for a church is received in Sunday offerings. Counting sheets are used to record the offerings in detail. Non-offering income for churches and other organizations should be receipted in detail.

Use of offering envelopes

Donors should be encouraged to donate by check and use offering envelopes for designated gifts and cash. Checks, payable to the church, are more difficult to steal than cash. And checks still provide proof of contributions for IRS purposes for single gifts of less than $250. The use of offering envelopes is essential when cash is given. Unless offering envelopes are used, loose cash could more easily be removed without detection during the cash collection and counting process. The money counters should verify that the contents of the offering envelopes are identical to any amounts written on the outside of the envelopes.

Some churches provide 52 numbered envelopes each year plus extra envelopes for special offerings. This system is ideal as a basis of posting contributions to church records. Other churches only provide blank envelopes in the pew racks. Either way, the recording of all gifts by donor with a periodic report of giving to each donor is necessary to provide adequate control over the money given.

Offering envelopes should be retained in the church office. Their retention is important if individual contributions need to be verified.

Bank deposits

Bank deposit slips should be prepared in duplicate with the original going to the bank and the copy kept for the organization's records. It is wise to deposit funds daily as funds are received. If the offering reports and other receipts have been properly prepared, it is generally not necessary to list each check on the deposit slips.

Revenue Flow Chart

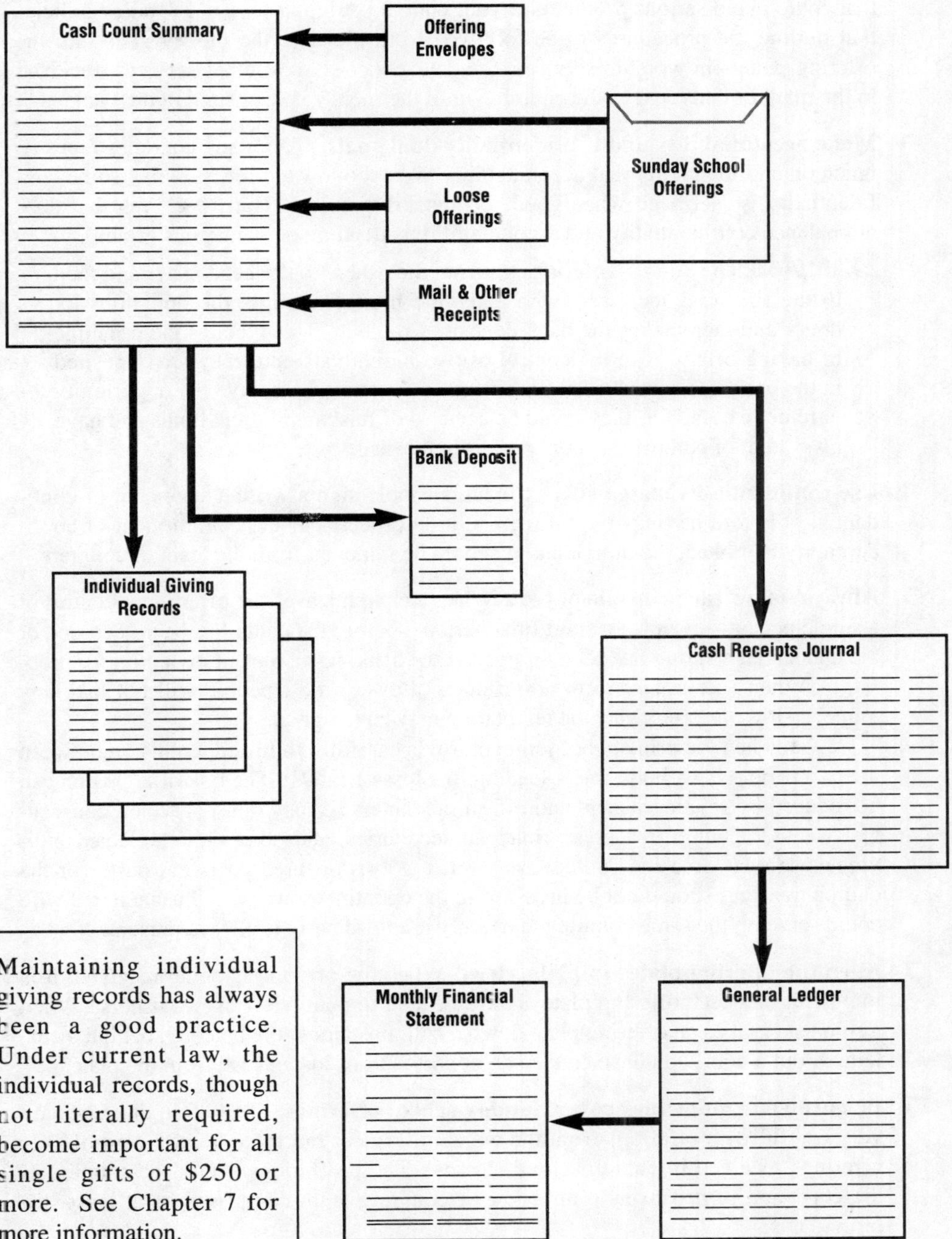

Maintaining individual giving records has always been a good practice. Under current law, the individual records, though not literally required, become important for all single gifts of $250 or more. See Chapter 7 for more information.

Guidelines for Processing Offerings

- ❐ **Adopt policies to prevent problems.** Written policies are the ounce-of-prevention that could avoid serious problems at your church. Adopt a series of detailed policies that outline the procedures to be followed from the time the money goes into the offering plate—in worship services, Sunday school classes, other services, received in the mail, or delivered to the church—until the money is deposited in the bank.

- ❐ **Make accountability and confidentiality dual goals.** Too many churches focus so much on confidentiality that accountability takes too low a priority. True, some confidentiality is sacrificed when good accountability exists. But the church that does not balance confidentiality and accountability is treading on dangerous ground.

  Example: The Sunday offerings go from the ushers to the head usher and then to the financial secretary, who takes the money, records the donations by donor and then makes the bank deposit. Problem: This violates the principle of having offerings in the control of two individuals until they are deposited in the bank. The head usher and financial secretary both have the opportunity to remove cash. Or, they could be accused of mishandling the funds and have no system of controls to support their innocence.

- ❐ **Use confidentiality statements.** Counters should sign a written statement of confidentiality before participating in the counting process. If the commitment of confidentiality is broken, the individual(s) should be removed from the team of counters.

- ❐ **Always follow the principle of two.** When a church leaves the offering in control of a single person—even for a short time period—before the count has been recorded or the uncounted offering has been dropped at the bank, it is a blatant invitation for problems. When sole access to the offering is allowed, most people will not take any money. However, for some, the temptation may be too great.

  Even when the principle of joint control is carefully followed, collusion between the two people is still possible—leading to a loss of funds. The risk of collusion can be reduced by rotating ushers and offering-counters so they don't serve on consecutive weeks. Church treasurers, financial secretaries, and other church-elected individuals should serve for limited terms, such as two or three years. A pastor or the church treasurer should not be involved in the counting process. A husband and wife could serve on the same counting team only if a third party is always present.

- ❐ **Keep the offering plates in plain view.** When the offering is being received, it is important that each offering plate always be kept in plain view of two ushers. When a solo usher takes an offering plate down a hall, upstairs to the balcony, behind a curtain, or out a door, you have created an opportunity of losing cash from the plate.

- ❐ **Be sure your guidelines cover Sunday school offerings.** Too often churches are very careful with offerings from the worship services but there is little control over offerings received in church school classes. These offerings should be counted in the class and turned over to an usher or counting team comprised of at least two individuals.

❒ **Encourage the use of offering envelopes.** Members should be encouraged to use offering envelopes. The envelopes provide a basis for recording contributions in the church's donor records.

Some churches emphasize this concept by providing each individual or church family with a series of pre-numbered offering envelopes to be used throughout the calendar year. The numbering system identifies the donor. This can ease the process of posting donations and is an excellent approach.

❒ **Count the offerings as soon as possible.** A frequent reason given by churches for not counting offerings immediately is that church members don't want to miss the service. This is very understandable. In many churches, the Sunday offerings are counted on Monday. Adequate control over the money is maintained by providing a secure place to store the funds, usually a safe, and carefully limiting access to the storage location.

However, the greater the length of time between receiving and counting the offering, the greater the potential for mishandling of funds. When offerings are immediately counted, secure storing of the funds is important but not as critical because an audit trail has been established.

❒ **Have counters complete offering tally sheets.** Tally sheets should be completed that separately account for loose checks and cash that was placed in offering envelopes. Checks or cash placed in blank, unidentified offering envelopes should be recorded with the loose funds. This separation of money serves as a control amount for the later posting to donor records.

❒ **Use a secure area for counting.** For safety of the counting team, confidentiality, and to avoid interruptions, provide a secure area in which the offering can be counted. (When offerings are significant, consider providing armed security when offerings are transported to the bank.) The counters should have an adding machine, coin wrappers, offering tally sheets, and other supplies. The adding machine should have a tape (instead of a paperless calculator) so the counting team can run two matching adding machine tapes of the offering.

❒ **Deposit all offerings intact.** Offerings should always be counted and deposited intact. Depositing intact means not allowing cash in the offering to be used for the payment of church expenses or to be exchanged for other cash or a check.

If offerings are not deposited intact, an unidentified variance between the count and the deposit could occur. Additionally, if an individual is permitted to cash a check from offering funds, the church may inadvertently provide the person with a cancelled check that could be used in claiming a charitable tax deduction.

❒ **Verify amounts on offering envelopes with the contents.** As the counting team removes the contents from offering envelopes, any amounts written on the envelope by the donors should be compared with the contents. Any variances should be noted on the envelope.

❒ **Properly identify donor-restricted funds.** All donor-restrictions should be carefully preserved during the counting process. These restrictions are usually noted on an offering envelope, but they can take the form of an instruction attached to a check or simply a notation on the check.

❒ **Use a restrictive endorsement for checks.** During the counting process, it is important to add a restrictive endorsement, with a "For Deposit Only" stamp, to the back of all checks.

❒ **Place offerings in a secure location when they are stored in the church.** If offerings are stored in the church, even for short periods of time, the use of a secure location is important. A safe implies security and an unlocked desk drawer connotes lack of security. But defining security is often not that easy.

Again, the principle is that no one person should have access to the funds at any time. This can be accomplished by

✓ obtaining a safe with two locks,

✓ changing the combination and distributing portions of the new combination to different people, or

✓ placing the safe in a locked room or building and placing the offerings in locked bags before locking them in the safe.

Ideally, offerings are counted during or after the service and a deposit is made immediately. Alternately, the cash portion of the offering is recorded and the uncounted offerings are immediately transported to the bank drop box by two people. When these two preferable options are not used, the offerings are generally stored at the church for a period of time on Sunday or perhaps until Monday morning. This process requires a secure storage location, preferably a safe, and highly structured controls over access to locked bank bags and the safe.

❒ **Use proper controls when dropping uncounted funds at the bank.** If your church drops uncounted offerings at the bank, several key principles should be followed:

✓ The funds should be placed in locked bank bags with careful control of the number of persons who have keys to the bags.

✓ Two individuals should transport the funds to the bank.

✓ Two people should pick up the funds from the bank on Monday morning.

❒ **Control deposit variances.** Provide written instructions to your bank concerning procedures to be followed if the bank discovers a discrepancy in the deposit. The notification should go to someone other than the individual(s) who participated in preparation of the deposit.

❒ **Segregate duties when recording individual contributions.** Someone other than a member of the counting team should record individual gifts in donor records. This segregation of duties reduces the possibility of misappropriation of gifts.

Cash Count Summary

March 6, 2000

	Sunday School	Sunday A.M.	Sunday P.M.	Received During Week	TOTAL
Coins	83.12	21.82	10.42		115.36
Currency	320.00	431.00	108.00		859.00
Checks	25.00	1,855.00	360.00	185.00	2,425.00
TOTALS	428.12	2,307.82	478.42	185.00	3,399.36

Breakdown By Type Of Gift

Regular Tithes and Offerings		1,942.82	368.42	140.00	2,451.24
Sunday School	428.12				428.12
Building Fund		85.00	50.00	15.00	150.00
Missions		100.00	30.00	20.00	150.00
Other Designated Funds:					
Benevolence Fund		40.00			40.00
School Project		30.00	10.00		40.00
Choir Robes		50.00			50.00
Youth Trip		40.00	20.00	10.00	70.00
Parking Lot		20.00			20.00
TOTALS	428.12	2,307.82	478.42	185.00	3,399.36

Counted by: Mike Anderson
Helen David
Bob Wells

Deposited on: March 7, 2000

Contributions By Donor

March 6, 2000 (×) A.M. ( ) P.M. ( ) ______

Name of Contributor	Regular Tithes & Offerings	Sunday School	Building Fund	Missions	Other: Description	Other: Amount
M/M Mark Wilson	50.00		10.00	20.00		
Frank Young	35.00					
Ellen Jackson	60.00		15.00			
Lori Avery	40.00					
M/M Mike Floyd	100.00	10.00			Benevolence	40.00
M/M Harold Long	45.00		5.00			
Mary Martin	75.00			10.00		
M/M Steve Ross	80.00			20.00		
M/M Joe Harris	65.00		5.00		School Project	30.00
Kelly York	50.00					
Peggy Walker	30.00					
M/M Bob Franklin	75.00	5.00		15.00		
Don Gilles	40.00		10.00			
Lou Shields	200.00					
M/M Ron White	80.00			20.00		
Art Howe	100.00		20.00		Choir Robes	50.00
M/M Stan Plunkett	60.00	10.00				
Nancy Robbins	75.00				Youth Trip	40.00
M/M Bill Lyon	50.00			5.00		
M/M David Clark	80.00		20.00			
James Bowers	40.00				Parking Lot	20.00
Cindy Bowers	60.00			10.00		
TOTALS	1,490.00	25.00	85.00	100.00		180.00

The Money Goes Out

Payment of expenses

One of the most important principles of handling funds is to pay virtually all expenses by check. The use of the petty cash fund should be the only exception to payment by check. Cash from a deposit should never be used to pay expenses.

If checks are prepared manually, a large desk-type checkbook is often helpful. Such a checkbook usually has three checks to a page and large stubs on which to write a full description of each expenditure. Computer-prepared checks should generally have a stub with adequate space to identify the type of expense and account number(s) charged.

Use preprinted, consecutively numbered checks. All spoiled checks should be marked "void" and kept on file with the cancelled checks.

In some instances, it may be wise to require two signatures on every check or on checks over a certain amount. In other situations, one signature may be appropriate. The level of controls over the funds will help you determine if more than one signature is necessary. Access to a checking account should generally be limited to no more than two or three individuals. A church pastor should not have access to the checking account. Checks should never be signed and delivered to anyone without completing the payee and the amount.

Checks should not be written until near the time there are funds available to cover them. Some organizations write checks when bills are due without regard to available cash. Checks are held for days, weeks, or sometimes months until they are released for payment. This is an extremely confusing practice that makes it very difficult to determine the actual checkbook balance.

Every check should have some type of written document to support it—an invoice, petty cash receipt, payroll summary, and so on. If such support is not available for some good reason, a memo should be written to support the expenditure. For example, an honorarium paid to a visiting speaker would not be supported by an invoice but should be documented by indicating the date of the speaking engagement and the event.

Occasionally it may be necessary to advance funds before supporting documentation is available (for example, a travel advance for future travel). In these instances, the treasurer must devise a system to ensure documentation is provided on a timely basis and any excess funds are returned.

Payments to venders should be based on *original* copies of invoices. Payments should not be based on month-end statements that do not show the detail of the service or products provided. After payment has been made, all supporting material should be filed in a paid-bills file in alphabetical order by payee.

It is important that a treasurer never mix personal funds with organization funds.

Example of Computer-Generated Cash Receipts Journal

Date	Reference	Entry Description	Account No.	Account Name	Amount Debit	Amount Credit
6/06/99	CR1	Weekly receipts	301-000	Regular Offerings		2,511.12
			302-000	Sunday School		304.78
			303-000	Missions		484.11
			304-000	Building Fund		241.50
			305-000	Benevolence Fund		148.70
			101-000	Valley View Bank	3,690.21	
6/13/99	CR2	Weekly receipts	301-000	Regular Offerings		2,604.80
			302-000	Sunday School		411.12
			303-000	Missions		389.00
			304-000	Building Fund		211.00
			306-000	Camp Fund		43.00
			307-000	Choir Fund		30.00
			308-000	School Fund		50.00
			101-000	Valley View Bank	3,738.92	
6/20/99	CR3	Weekly receipts	301-000	Regular Offerings		2,383.70
			302-000	Sunday School		391.42
			303-000	Missions		411.00
			304-000	Building Fund		305.00
			305-000	Benevolence Fund		30.00
			308-000	School Fund		25.00
			101-000	Valley View Bank	3,546.12	
6/27/99	CR4	Weekly receipts	301-000	Regular Offerings		2,780.12
			302-000	Sunday School		393.23
			303-000	Missions		305.00
			304-000	Building Fund		283.00
			305-000	Benevolence Fund		45.00
			307-000	Choir Fund		20.00
			308-000	School Fund		45.00
			101-000	Valley View Bank	3,871.35	
					14,846.60	14,846.60

Example of Computer-Generated General Ledger with Entries Posted from Cash Receipts Journal

Source	Acct. No./ Date	Reference	Description	Beginning Balance	Current Entries	Ending Balance
	301-000		**Regular Offerings**	**65,211.12-**		
CR	6/06/99	CR1	Weekly receipts		2,511.12-	
CR	6/13/99	CR2	Weekly receipts		2,604.80-	
CR	6/20/99	CR3	Weekly receipts		2,383.70-	
CR	6/27/99	CR4	Weekly receipts		2,780.12-	
					10,279.74-	75,490.86-
	302-000		**Sunday School Offerings**	**7,511.82-**		
CR	6/06/99	CR1	Weekly receipts		304.78-	
CR	6/13/99	CR2	Weekly receipts		411.12-	
CR	6/20/99	CR3	Weekly receipts		391.42-	
CR	6/27/99	CR4	Weekly receipts		393.23-	
					1,500.55-	9,012.37-
	303-000		**Missions Offerings**	**10,211.80-**		
CR	6/06/99	CR1	Weekly receipts		484.11-	
CR	6/13/99	CR2	Weekly receipts		389.00-	
CR	6/20/99	CR3	Weekly receipts		411.00-	
CR	6/27/99	CR4	Weekly receipts		305.00-	
					1,589.11-	11,800.91-
	304-000		**Building Fund**	**5,612.70-**		
CR	6/06/99	CR1	Weekly receipts		241.50-	
CR	6/13/99	CR2	Weekly receipts		211.00-	
CR	6/20/99	CR3	Weekly receipts		305.00-	
CR	6/27/99	CR4	Weekly receipts		283.00-	
					1,040.50-	6,653.20-
	305-000		**Benevolence Fund**	**1,411.70-**		
CR	6/06/99	CR1	Weekly receipts		148.70-	
CR	6/20/99	CR3	Weekly receipts		30.00-	
CR	6/27/99	CR4	Weekly receipts		45.00-	
					223.70-	1,635.40-

Expense approval and recording

If funds are approved in a church or other organization budget, this may be sufficient authority for the treasurer to pay the bills. In other instances, the approval of department heads or supervising personnel may be appropriate. Expenses that exceed the budget may need specific approval.

Although every organization should have a budget, many do not. Even without a budget, routine expenses for utilities, salaries, and mortgage payments normally do not need specific approval before payment by the treasurer.

All checks should be recorded in a cash disbursements journal. The type of expense is reflected in the proper column in a manually prepared journal. Expense account numbers are used to identify the type of expense in a computerized journal. Expenses should be categorized in sufficient detail to provide an adequate breakdown of expenses on the periodic financial statements.

Petty cash system

To avoid writing numerous checks for small amounts, it is wise to have a petty-cash fund (with a fixed base amount) from which to make small payments. For example, if the church office needs a roll of stamps, the use of the petty cash fund for the expense is more efficient than writing a check for the minor amount.

A petty cash fund of $50 or $100 is often adequate for small organizations. Large organizations may have multiple petty cash funds in various departments. The amount of the fund may vary based on need.

As funds are disbursed from the petty cash fund, a slip detailing the expense is completed and placed in the petty cash box. If an invoice or receipt is available, it should be attached to the petty cash slip for filing. The petty cash slips are kept with the petty cash. At all times, the total of the unspent petty cash and the petty cash slips should equal the fixed amount of the petty cash fund.

When the cash in the fund is getting low, a check is written payable to "Petty Cash Fund" for an amount equal to the expense slips plus or minus any amounts the fund is out-of-balance. The check is cashed and the cash returns the fund to the fixed balance. Expenses are allocated and recorded based on the purposes reflected on the slips.

Accounting Records

Accounting systems differ in shape, size, complexity, and efficiency. The objectives of the system should be to measure and control financial activities and to provide financial information to the church governing body, the congregation, and donors. In choosing the accounting records for your organization, the most important consideration is the ability of the individual(s) keeping the records.

Disbursements Flow Chart

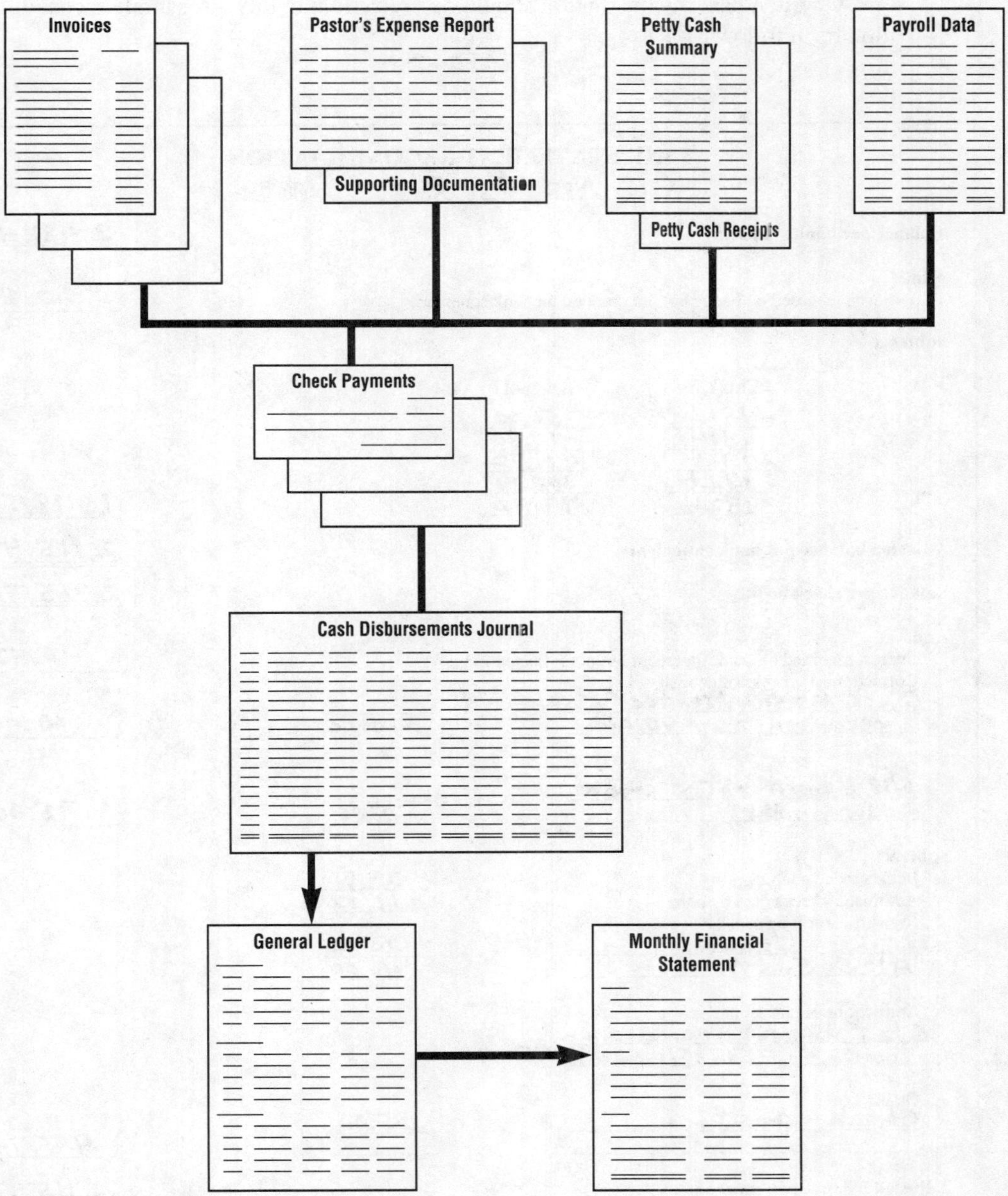

Bank reconciliation

A written bank reconciliation should be prepared monthly. A sample reconciliation form follows:

BANK STATEMENT RECONCILIATION

As of March 31, 2000

Balance per bank statement		2,481.40
Add:		
Deposits recorded on books but not credited on bank statement		1,012.80
Subtract:		
Outstanding checks		

Check No.	Amount
1312	50.00
1314	17.80
1318	411.72
1321	108.14
1324	791.12

		1,378.78
Adjusted balance per bank statement		2,115.42
Balance per check book		2,365.74
Add:		
Interest recorded on bank statement but not reflected in books		10.42
Corrections of checks or deposits:		
Check #1250 written for $80.00/ recorded as $90.00	10.00	10.00
Other:		
6/18 deposit not recorded in books	175.00	175.00
Subtract:		
Bank service charges	29.80	
Automatic checks paid by bank	311.12	
Nonsufficient fund checks:		
Mike Brown	20.00	
Alex Smith	40.00	
Corrections of checks or deposits:		
6/25 deposit recorded on books as $511.80/should be $501.98	9.82	
Other:		
Check printing	35.00	
		445.74
Adjusted balance per checkbook		2,115.42

These items should be recorded in the checkbook and the cash receipts or disbursements journals after the reconciliation is completed.

Using double entry accounting

Double-entry bookkeeping is necessary for most organizations. It shows a twofold effect by recording every transaction twice—as a debit entry in one account and as a credit entry in another. Either or both of the entries may be broken down into several items, but the total of the amounts entered as debits must equal the total of the amounts entered as credits.

As the following table shows, when you pay an expense, the amount paid is entered as a debit to expense and as a credit to your cash account (an asset). When you receive a gift, an asset is debited (cash) and an income account is credited.

Type of account	If the transaction will decrease the account, enter it as a —	If the transaction will increase the account, enter it as a —	Typical balance
Asset	credit	debit	debit
Liability	debit	credit	credit
Capital	debit	credit	credit
Income	debit	credit	credit
Expense	credit	debit	debit

Cash and accrual methods

Most small churches and nonprofit organizations use the cash basis of accounting. Other organizations frequently use the accrual method. A common rule of thumb is that organizations with annual revenue of $250,000 and larger probably need to use the accrual method of accounting.

Advantages of cash method

Under this method, revenue is recorded only when cash is received, and expenses are recorded when they are paid. For example, office supplies expense is shown in the month when the bill is paid, even though the supplies were received and used in the previous month.

The primary advantage of the cash method is its simplicity. It is easier for nonaccountants to understand and keep records on this basis. When financial statements are required, the treasurer just summarizes the transactions from the checkbook stubs or runs the computer-prepared financial statements with fewer adjusting entries required. For smaller organizations, the difference between financial results on the cash and on the accrual basis are often not significantly different.

Advantages of accrual method

Many organizations use the accrual method of accounting when the cash basis does not accurately portray the financial picture. Under the accrual method, revenue

PETTY CASH RECONCILIATION

DEPARTMENT Youth DATE June 30, 2000

Cash On Hand		Payments from Petty Cash — Reconciliation Period From 6/1/00 To 6/30/00									
Currency	Amount	Account	Date	Amount	Date	Amount	Date	Amount	Date	Amount	Total
$20.00 Bills	100 00	626-010	6/2	3 10	6/16	2 00					5 10
10.00 Bills	10 00	633-021	6/10	5 50							5 50
5.00 Bills	20 00	634-120	6/8	1 30	6/20	4 00	6/29	1 00			6 30
2.00 Bills		636-041	6/18	12 89							12 89
1.00 Bills	10 00	637-910	6/4	6 00							6 00
Checks		644-002	6/21	13 80							13 80
$1.00 Coins		645-001	6/10	2 50	6/12	2 00	6/18	1 50			6 00
.50 Coins		647-102	6/26	11 91							11 91
.25 Coins	3 75	649-023	6/19	5 50							5 50
.10 Coins	2 20	651-101	6/3	8 10							8 10
.05 Coins	80	653-001	6/12	12 40							12 40
.01 Coins	36	655-012	6/14	7 12							7 12
SUMMARY		660-001	6/2	1 02	6/8	2 04	6/12	3 11	6/20	4 00	10 17
		663-004	6/8	7 00	6/21	4 00					11 00
1. Total Cash	147 11	665-012	6/29	16 40							16 40
2. Total Petty Cash Slips	150 89	670-080	6/12	4 70	6/20	8 00					12 70
3. Subtotal (1+2)	298 00										
4. Petty Cash Fund	300 00										
5. Overage (3-4)											
6. Shortage (4-3)	2 00										
7. To be reimbursed (2+6 or 2-5)	152 89										
										TOTAL PETTY CASH SLIPS	150 89

7/2/00
Date

Dave Mason
Signature of Person Reconciling

When the cash in the petty cash fund is about used up, the custodian summarizes the petty cash receipts on a form like the one illustrated above. A check is then written to replenish the fund.

PETTY CASH RECEIPT

Date June 7, 2000

DESCRIPTION OF ITEM / SERVICE PURCHASED	AMOUNT
Office Supplies:	
Pens (1 doz.)	4 90
Envelopes 9x12 (2 doz.)	8 40
Receipt from Complete	
Office Supply is attached	
CHARGE TO ACCOUNT 652-001 TOTAL	13 30

Mary Moore
Money Received By

Dave Mason
Approved By

CASH EXPENSE REPORT

Name: Pastor Frank Morris

Address: 3801 North Florida Avenue
Miami, Florida 33168

Period Covered: From: 6/1/00 To: 6/15/00

DATE	TRAVEL City	Purpose of Travel	Brkfast	Lunch	Dinner	Snack	Lodging	Trans.	OTHER * Description	Amount	ACCOUNT TO BE CHARGED
6/2/99									Lunch w/Bob Cox	18.21	641-002
6/6/99	Atlanta, GA	Continuing Ed Seminar		10.80	13.40	2.10	90.50	281.00	Tips	8.00	644-010
6/6/99	✓ ✓	✓ ✓	6.40								644-010
6/8/99									Lunch w/Al Lane	12.80	641-002
6/14/99									Lunch w/Sam Lee	11.10	641-002
	TOTAL CASH EXPENSES		6.40	10.80	13.40	2.10	90.50	281.00		50.11	

*If this is entertainment, please use the entertainment worksheet on the back of this form.

Total cash expenses	454.31
Personal auto business mileage (Complete worksheet on the back of this form.) 221 miles X 31.0 per mile	68.51
Less travel advance	<300.00>
Balance due	222.82
Refund due organization	

Frank Morris — Signature (person requesting reimbursement) — Date 6/16/00

Bob Davis — Approved by — Date 6/16/00

PERSONAL AUTO BUSINESS MILEAGE			
Date	Purpose/Destination	Miles	Account to be charged
6/1/00	Calls/Valley View Rest Home	23	638-000
6/2/00	Brown Funeral Home / Harold Boone	18	✓
6/3/00	Calls / Various Homes	20	✓
6/4/00	Calls / Memorial Hospital	15	✓
6/5/00	Kiwanis Speaker / Pat's Cafeteria	25	✓
6/7/00	Calls / Various Homes	10	✓
6/8/00	Calls / St. Luke's Hospital	17	✓
6/9/00	Calls / Cannon Nursing Home	12	✓
6/10/00	Calls / Various Homes	8	✓
6/12/00	Calls / Memorial Hospital	15	✓
6/15/00	Ministerial Convention / Webb City	58	✓
	TOTAL MILES TRAVELED	221	

ENTERTAINMENT WORKSHEET (Expenses paid in behalf of individual(s) other than the person filing this expense report.)				
Date	Persons Entertained	Purpose of Entertainment	Place	Amount
6/2/00	M/M Bob Cox	Prospective Members	Olive Garden	18.21
6/8/00	Frank Lane	Discuss church bldg. plans	Chi Chi's	12.80
6/14/00	Sam Lee	Church goals w/board chair.	Damon's	11.10
			TOTAL AMOUNT SPENT	42.11

To mileage summary on page one

To "other" expense column on page one

Example of Computer-Generated Cash Disbursements Journal

Date	Reference	Entry Description	Account No.	Account Name	Amount Debit	Amount Credit
6/01/99	1025	Rev. Glenn Phillips	501-000	Pastor Salary	1,500.00	
			211-000	Income Tax W/H		200.00
6/01/99	1026	Mary Brown	505-000	Secretary Salary	750.00	
			211-000	Income Tax W/H		50.00
			212-000	FICA W/H		57.37
6/03/99	1027	Postmaster	649-000	Postage	29.00	
6/04/99	1028	Bell Telephone	663-000	Telephone	83.92	
6/04/99	1029	City Power & Light	664-000	Utilities	173.12	
6/06/99	1030	Gas Service Co.	664-000	Utilities	20.11	
6/09/99	1031	Harold Reynolds	810-000	Benevolence Expense	50.00	
6/11/99	1032	Blair Insurance	690-000	Insurance Expense	342.00	
6/13/99	1033	Franklin Printing	651-000	Literature & Prtg.	83.29	
6/14/99	1034	Postmaster	649-000	Postage	142.00	
6/15/99	1035	Rev. Glenn Phillips	501-000	Pastor Salary	1,500.00	
			211-000	Income Tax W/H		200.00
6/15/99	1036	Mary Brown	505-000	Secretary Salary	750.00	
			211-000	Income Tax W/H		50.00
			212-000	FICA W/H		57.37
6/20/99	1037	Valley View Bank	505-000	Income Tax W/H	500.00	
			211-000	FICA W/H	114.74	
			212-000	FICA Expense	114.74	
6/20/99	1038	ABC Church Supply	651-000	Literature & Prtg.	200.00	
6/30/99			101-000	Valley View Bank		5,738.18
					6,352.92	6,352.92

Example of Computer-Generated General Ledger with Entries Posted from Cash Disbursements Journal

Source	Acct. No./ Date	Reference	Description	Beginning Balance	Current Entries	Ending Balance
	649-000		**Postage**	316.61		
CD	6/07/99	1027	Postmaster		29.00	
CD	6/14/99	1034	Postmaster		142.00	
					171.00	487.61
	651-000		**Literature & Printing**	702.58		
CD	6/13/99	1033	Franklin Printing		83.29	
CD	6/20/99	1038	ABC Church Supply		200.00	
					283.29	985.87
	653-000		**Kitchen Supplies**	53.72		53.72
	663-000		**Telephone**	648.12		
CD	6/14/99	1028	Bell Telephone		83.92	
					83.92	732.04
	664-000		**Utilities**	1,401.43		
CD	6/04/99	1029	City Power & Light		173.12	
CD	6/06/99	1030	Gas Service Co.		20.11	
					193.23	1,594.66
	810-000		**Benevolence Expense**	200.00		
CD	6/09/99	1031	Harold Reynolds		50.00	
					50.00	250.00
	850-000		**Missions Expense**	2,411.80		2,411.80
	865-000		**Camp Expense**	1,012.80		1,012.80

is recorded when earned. For example, a church charges a fee for the use of the fellowship hall for a wedding.

Under accrual accounting, the revenue is recorded in the month earned even though the cash might not be received until a later month. Under accrual accounting, expenses are recorded when incurred. For example, telephone expense is recorded in the month when the service occurs although the bill may not be paid until the next month.

Generally accepted accounting principles for nonprofit organizations require the use of accrual basis accounting. Organizations that have their books audited by Certified Public Accountants, and want the CPAs to report that the financial statement appear according to "generally accepted accounting principles (GAAP)," must either keep their records on the accrual basis or make the appropriate adjustments at the end of the year to convert to this basis. Financial statements prepared on a cash or other comprehensive basis may qualify under GAAP if the financial statements are not materially different from those prepared on an accrual basis.

Modified cash method

The modified cash method of accounting is a combination of certain features of the cash and accrual methods. For example, accounts payable may be recorded when a bill is received although other payables or receivables are not recorded. The modified cash method portrays the financial picture more accurately than the cash method but not as well as the full accrual method.

Some organizations use the modified cash accounting method during the year and then make entries at year-end to convert the accounting data to a full accrual basis for audit purposes. This method simplifies the day-to-day bookkeeping process with interim reports focused on cash management.

Fund accounting

Fund accounting (or accounting by classes of net assets) provides an excellent basis for stewardship reporting. It is a system of accounting in which separate records are kept for resources donated to an organization which are restricted by donors or outside parties to certain specified purposes or use.

GAAP requires that net assets be broken down into the following three classes, based on the presence or absence of donor-imposed restrictions and their nature:

- ✓ **Permanently restricted.** These assets are not available for program expenses, payments to creditors, or other organizational needs. An example is an endowment gift with a stipulation that the principal is permanently not available for spending but the investment income from the principal may be used in current operations.

- ✓ **Temporarily restricted.** These assets may be restricted by purpose or time, but the restrictions are not permanent. An example of the purpose-restricted gift is a gift for a certain project or for the purchase of some equipment. An example of a time-restricted gift is a contribution in the form of a trust, annuity, or term endowment (principal of the gift is restricted for a certain term of time).

✓ **Unrestricted.** These net assets may be used for any of the organization's purposes. According to accounting standards, "the only limits on unrestricted net assets are broad limits resulting from the nature of the organization and the purposes specified in its articles of incorporation or bylaws."

Donor-imposed restrictions normally apply to the use of net assets and not to the use of specific assets. Only donors or outside parties may "restrict" funds given to a nonprofit organization. The organization's board may not "restrict" monies—they may only "designate" funds. For example, if a donor gives money for a new church organ, the funds should be placed in a restricted fund. If the church board sets funds aside in a debt retirement fund, this is a designated fund.

Fund accounting does not necessarily require multiple bank accounts. One bank account is all that is usually necessary. However, it may be appropriate to place restricted funds into a separate bank account to ensure that the funds are not inadvertently spent for other purposes.

Depreciation

Some organizations charge-off or record land, buildings, and equipment as expense at the time of purchase. Other organizations capitalize land, buildings, and equipment at cost and do not record depreciation. Other organizations record land, buildings, and equipment at cost and depreciate them over their estimated useful life. GAAP requires this last method. Depreciation is not required for financial statement presentation on any other basis of accounting.

Organizations may set dollar limits for the recording of buildings and equipment as assets. For example, one organization might properly expense all equipment purchases of less than $2,000 per item and record items as assets above that amount.

Chart of accounts

The chart of accounts lists all ledger accounts and their account number to facilitate the bookkeeping process. Assets, liabilities, net assets, support and revenue, and expense accounts are listed. For a sample chart of accounts for a church, see page 127.

Account numbers are used to indicate the source of support and revenue or the object of expense. In computerized accounting systems, the account number is used to post an entry to the general ledger. The same concept can be used in a manually-prepared accounting system to avoid writing out the account name each time.

Church management software

The accounting records for most organizations are maintained on computers. Even many small churches have a personal computer that is primarily used for word processing. This computer can be used to run software to process church financial data. Many accounting software packages designed for small businesses can be easily adapted for nonprofit use. Most of these packages include the double-entry process. There are also many software packages designed specifically for churches. An excellent summary of church management software prepared by Nick B. Nicholaou, President, Ministry Business Services, Inc., P.O. Box 1567, Huntington Beach, CA 92647 (Tel. 714-840-5900) is reprinted with permission on the following four pages. Feel free to contact the church management software providers.

A compilation of their responses is summarized on the chart on page 122. The symbol ■ is used on those options currently available and that they provide directly. The symbol ☒ is used on those options the provider offers from an outside source. The symbol □ is used on those options the provider is working on, but was not ready to offer at press time. If an item on the contact portion of the list was not answered, "n/a" is shown.

Financial Reports

In preparing financial reports, there is one basic rule: prepare different reports for different audiences. For example, a church board would normally receive a more detailed financial report than the church membership. Department heads in a nonprofit organization might receive reports that only relate to their department.

Financial statements should

- ✓ be easily comprehensible so that any person taking the time to study them will understand the financial picture;
- ✓ be concise so that the person studying them will not get lost in detail;
- ✓ be all-inclusive in scope and should embrace all activities of the organization;
- ✓ have a focal point for comparison so that the person reading them will have some basis for making a judgment (usually this will be a comparison with a budget or data from the corresponding period of the previous year); and
- ✓ be prepared on a timely basis (the longer the delay after the end of the period, the longer the time before corrective action can be taken).

For additional reading on this topic, see the *Accounting and Financial Reporting Guide for Christian Ministries* (published by the Evangelical Joint

Church Management Software Comparison Chart

Compiled by
Ministry Business Services, Inc.

Feature	AlphaOmega InfoSystems	Automated Church System (ACS)	Blackbaud Microsystems	By the Book	Church Windows/Computer Helper	Diakonia	Focus on Business	Greentree Applied Systems	Hunter Systems	Icon Systems	J.S. Paluch Co.	Lieberman Consulting Group
Congregation Database	■	■	■	■	■	■	■	■	■	■	■	■
Attendance Tracker	■	■		■	■	■	■	■	■	■	■	
Contributions Tracker	■	■	■	■	■	■	■	■	■	■	■	■
Can Add/Modify Fields	■	■	■	■	■	■		■	■	■	■	■
Photos by Individual/Family	■	■	■	■	■	■		■	■	■		
Mail Merge Interface	■	■	■	■	■	■	■	■	■	■	■	■
Bulk Mail Bar Codes		■	■	■	■			■	■	■		
Bulk Mail CASS Certification		■		■	■			■	■	■		
Telephony Services Link	■					■			■			
Facility Scheduler		■					■					
Equipment Scheduler		■					■					
Retreat Registrations & A/R		■										
General Ledger	■	■	■		■		■	■	■	☒	■	
GAAP Compliant		■	■		■			■	■			
Full Audit Trail		■			■		■	■	■			
Fixed Budget Tracker		■	■		■		■	■	■			
Variable Budget Tracker		■			■			■	■		■	
Graphic Analysis		■	■		■							
Accounts Payable	■	■	■		■		■	■	■	☒	■	
Accrual Basis Capable		■	■		■		■	■	■			
Cash Basis Capable		■	■		■		■		■			
Annual 1099's		■	■		■		■	■	■			
Laser Checks	■	■	■		■		■	■	■		■	
Dot Matrix Checks		■	■		■		■	■	■			
Payroll		■	■		■		■	■	■	☒		
Minister's Salary Capable		■			■		■	■	■			
ACH Direct Deposit Capable												
Quarterly 941's		■	■		■		■	■	■			
Annual W2's		■	■		■		■	■	■			
Workers' Comp Audit		■			■							
Laser Checks	■	■	■		■		■	■	■			
Dot Matrix Checks		■	■		■		■	■	■			
Tracks Vacation & Sick		■	■		■		■	■	■			
IBM PC - DOS		■	■				■		■			
IBM PC - Windows	■	■	■	■		■	■	■	■	■	■	■
Macintosh / Power Mac	■			■		■				■		
Unix / Xenix												
Midrange System												
Novell Networks	■	■	■	■	■	■		■	■	■	■	■
NT Networks	■	■	■	■	■	■		■	■	■	■	■
Other Networks	■	■		■	■	■			■	■		■
Year 2000 Certified	■	■	■	■	■	■	□	■	■	■	□	□

Feature	Logos Management Software	Membership Services (MSI)	Micro Information Products	Parish Data Systems	Parsons Technology	PowerChurch Software	RDS Publishing	SaintSaver	Servant PC Resources, Inc.	Shelby Systems	Shepherd's Staff
Congregation Database	■	■		■	■	■	■	■	■	■	■
Attendance Tracker	■	■		■	■	■	■	■	■	■	■
Contributions Tracker	■	■		■	■	■	■	■	■	■	■
Can Add/Modify Fields	■	■		■	■		■	■	■	■	■
Photos by Individual/Family	■				■	■	■		■	■	■
Mail Merge Interface	■	■		■	■	■	■	■	■	■	■
Bulk Mail Bar Codes	■	■		■	■	■	■		■	■	■
Bulk Mail CASS Certification	■	■		■		■	■			■	
Telephony Services Link	■	■			■		■			■	
Facility Scheduler	■	■		■			■				
Equipment Scheduler	■	■					■				
Retreat Registrations & A/R	■	■								■	
General Ledger	■	■	■	■	■	■	■	■	■	■	■
GAAP Compliant	■	■	■			■	■		■	■	■
Full Audit Trail	■	■	■		■	■	■	■	■	■	■
Fixed Budget Tracker	■	■	■	■	■	■	■	■	■	■	■
Variable Budget Tracker	■	■	■	■	■		■	■	■	■	■
Graphic Analysis	■	■			■	■	☒	■	☒	■	
Accounts Payable	■	■	■	■	■	■	■	■	■	■	□
Accrual Basis Capable	■	■	■				■	■	■	■	□
Cash Basis Capable	■	■	■	■	■	■	■	■	■	■	■
Annual 1099's	■	■	■	■			■		■	■	☒
Laser Checks	■	■	■	■	■	■	■		■	■	■
Dot Matrix Checks		■	■	■	■	■	■		■	■	■
Payroll	■	■	■	■		■	■		■	■	□
Minister's Salary Capable	■	■	■	■		■	■		■	■	■
ACH Direct Deposit Capable	■	■	■				■			■	
Quarterly 941's	■	■		■			■		■	■	□
Annual W2's	■	■	■	■		■	■		■	■	■
Workers' Comp Audit	■	■	■				■		■	■	
Laser Checks	■	■	■	■		■	■		■	■	■
Dot Matrix Checks		■	■	■		■	■		■	■	
Tracks Vacation & Sick	■	■	■	■			■		■	■	
IBM PC - DOS	■	■	■	■			■			■	■
IBM PC - Windows	■	■	■	■	■	■	■		■	■	■
Macintosh / Power Mac	■	■						■			
Unix / Xenix		■					■			■	
Midrange System		■								■	
Novell Networks	■	■	■	■	■	■	■		■	■	■
NT Networks	■	■	■	■	■	■	■		■	■	■
Other Networks	■	■		■	■	■	■		■	■	■
Year 2000 Certified	■	■	■	■	■	■	■	■	■	■	■

Feature	Software for Ministry	Software Library	Specialty Software	Summit Systems	Suran Systems	Titus Information Systems	TLC Communications, Inc.	Torbert Data Systems	Vian	Yaffey Software Development, Inc.
Congregation Database	■	■	■	■	■	■	■	■	■	■
Attendance Tracker	■	■	■	■	■	■		■		
Contributions Tracker	■	■	■	■	■	■	■	■	■	■
Can Add/Modify Fields	■	■	■	■	■		■	■		
Photos by Individual/Family	□	■	■		■		■			
Mail Merge Interface	■	■	■	■	■	■	■	■	■	■
Bulk Mail Bar Codes	■	■	■		■	■	■	■	■	
Bulk Mail CASS Certification	■	■	■		■	■				
Telephony Services Link					■					
Facility Scheduler		■		■			■	■		
Equipment Scheduler							■	■		
Retreat Registrations & A/R					■					
General Ledger		■	■	■	■	■		■	■	
GAAP Compliant		■	■	■	■			■		
Full Audit Trail		■	■	■	■	■		■	■	
Fixed Budget Tracker		■	■	■	■	■		■	■	
Variable Budget Tracker		■	■	■	■	■		■		
Graphic Analysis		■	■							
Accounts Payable		■	■	■	■	■		■	■	
Accrual Basis Capable		■		■	■	■		■		
Cash Basis Capable		■	■	■	■	■		■	■	
Annual 1099's		■	■	■	■	■				
Laser Checks		■	■	■	■	■		■	■	
Dot Matrix Checks		■	■	■	■	■		■		
Payroll		■	■	■	■	■				
Minister's Salary Capable		■	■	■	■	■			■	
ACH Direct Deposit Capable						■				
Quarterly 941's		■	■	■	■	■				
Annual W2's		■	■	■	■	■				
Workers' Comp Audit		■				■				
Laser Checks		■	■	■	■	■			■	
Dot Matrix Checks		■	■	■	■	■				
Tracks Vacation & Sick		■		■		■				
IBM PC - DOS	■		■			■	■	■		
IBM PC - Windows	■	■	■	■	■		■	■	■	■
Macintosh / Power Mac			■		■					
Unix / Xenix										
Midrange System										
Novell Networks		■		■	■	■			■	
NT Networks		■	■	■	■		■		■	
Other Networks				■	■				■	■
Year 2000 Certified	■	■	■	■	■	■	■	■	■	■

Church Management Software Providers

Compiled by Ministry Business Services, Inc.

AlphaOmega InfoSystems
2400 Boston St. #327
Baltimore, MD 21224
Voice: (888) CH-WORKS (249-6757)
Fax: (410) 327-8912
Email: churchwrks@aol.com
Web: www.aois.com
Company Founded: 1993
Years Marketing CMS: 5
Active Installed User Base: 5000
Number of Employees: 15
Tech Support Hours: 10a-4p
Last Major Release Date: 1/98
Number of Updates / Year: 1

Automated Church System (ACS)
PO Box 202010
Florence, SC 29502-2010
Voice: (800) 736-7425
Fax: (800) 227-5990
Email: info@acshome.com
Web: www.acshome.com
Company Founded: 1978
Years Marketing CMS: 21
Active Installed User Base: 10,000
Number of Employees: 130
Tech Support Hours: 8a-8p (-6p F)
Last Major Release Date: 4/99
Number of Updates / Year: 2

Blackbaud Microsystems
4401 Belle Oaks Dr.
Charleston, SC 29405
Voice: (800) 443-9441
Fax: (843) 740-5410
Email: sales@blackbaud.com
Web: www.blackbaud.com
Company Founded: 1981
Years Marketing CMS: 15
Active Installed User Base: 12,000
Number of Employees: 609
Tech Support Hours: 8:30a-11p
Last Major Release Date: 10/97
Number of Updates / Year: 2-3

By The Book
3900 E Grace Blvd.
Highlands Ranch, CO 80126-7801
Voice: (800) 554-9116
Fax: (303) 791-1032
Email: orders@bythebook.com
Web: www.bythebook.com
Company Founded: 1991
Years Marketing CMS: 8
Active Installed User Base: 550
Number of Employees: 3
Tech Support Hours: 9a-5p
Last Major Release Date: 4/99
Number of Updates / Year: 1

Church Windows/ Computer Helper
PO Box 30191
Columbus, OH 43230-0191
Voice: (800) 533-5227
Fax: (614) 478-0625
Email: info@churchwindows.com
Web: www.churchwindows.com
Company Founded: 1986
Years Marketing CMS: 12
Active Installed User Base: 3000
Number of Employees: 20
Tech Support Hours: 9a-5p
Last Major Release Date: 12/99
Number of Updates / Year: 1-3

Diakonia
PO Box 5647
Diamond Bar, CA 91765
Voice: (909) 861-8787
Fax: (909) 861-0335
Email: diakonia@compuserve.com
Web: ourworld.compuserve.com/homepages/diakonia
Company Founded: 1992
Years Marketing CMS: 6
Active Installed User Base: classified info
Number of Employees: classified info
Tech Support Hours: 9a-5p
Last Major Release Date: 4/99
Number of Updates / Year: varies

Focus On Business
116 SW 19th St.
Guthrie, OK 73044
Voice: (405) 282-1143
Fax: (405) 282-1700
Email: magnum_sos@aol.com
Web: none
Company Founded: 1985
Years Marketing CMS: 12
Active Installed User Base: 500
Number of Employees: 6
Tech Support Hours: 8a-5p
Last Major Release Date: 10/98
Number of Updates / Year: 2

Greentree Applied Systems
157 Propserous PL #1A
Lexington, KY 40509
Voice: (800) 928-6388
Fax: (606) 263-9824
Email: info@greentreeky.com
Web: www.greentreeky.com
Company Founded: 1982
Years Marketing CMS: 3
Active Installed User Base: 500
Number of Employees: 10
Tech Support Hours: 9a-5p
Last Major Release Date: 10/98
Number of Updates / Year: 6

Hunter Systems
100 Century Park South #206
Birmingham, AL 35226
Voice: (800) 326-0527
Fax: (205) 979-3389
Email: sales@huntersystems.com
Web: www.huntersystems.com
Company Founded: 1986
Years Marketing CMS: 13
Active Installed User Base: 400
Number of Employees: 50
Tech Support Hours: 8:30a-5:30p
Last Major Release Date: 1997
Number of Updates / Year: 1-2

Icon Systems
3704 Westmoor Dr.
Moorhead, MN 56560
Voice: (800) 596-4266
Fax: (218) 236-0235
Email: revelations@corpcomm.net
Web: www.revelations.com
Company Founded: 1992
Years Marketing CMS: 5
Active Installed User Base: 1500
Number of Employees: classified info
Tech Support Hours: 8:30a-4:30p
Last Major Release Date: 8/98
Number of Updates / Year: 2

J.S. Paluch Co.
3825 N Willow Rd.
Schiller Park, IL 60176
Voice: (800) 621-6732
Fax: (847) 928-5812
Email: pcmsupport@jspaluch.com
Web: www.jspaluch.com
Company Founded: 1913
Years Marketing CMS: 14
Active Installed User Base: 600
Number of Employees: 490
Tech Support Hours: 8a-4:30p
Last Major Release Date: 12/97
Number of Updates / Year: 3

Lieberman Consulting Group
2253 South Ave.
Scotch Plains, NJ 07090-4688

Church Management Software Providers *(continued)*

Compiled by Ministry Business Services, Inc.

Voice: (925) 283-3289
Fax: (925) 283-3289
Email: sales@lieberware.com
Web: www.lieberware.com/mem-info
Company Founded: 1982
Years Marketing CMS: 3
Active Installed User Base: 14
Number of Employees: 2
Tech Support Hours: 9a-5p PST
Last Major Release Date: 1/99
Number of Updates / Year: 2

Logos Management Software

15500 W Telegraph Rd.
Santa Paula, CA 93060
Voice: (800) 266-3311
Fax: (805) 525-6161
Email: info@logoslbe.com
Web: logoslbe.com
Company Founded: 1980
Years Marketing CMS: 18
Active Installed User Base: 3500
Number of Employees: classified info
Tech Support Hours: 7a-5p
Last Major Release Date: 1/99
Number of Updates / Year: 1

Membership Services (MSI)

PO Box 152130
Irving, TX 75038
Voice: (800) 955-0805
Fax: (972) 594-8100
Email: msi@dallas.net
Web: www.members.aol.com/msidot
Company Founded: 1966
Years Marketing CMS: 32
Active Installed User Base: 1100
Number of Employees: 14
Tech Support Hours: 7a-5p
Last Major Release Date: 1998
Number of Updates / Year: 6

Micro Information Products

313 E Anderson Ln. #200
Austin, TX 78752
Voice: (800) 647-3863
Fax: (512) 454-2254
Email: info@mip.com
Web: www.mip.com
Company Founded: 1982
Years Marketing CMS: 17
Active Installed User Base: 4100
Number of Employees: 90
Tech Support Hours: 8a-6p
Last Major Release Date: 9/98
Number of Updates / Year: 3

Parish Data Systems, Inc.

14425 N 19th Ave.
Phoenix, AZ 85023
Voice: (602) 789-0595
Fax: (602) 789-0597
Email: pdsphx@parishdatainc.com
Web: www.parishdatainc.com
Company Founded: 1978
Years Marketing CMS: 20
Active Installed User Base: 10,000
Number of Employees: 16
Tech Support Hours: 8a-5p
Last Major Release Date: 11/98
Number of Updates/Year: as needed

Parsons Technology

1700 Progress Dr.
Hiawatha, IA 52233
Voice: (800) 644-6344
Fax: (319) 378-0335
Email: none
Web: www.quickverse.com
Company Founded: 1984
Years Marketing CMS: 9
Active Installed User Base: 25,000
Number of Employees: 500
Tech Support Hours: 6a-8p
Last Major Release Date: 6/98
Number of Updates/Year: as needed

PowerChurch Software

208 Ridgefield Ct.
Asheville, NC 28806-2262
Voice: (800) 486-1800
Fax: (828) 665-1999
Email: info@pchurch.com
Web: www.pchurch.com
Company Founded: 1984
Years Marketing CMS: 15
Active Installed User Base: 12,000
Number of Employees: classified info
Tech Support Hours: 9a-6p
Last Major Release Date: 6/98
Number of Updates / Year: 1

RDS Publishing

6801 N Broadway #120
Oklahoma City, OK 73116
Voice: (405) 840-5177
Fax: (405) 840-0468
Email: rds@rdsadvantage.com
Web: www.rdsadvantage.com
Company Founded: 1983
Years Marketing CMS: 16
Active Installed User Base: classified info
Number of Employees: classified info
Tech Support Hours: 8a-5p
Last Major Release Date: 10/98
Number of Updates / Year: 1

SaintSaver

9150 Russell Ave. S
Bloomington, MN 55431-2120
Voice: (612) 881-7324
Fax: none
Email: gary@mumac.org
Web: www.mumac.org/saintsaver.html
Company Founded: 1992
Years Marketing CMS: 7
Active Installed User Base: 100
Number of Employees: classified info
Tech Support Hours: 24 hours
Last Major Release Date: 1994
Number of Updates / Year: no updates

Servant PC Resources, Inc.

3342 Nichols Run Rd.
Jersey Shore, PA 17740
Voice: (800) 773-7570
Fax: (570) 398-2501
Email: servantpc@servantpc.com
Web: www.servantpc.com
Company Founded: 1994
Years Marketing CMS: 5
Active Installed User Base: 5000
Number of Employees: 13
Tech Support Hours: 9a-6p
Last Major Release Date: 4/98
Number of Updates / Year: 1

Shelby Systems

65 Germantown Ct. #303
Cordova, TN 38018
Voice: (800) 877-0222
Fax: (901) 759-3682
Email: mktg@shelbyinc.com
Web: www.shelbyinc.com
Company Founded: 1976
Years Marketing CMS: 22
Active Installed User Base: 5000
Number of Employees: 75
Tech Support Hours: 8a-6p
Last Major Release Date: 9/97
Number of Updates / Year: 4-5

Church Management Software Providers *(continued)*

Compiled by Ministry Business Services, Inc.

Shepherd's Staff
3558 S. Jefferson Ave.
St. Louis, MO 63118-3968
Voice: (800) 325-2399
Fax: (800) 496-2641
Email: softwaresales@cphnet.org
Web: support.cphnet.com
Company Founded: 1869
Years Marketing CMS: 17
Active Installed User Base: 7000
Number of Employees: 350
Tech Support Hours: 7:30a-5:30p
Last Major Release Date: 10/98
Number of Updates / Year: 1-3

Software For Ministry
PO Box 1165
Yucaipa, CA 92399
Voice: (707) 965-3225
Fax: (707) 965-3541
Email: 74617.1146@compuserve.com
Web: www.softwareforministry.com
Company Founded: 1983
Years Marketing CMS: 15
Active Installed User Base: 1250
Number of Employees: 2
Tech Support Hours: 9a-5p
Last Major Release Date: 2/98
Number of Updates / Year: 1-2

Software Library
3300 Bass Lake Rd. #304
Brooklyn Center, MN 55429
Voice: (800) 247-8044
Fax: (612) 566-2250
Email: cms@softwarelib.com
Web: www.softwarelib.com
Company Founded: 1985
Years Marketing CMS: 12
Active Installed User Base: 2000
Number of Employees: 10
Tech Support Hours: 8a-7p
Last Major Release Date: 12/98
Number of Updates / Year: 1

Specialty Software
PO Box 5494
Evansville, IN 47716
Voice: (800) 568-6350
Fax: (407) 728-1077
Email: info@specialtysoftware.com
Web: www.specialtysoftware.com
Company Founded: 1983
Years Marketing CMS: 16
Active Installed User Base: 5000
Number of Employees: 10
Tech Support Hours: 9a-5p
Last Major Release Date: 1/99
Number of Updates / Year: 1

Summit Systems
2163 Amicks Ferry Rd.
Chapin, SC 29036
Voice: (800) 228-5857
Fax: (803) 345-3940
Email: sumsys@juno.com
Web: www.intraweb.com/summit.htm
Company Founded: 1984
Years Marketing CMS: 15
Active Installed User Base: 850
Number of Employees: 5
Tech Support Hours: 8a-5:30p
Last Major Release Date: 12/98
Number of Updates / Year: 2

Suran Systems
695 Craigs Creek Rd.
Versailles, KY 40383-8909
Voice: (800) 557-8726
Fax: (606) 873-0308
Email: randy@suran.com
Web: www.suran.com
Company Founded: 1986
Years Marketing CMS: 13
Active Installed User Base: 2000
Number of Employees: 12
Tech Support Hours: 9a-7p
Last Major Release Date: 3/98
Number of Updates / Year: 1

Titus Information Systems
1528 E Missouri #161
Phoenix, AZ 85014
Voice: (602) 234-8969
Fax: (602) 234-8927
Email: titusinfo@mindspring.com
Web: none
Company Founded: 1979
Years Marketing CMS: 17
Active Installed User Base: 6
Number of Employees: 1
Tech Support Hours: 8a-5p
Last Major Release Date: 8/97
Number of Updates / Year: as needed

TLC Communications, Inc.
1045 Wildwood Blvd. SW
Issaquah, WA 98027-4506
Voice: (425) 392-9592
Fax: (425) 392-9592
Email: tlccomm@msn.com
Web: www.tlccommunications.com
Company Founded: 1984
Years Marketing CMS: 2
Active Installed User Base: 50
Number of Employees: 4
Tech Support Hours: 7a-6p
Last Major Release Date: 12/99
Number of Updates / Year: 1

Torbert Data Systems
PO Box 9218
Chesapeake, VA 23321
Voice: (800) 755-2641
Fax: none
Email: tds@churchsoftware.com
Web: www.churchsoftware.com
Company Founded: 1990
Years Marketing CMS: 9
Active Installed User Base: 1150
Number of Employees: 4
Tech Support Hours: 8a-5p, Sat 9-1
Last Major Release Date: 3/99
Number of Updates / Year: 2

Vian
452 W Hill Rd.
Glen Gardner, NJ 08826-3253
Voice: (908) 537-4642
Fax: none
Email: vian@vian.com
Web: www.vian.com
Company Founded: 1982
Years Marketing CMS: 14
Active Installed User Base: 1982
Number of Employees: classified info
Tech Support Hours: 4:30p-6:00p
Last Major Release Date: 1/99
Number of Updates / Year: varies

Yaffey Software Development, Inc.
435 Walhalla Rd.
Columbus, OH 43202-1474
Voice: (614) 268-6353
Fax: none
Email: cyaffey@columbus.rr.com
Web: home.columbus.rr.com/cyaffey
Company Founded: 1990
Years Marketing CMS: 8
Active Installed User Base: 6
Number of Employees: 1
Tech Support Hours: 9a-5p
Last Major Release Date: 10/98
Number of Updates / Year: varies

CROSS REFERENCE

Accounting Committee and available at 800-3BE-WISE) and *Financial and Accounting Guide for Not-for-Profit Organizations* by Melvin J. Gross, Jr., and Richard F. Larkin (John Wiley & Sons).

Statement of activity

The statement of activity (also referred to as a statement of revenues and expenses) reflects an organization's support and revenue, expenses, and changes in net assets for a certain period of time. It shows the sources of an organization's income and how the resources were used. The form of the statement will depend on the type of organization and accounting method used. But the statement must present the change in unrestricted, temporarily restricted, permanently restricted, and total net assets.

Many smaller organizations will have several lines for support and revenue such as contributions, sales of products, investment income, and so on. Expenses are often listed by natural classification such as salaries, fringe benefits, supplies, and so on.

Organizations desiring to meet GAAP accounting standards must reflect functional expenses (for example, by program, management and general, fund raising, and membership development) in the statement of activity or footnotes. Smaller organizations will tend to show expenses by natural classification in the statement of activity and functional expenses in the footnotes. The reverse approach will generally be true of larger organizations. While the reporting of expenses by natural classification is not generally required under GAAP, readers of the financial statements will often find the additional reporting very helpful.

Statement of financial position

A statement of financial position shows assets, liabilities, and net assets as of the end-of-period date. This statement is also called a balance sheet because it shows how the two sides of the accounting equation (assets minus liabilities equal net assets) "balance" in your organization.

Anything an organization owns that has a money value is an asset. Cash, land, buildings, furniture, and fixtures are examples of assets. Anything the organization owes is a liability. Liabilities might include amounts owed to supplies (accounts payable) or to the bank (notes payable, and other amounts due).

Statement of cash flows

The statement of cash flows provides information about the cash receipts and disbursements of your organization and the extent to which resources were obtained from, or used in, operating, investing, or financing activities. The direct method of presenting a cash flow statement starts by listing all sources of cash from operations during the period and deducts all operating outflows of cash to arrive at the net cash flow. The indirect method begins with the change in net assets and adjusts backwards to reconcile the change in net assets to net cash flows. The financial Accounting Standards Board encourages the use of the direct presentation method.

SAMPLE CHART OF ACCOUNTS FOR A CHURCH

Assets
- Cash and cash equivalents
- Prepaid expenses
- Short-term investments
- Land, buildings, and equipment:
  - Church buildings
  - Parsonage
  - Furnishings
- Long-term investments

Liabilities
- Accounts payable
- Notes payable
- Long-term debt

Revenues and Support
- Contributions
  - Regular offerings
  - Sunday school offerings
  - Missions offerings
  - Building fund offerings
  - Other offerings
- Investment income
  - Interest income
  - Rental income
- Other income
  - Tape sales
  - Other sales
  - Other income

Expenses
- Salaries and wages
  - Salary including cash housing allowance
  - Tax deferred payments (TSA/IRA)
- Benefits
  - Pension
  - Social security (SECA) reimbursement
  - Social Security (FICA)
  - Medical expense reimbursement
  - Insurance premiums
- Supplies
  - Postage
  - Literature and printing
  - Office supplies
  - Maintenance supplies
  - Food
  - Kitchen supplies
  - Flowers
  - Other supplies
- Travel and entertainment
  - Auto expense reimbursements
  - Vehicle rental
  - Other travel expense
- Continuing education
- Insurance
  - Workers' Compensation
  - Health insurance
  - Property insurance
  - Other insurance
- Benevolences
  - Denominational budgets
  - Other benevolences
- Services and professional fees
  - Speaking honoraria
  - Custodial services
  - Legal and audit fees
  - Other fees
- Office and occupancy
  - Rent
  - Telephone
  - Utilities
  - Property taxes
  - Other office and occupancy
- Depreciation
- Interest expense
- Other
  - Banquets
  - Advertising

Suffix digits may be used to indicate the functional expense category such as

- 10	Program expenses
- 11	Pastoral
- 12	Education
- 121	Sunday school
- 122	Vacation Bible school
- 123	Camps and retreats
- 13	Music and worship
- 14	Missions
- 15	Membership and evangelism
- 16	Youth
- 17	Singles
- 18	Seniors
- 20	Management and general
- 21	Church plant
- 22	Parsonages
- 23	Office
- 30	Fund raising

Fall Creek Church
Statement of Activity
Year Ended June 30, 1999

	Unrestricted	Temporarily Restricted	Permanently Restricted	Total
Support and revenues				
Contributions				
Regular offerings	$260,000			$260,000
Sunday school offerings	45,000			45,000
Missions offerings	50,000			50,000
Other offerings	25,000	$10,000		35,000
Investment income				
Interest income	1,000		$2,000	3,000
Rental income	3,000			3,000
Total revenues	384,000	10,000	2,000	396,000
Expenses				
Program expenses				
Worship	25,000	9,000		34,000
Sunday school	35,000			35,000
Youth	30,000			30,000
Management and general	296,000			296,000
Fund-raising	5,000			5,000
Total expenses	391,000	9,000		400,000
Change in net assets	(7,000)	1,000	2,000	(4,000)
Net assets at beginning of year	645,000	4,000	18,000	667,000
Net assets at end of year	$ 638,000	$ 5,000	$ 20,000	$ 663,000

Expenses incurred were for:

	Total	Worship	Sunday School	Youth	Mgt. & Gen.	Fund Raising
Salaries, wages, and benefits	$142,000	$5,000	$6,000		$131,000	
Supplies	73,000	25,000	24,000	$24,000		
Travel	16,000			1,000	10,000	$5,000
Insurance		20,000				20,000
Benevolences						
Denominational budgets	20,000				20,000	
Other benevolences	50,000				50,000	
Services and professional fees	14,000	4,000	5,000	5,000		
Office and occupancy	30,000				30,000	
Depreciation		10,000				10,000
Interest		25,000				25,000
	$400,000	$ 34,000	$ 35,000	$ 30,000	$296,000	$ 5,000

Note: This is a multi-column presentation of a statement of activity. Reporting of expenses by natural classification (at bottom of page), though often useful, is not required.

Castle Creek Church
Statement of Activity
Year Ended June 30, 1999

Changes in unrestricted net assets:	
Revenues:	
Contributions	$ 141,000
Fees	6,250
Income on long-term investments	5,400
Other	20,100
Total unrestricted revenues	172,500
Expenses (Note A)	
Salaries, wages, and benefits	90,500
Supplies	3,000
Travel	5,000
Insurance	7,500
Benevolences	
Denominational budgets	10,000
Other benevolences	20,000
Services and professional fees	8,000
Office and occupancy	7,000
Depreciation	5,000
Interest	20,000
Total expenses	176,000
Net assets released from restrictions:	
Satisfaction of program restrictions	2,000
Expiration of time restrictions	3,000
Total net assets released from restrictions	5,000
Increase in unrestricted net assets	2,500
Changes in temporarily restricted net assets:	
Contributions	23,000
Net assets released from restrictions	(5,000)
Increase in temporarily restricted net assets	19,500
Changes in permanently restricted net assets:	
Contributions	5,000
Increase in permanently restricted net assets	7,000
Increase in net assets	29,000
Net assets at beginning of year	910,000
Net assets at end of year	$941,000

Note A:
Functional expense breakdown:

Program expenses:	
Worship	$16,000
Sunday school	7,000
Youth	5,000
Management and general	145,500
Fund-raising	2,500
Total expenses	$176,000

Note: This is an alternate, single-column, presentation of a statement of activity. If the natural classification of expenses is shown in the body of the statement, the functional expenses must be reflected in a footnote to meet accounting standards.

Fall Creek Church
Statement of Financial Position
June 30, 1999 and 1998

	1998	1997
Assets:		
Cash and cash equivalents	$20,000	$15,000
Prepaid expenses	5,000	4,000
Short-term investments	10,000	8,000
Land, buildings, and equipment:		
Church buildings	525,000	525,000
Parsonage	110,000	110,000
Furnishings	175,000	160,000
Long-term investments	30,000	25,000
Total assets	875,000	847,000
Liabilities and net assets:		
Accounts payable	$8,000	$7,000
Notes payable	9,000	10,000
Long-term debt	195,000	205,000
Total liabilities	212,000	222,000
Net assets:		
Unrestricted	638,000	601,000
Temporarily restricted (Note 1)	5,000	4,000
Permanently restricted (Note 2)	20,000	20,000
Total net assets	663,000	625,000
Total liabilities and net assets	$875,000	$847,000

Note 1: Restricted net assets result when a donor has imposed a stipulation to use the funds or assets contributed in a manner which is more limited than the broad purpose for which tax-exempt status is granted for an organization. For example, a church may receive a contribution to establish a scholarship fund with the principal and earnings available for scholarship payments. This gift is a temporarily restricted contribution. If the scholarship funds were all expended in the church's fiscal year when the gift was received, the contribution would be unrestricted.

Note 2: Permanently restricted contributions are those which contain a stipulation which will always be present. For example, if a scholarship gift is made with the stipulation that only the earnings from the fund may be spent for scholarships, this is a permanently restricted net asset.

The financial statements illustrated on pages 128-30 are presented based on Statement No. 117 issued by the Financial Accounting Standards Board (FASB) of the American Institute of Certified Public Accountants.

Budgeting

It is possible for a small church or nonprofit organization to operate without a budget. But a budget is an effective tool for allocating financial resources and planning and controlling your spending even for smaller organizations. For larger organizations, a budget is essential.

A budget matches anticipated inflows of resources with outflows of resources. Preparing a budget requires considerable effort. It includes looking back at revenue and expense trends. Projected plans and programs must be converted into estimated dollar amounts. Too many organizations budget expenses with some degree of precision and then set the income budget at whatever it takes to cover the total expenses. This is often a disastrous approach.

Ideally, separate budgets should be prepared for all funds of an organization. Even capital and debt-retirement funds should be budgeted. The separate budgets are then combined into a unified budget.

Line-item budgets within each fund reflect the projected cost of salaries, fringe benefits, utilities, maintenance, debt retirement, and other expenses. The line-item approach is generally used by a treasurer in reporting to department heads or other responsible individuals.

Program budgets are often presented to the board of a nonprofit organization or a church's membership. In this approach, the cost of a program is reflected rather than the cost of specific line-items such as salaries or fringe benefits.

A good budgeting approach is to divide the budget into quarterly or monthly segments. If a monthly budget is used, the budget for each month is not necessarily one-twelfth of the annual amount. For example, if gifts are typically lower in summer months, the monthly budgets for the summer reflect the projected lower income. When actual activity is compared to monthly or quarterly budgets, it may be possible to make program adjustments as the year progresses.

Audit Guidelines

An annual audit of the organization's records is a must. External audits are performed by an independent auditor that has no impairing relationship to the organization and can review the data procedures with maximum objectivity. Internal audits are generally performed by members or those closely associated with the organization.

External audits

The ideal is to have an annual audit performed by independent CPAs. However, only medium to large nonprofits generally can afford this extra expense. External audits of smaller organizations are often done on a non-GAAP basis—the statements do not conform to the full accrual method with depreciation recognized.

Non-GAAP audits of smaller organizations are often acceptable to banks and other agencies that require audited financial statements.

Internal audits

Members of the organization may form an audit committee to perform an internal audit to determine the validity of the financial statements. (Sample internal audit guidelines for churches are shown on pages 133-36.) If the committee takes its task seriously, the result may be significant improvements in internal control and accounting procedures. Too often, the internal audit committee only conducts a cursory review, commends the treasurer for a job well done, and provides the organization with a false sense of security.

Key Concepts

- Good accounting records and good stewardship go hand in hand.
- Your organization is the trustee of the money it receives—handle it carefully.
- Tailor meaningful financial statements for your organization.
- Prepare timely financial reports covering all of your funds—not just the operating fund.
- An annual audit—either external or internal—is a must.

Church Internal Audit Guidelines

Financial statements

- ✓ Are monthly financial statements prepared on a timely basis and submitted to the organization's board?
- ✓ Do the financial statements include all funds (unrestricted, temporarily restricted, and permanently restricted)?
- ✓ Do the financial statements include a statement of financial condition and statement of activity?
- ✓ Are account balances in the financial records reconciled with amounts presented in financial reports?

Cash receipts

✓ **General**

- Are cash handling procedures in writing?
- Has the bank been notified to never cash checks payable to the church?
- Are Sunday school offerings properly recorded and delivered to the money counters?
- Are procedures established to care for offerings and monies delivered or mailed to the church office between Sundays?

✓ **Offering counting**

- Are at least two members of the counting committee present when offerings are counted? (The persons counting the money should not include a pastor of a church or the church treasurer.)
- Do money counters verify that the contents of the offering envelopes are identical to the amounts written on the outside of the envelopes?
- Are all checks stamped with a restrictive endorsement stamp immediately after the offering envelope contents are verified?
- Are money counters rotated so the same people are not handling the funds each week?

- Are donor-restricted funds properly identified during the process of counting offerings?

✓ **Depositing of funds**

- Are two members of the offering counting team in custody of the offering until it is deposited in the bank, placed in a night depository, or the church's safe?
- Are all funds promptly deposited? Compare offering and other receipt records with bank deposits.
- Are all receipts deposited intact? Receipts should not be used to pay cash expenses.

✓ **Restricted funds**

- Are donations for restricted purposes properly recorded in the accounting records?
- Are restricted funds held for the intended purpose(s) and not spent on operating needs?

Donation records/receipting

✓ Are individual donor records kept as a basis to provide donor acknowledgments for all single contributions of $250 or more?

✓ If no goods or services were provided (other than intangible religious benefits) in exchange for a gift, does the receipt include a statement to this effect?

✓ If goods or services (other than intangible religious benefits) were provided in exchange for a gift, does the receipt

- inform the donor that the amount of the contribution that is deductible for federal income tax purposes is limited to the excess of the amount of any money and the value of any property contributed by the donor over the value of the goods and services provided by the organization, and
- provide the donor with a good faith estimate of the value of such goods and services?

✓ Are the donations traced from the weekly counting sheets to the donor records for a selected time period by the audit committee?

Cash disbursements

- ✓ Are all disbursements paid by check except for minor expenditures paid through the petty cash fund?
- ✓ Is written documentation available to support all disbursements?
- ✓ If a petty cash fund is used, are vouchers prepared for each disbursement from the fund?
- ✓ Are pre-numbered checks used? Account for all the check numbers including voided checks.
- ✓ Are blank checks ever signed in advance? This should never be done.

Petty cash funds

- ✓ Is a petty cash fund used for disbursements of a small amount? If so, is the fund periodically reconciled and replenished based on proper documentation of the cash expenditures?

Bank statement reconciliation

- ✓ Are written bank reconciliations prepared on a timely basis? Test the reconciliation for the last month in the fiscal year. Trace transactions between the bank and the books for completeness and timeliness.
- ✓ Are there any checks that have been outstanding over three months?
- ✓ Are there any unusual transactions in the bank statement immediately following year-end? Obtain the bank statement for the first month after year-end directly from the bank for review by the audit committee. Otherwise, obtain the last bank statement (unopened) from the church treasurer.

Savings and investment accounts

- ✓ Are all savings and investment accounts recorded in the financial records? Compare monthly statements to the books.
- ✓ Are earnings or losses from savings and investment accounts recorded in the books?

Land, buildings, and equipment records

- ✓ Are there detailed records of land, buildings, and equipment including date acquired, description, and cost or fair market value at date of acquisition?
- ✓ Was an equipment physical inventory taken at year-end?
- ✓ Have the property records been reconciled to the insurance coverages?

Accounts payable

- ✓ Is there a schedule of unpaid invoices including vendor name, invoice date, and due date?
- ✓ Are any of the accounts payable items significantly past-due?
- ✓ Are there any disputes with vendors over amounts owed?

Insurance policies

- ✓ Is there a schedule of insurance coverage in force? Reflect effective and expiration dates, kind and classification of coverages, maximum amounts of each coverage, premiums and terms of payment.
- ✓ Is Workers' Compensation insurance being carried as provided by law in most states? Are all employees (and perhaps some independent contractors) covered under the Workers' Compensation policy?

Amortization of debt

- ✓ Is there a schedule of debt such as mortgages and notes?
- ✓ Have the balances owed to all lenders been confirmed directly in writing?
- ✓ Have the balances owed to all lenders been compared to the obligations recorded on the balance sheet?

Securities and other negotiable documents

- ✓ Does the church own any marketable securities or bonds? If so, are they kept in a safety deposit box, and are two signatures (excluding a pastor) required for access?
- ✓ Have the contents of the safety deposit box been examined and recorded?

CHAPTER SEVEN

Charitable Gifts

In This Chapter

- Percentage limitations
- Charitable gift options
- Charitable gift timing
- Charitable contribution acknowledgments
- Gifts that may not qualify as contributions
- Reporting to the IRS
- Quid pro quo disclosure requirements
- Special charitable contribution issues

While most donors care more about the reason for giving than they do about the tax implications, the spirit of giving should never be reduced by unexpected tax results.

A gift is the voluntary transfer of cash or property motivated by something other than "consideration." Consideration is something being received in return for a payment. The mere transfer of funds to a church or charitable nonprofit is not necessarily a gift. Thus, when a parent pays the college tuition for a child, there is no gift or charitable deduction.

If payments are made to a church or other nonprofit organization to receive something in exchange, the transaction is more in the nature of a purchase. The tax law states that a transfer to a nonprofit is not a contribution when made "with a reasonable expectation of financial return commensurate with the amount of the transfer." When one transfer comprises both a gift and a purchase, only the gift portion is deductible.

The two broad categories of charitable gifts are *outright* gifts and *deferred* gifts. Outright gifts require that the donor immediately transfer possession and use of the gift property to the donee. In deferred giving, the donor also makes a current gift, but the gift is of a future interest. Accordingly, actual possession and use of the gift property by the donee is deferred until the future.

Charitable contributions are deductible if given "to and for the use" of a "qualified" tax-exempt organization to be used under its control to accomplish its exempt purposes. ("Qualified" organizations are churches and other domestic 501(c)(3) organizations.) To be deductible, contributions must be unconditional and without personal benefit to the donor.

Three types of gifts commonly given to a church or other nonprofit organization are:

CAUTION

- ✓ **Gifts without donor stipulations.** Contributions received without donor restriction are generally tax-deductible.

- ✓ **Donor restricted gifts.** Contributions may be designated (*also referred to as restricted*) by the donor for a specific exempt purpose of the organization rather than being given without donor stipulation. If the gifts are in support of the organization's exempt program activities and not designated or restricted for an individual, they are generally tax-deductible.

  If gifts are designated or earmarked for a specific individual, no tax deduction is generally allowed unless the church or nonprofit organization exercises full administrative control over the funds and they are spent for program activities of the organization.

- ✓ **Personal gifts.** Gifts made through an organization to an individual, where the donor has specified, by name, the identity of the person who is to receive the gift, are not tax-deductible. Processing of personal gifts through a church or nonprofit organization should be discouraged by the organization unless it is done as a convenience to donors and the ultimate recipients where communication between the two parties might otherwise be difficult (e.g., a missionary supported by the organization who is serving in a foreign country).

Tax-deduction receipts should not be issued to a donor for personal gifts and the organization should affirmatively advise donors that the gifts are not tax-deductible.

Percentage Limitations

Charitable deductions for a particular tax year are limited by certain percentages of an individual's adjusted gross income (AGI). These are the limitations:

- ✓ Gifts of cash and ordinary income property to public charities and private operating foundations are limited to 50% of AGI. Any excess may generally be carried forward up to five years.

- ✓ Gifts of long-term (held 12 months or more) capital gain property to public charities and private operating foundations are limited to 30% of AGI. The same five-year carry-forward is possible.

- ✓ Donors of capital gain property to public charities and private operating foundations may use the 50% limitation, instead of the 30% limitation, where the amount of the contribution is reduced by all the unrealized appreciation (nontaxed gain) in the value of the property.

- ✓ Gifts of cash, short-term (held less than 12 months) capital gain property, and ordinary income property to private foundations and certain other charitable donees (other than public charities and private operating foundations) are generally limited to the item's cost basis and 30% of AGI. The carry-forward rules apply to these gifts.

- ✓ Gifts of long-term (held 12 months or more) capital gain property to private foundations and other charitable donees (other than public charities and private operating foundations) are generally limited to 20% of AGI. There is no carry-forward for these gifts.

- ✓ Charitable contribution deductions by corporations in any tax year may not exceed 10% of pretax net income. Excess contributions may be carried forward up to five years.

Charitable Gift Options

Irrevocable nontrust gifts

- ✓ **Cash.** A gift of cash is the simplest method of giving. The value of the gift is easily known. A cash gift is deductible within the 50% or 30% of adjusted gross income limitations, depending on the type of the recipient organization. Generally the 50% limit applies.

- ✓ **Securities.** The contribution deduction for stocks and bonds held long-term (held 12 months or more), is the mean between the highest and lowest selling prices on the date of the gift where there is a market for listed securities. The contribution deduction is limited to cost for securities held short-term.

  Example: An individual taxpayer plans to make a gift of $50,000 to a college. To provide the capital, the taxpayer planned to sell stock that had cost $20,000 some years earlier yielding a long-term capital gain of $30,000. The taxpayer decides to donate the stock itself instead of the proceeds of its sale. The taxpayer receives a contribution deduction of $50,000 and the unrealized gain on the stock is not taxable. By contributing the stock, the taxpayer's taxable income is $30,000 less than if the stock were sold.

- ✓ **Real estate.** The contribution deduction for a gift of real estate is based on the fair market value on the date of the gift. If there is a mortgage on the property, the value must be reduced by the amount of the debt.

✓ **Life insurance.** The owner of a life insurance policy may choose to give it to a charitable organization. The gift will produce a tax deduction equal to one of several amounts. The deduction may equal the cash surrender value of the policy, its replacement value, its tax basis or its "interpolated terminal reserve" value (a value slightly more than cash surrender value). The deduction cannot exceed the donor's tax basis in the policy.

✓ **Bargain sale.** A bargain sale is part donation and part sale. It is a sale of property in which the amount of the sale proceeds is less than the property's fair market value. The excess of the fair market value of the property over the sale's price represents a charitable contribution to the organization. Generally each part of a bargain sale is a reportable event so the donor reports both a sale and a contribution.

✓ **Remainder interest in a personal residence or life estate.** A charitable contribution of the remainder interest in a personal residence (including a vacation home) or farm creates an income tax deduction equal to the present value of that future interest.

✓ **Charitable gift annuity.** With a charitable gift annuity, the donor purchases an annuity contract from a charitable organization for more than its fair value. This difference in values between what the donor could have obtained and what the donor actually obtained represents a charitable contribution. The contribution is tax-deductible in the year the donor purchases the annuity.

✓ **Deferred charitable gift annuity.** A deferred gift annuity is similar to an immediate payment annuity except that the annuity payments begin at a future date. This date is determined by the donor at the time of the gift.

Irrevocable gifts in trust

✓ **Charitable remainder annuity trust.** With an annuity trust, the donor retains the right to a specified annuity amount for a fixed period or the lifetime of the designated income beneficiary. The donor fixes the amount payable by an annuity trust at the inception of the trust.

✓ **Charitable remainder unitrust.** The unitrust and annuity trust are very similar with an important difference—the determination of the payment amount. The unitrust payout rate is applied to the fair market value of the net trust assets, determined annually, to establish the distributable amount each year.

✓ **Charitable lead trust.** The charitable lead trust is the reverse of the charitable remainder trust. The donor transfers property into a trust, creating an income interest in the property in favor of the charitable organization for a period of years or for the life or lives of an individual or individuals. The remainder interest is either returned to the donor or given to a noncharitable beneficiary (usually a family member).

✓ **Pooled income fund.** A pooled income fund consists of separate contributions of property from numerous donors. A pooled income fund's payout to its income beneficiaries is not a fixed percentage. The rate of return that the fund earns each year determines the annual payout.

Revocable gifts

✓ **Trust savings accounts.** A trust savings account may be established at a bank, credit union, or savings and loan. The account is placed in the name of the depositor "in trust for" a beneficiary, a person, or organization other than the depositor.

The depositor retains full ownership and control of the account. The beneficiary receives the money in the account either when the depositor dies, or when the depositor turns over the passbook.

✓ **Insurance and retirement plan proceeds.** A nonprofit organization may be named the beneficiary of an insurance policy or retirement plan. The owner of the policy or retirement plan completes a form naming the nonprofit as the beneficiary, and the company accepts the form in writing. The gift may be for part or all the proceeds.

✓ **Bequests.** By a specific bequest, an individual may direct that, at death, a charity shall receive either a specified dollar amount or specific property. Through a residuary bequest, an individual may give to charity the estate portion remaining after the payment of other bequests, debts, taxes, and expenses.

Charitable Gift Timing

When donors make gifts near the end of the year, the question often arises: "Is my gift deductible this year?" A donor's charitable deduction, assuming deductions are itemized, depends on various factors:

CAUTION

✓ **Checks.** A donation by check is considered made on the date the check is delivered or mailed, as evidenced by its postmark, if the check subsequently clears the donor's bank in due course. That means a check that's mailed with a December 31 postmark and promptly deposited by the charity will be deductible by the donor in the year the check is written, even though the check clears the bank the following year. However, a postdated check is not deductible until the day of its date.

Example 1: Donor mails a check with a postmark of December 31, 1999. The charity does not receive the check until January 7, 2000. The charity deposits the check in its bank on January 7 and it clears the donor's bank on January 10. The gift is deductible by the donor in 1999.

Example 2: Donor delivers a check to the charity on December 31, 1999. The donor asks that the check be held for three months. Complying with the donor's request, the charity deposits the check on March 31, 2000. This gift is deductible by the donor in 2000.

Example 3: Donor delivers a check to the charity on January 5, 2000. The check is dated December 31, 1999. The gift is deductible by the donor in 2000.

✓ **Credit cards.** A contribution charged to a bank credit card is deductible by the donor when the charge is made, even though the donor does not pay the credit card charge until the next year.

✓ **Cyber gifts.** Donors can instruct their banks via phone or computer to pay contributions to your charity. If a donor uses this method to make a donation, it's deductible at the time payment is made by the bank.

✓ **Pledges.** A pledge is not deductible until payment or other satisfaction of the pledge is made.

✓ **Securities.** A contribution of stock is completed upon the unconditional delivery of a properly endorsed stock certificate to your charity or its agent. If the stock is mailed and is received by the charity or its agent in the ordinary course of the mail, the gift is effective on the date of mailing. If the donor delivers a stock certificate to the issuing corporation or to the donor's broker for transfer to the name of the charity, the contribution is not completed until the stock is actually transferred on the corporation's books.

✓ **Real estate.** A gift of real estate is deductible at the time a properly executed deed is delivered to the charity.

Charitable Contribution Acknowledgments

Contributors to your charity seeking a federal income tax charitable contribution deduction must produce, if asked, a written receipt from the charity if a single contribution's value if $250 or more.

Strictly speaking, the burden of compliance with the $250 or more rule falls on the donor. In reality, the burden and administrative costs fall on the charity, not the donor.

The IRS can fine a charity that deliberately issues a false acknowledgement to a contributor. The fine is up to $1,000 if the donor is an individual and $10,000 if the donor is a corporation.

A donor will not be allowed a charitable deduction for donations of $250 or more unless the donor has a receipt from your charity. This applies to any type of donation. For a single donation of $250 or more made by check, the cancelled check is not adequate substantiation.

If a donor makes multiple contributions of $250 or more to one charity, one acknowledgment that reflects the total amount of the donor's contributions to the charity for the year is sufficient. In other words, the charity can total all of the contributions for a donor and only show the total amount on the receipt.

✓ **Information to be included in the receipt.** The following information must be included in the gift receipt:

- the donor's name,
- if cash, the amount of cash contributed,
- if property, a description, but not the value, of the property,
- a statement explaining whether the church provided any goods or services to the donor in exchange for the contribution,
- if goods or services were provided to the donor, a description and good-faith estimate of their value and a statement that the donor's charitable deduction is limited to the amount of the payment in excess of the value of the goods and services provided, and if services were provided consisting solely of intangible religious benefits, a statement to that effect,
- the date the donation was made (except for out-of-pocket expenses, see below), and,
- the date the receipt was issued.

✓ **When receipts should be issued.** Donors must obtain their receipts no later than the earlier of the due date, plus any extension, of their income tax returns or the date the return is filed. If a donor receives the receipt after this date, the gift does not qualify for a contribution deduction even on an amended return.

If your charity is issuing receipts on an annual basis, you should try to get them to your donors by at least January 31 each year and earlier in January if possible. This will assist your donors in gathering the necessary data for tax return preparation.

✓ **Frequency of issuing receipts.** The receipts or acknowledgements can be issued gift-by-gift, monthly, quarterly, annually, or any other frequency. For

Sample Charitable Gift Receipt

Received from: Jackie J. Burns

Cash received as an absolute gift:

Received on March 6, 1999 $300.00

Property received described as follows:

Received on May 1, 1999, one 1994 Honda Civic, 4-door sedan LX, automatic transmission, 64,231 miles, vehicle ID #1BFHP53L2NH440968.

(*Note:* No value is shown for the property. Valuation of property is the responsibility of the donor.)

Any goods or services you may have received in connection with this gift were solely intangible religious benefits. (*Note:* It is very important for a religious organization to use wording of this nature when no goods or services were given in exchange for the gift.)

This document is necessary for any available federal income tax deduction for your contribution. Please retain it for your records.

Receipt issued on: January 31, 2000

Receipt issued by: Harold Morrison, Treasurer
Castleview Church
1008 High Drive
Dover, DE 19901

Note: 1. This sample receipt is based on the following assumptions:

A. No goods or services were provided in exchange for the gift(s) other than intangible religious benefits.

B. The receipt is issued for a single gift (versus one receipt for multiple gifts).

2. Receipts should be numbered consecutively for control and accounting purposes.

Sample Charitable Gift Receipt

Received from: Howard K. Auburn

Cash received as an absolute gift:

Date Cash Received	Amount Received
1/2/99	$250.00
1/16/99	50.00
3/13/99	300.00
3/27/99	100.00
6/12/99	500.00
7/10/99	150.00
8/21/99	200.00
10/16/99	400.00
11/20/99	350.00
	$2,300.00

Property received described as follows:

Received on May 1, 1999, one 1994 Honda Civic, 4-door sedan LX, automatic transmission, 64,231 miles, vehicle ID# IBFHP53L2NH440968. (***Note:*** No value is shown for the property. Valuation of property is the responsibility of the donor.)

Any goods or services you may have received in connection with this gift were solely intangible religious benefits. (***Note:*** It is very important for a religious organization to use wording of this nature when no goods or services were given in exchange for the gift.)

This document is necessary for any available federal income tax deduction for your contribution. Please retain it for your records.

Receipt issued on: January 10, 2000
Receipt issued by: Harold Morrison, Treasurer
Castleview Church
1008 High Drive
Dover, DE 19901

Note: 1. This sample receipt is based on the following assumptions:

A. No goods or services were provided in exchange for the gifts other than intangible religious benefits.

B. The receipt is issued on a periodic or annual basis for all gifts whether over or under $250.

2. Receipts should be numbered consecutively for control and accounting purposes.

ease of administration, many charities provide a receipt for all gifts, whether over or under $250.

✓ **Form of receipts.** No specific design of the receipt is required. The IRS has not issued any sample receipts to follow.
The receipt can be a letter, a postcard, or a computer-generated form. It does not have to include the donor's social security number or other taxpayer identification number.

✓ **Separate gifts of less than $250.** If a donor makes separate gifts during a calendar year of less than $250, there is no receipting requirement since each gift is a separate contribution. The donor's cancelled check will provide sufficient substantiation. However, most charities receipt all gifts with no distinction between the gifts under or over $250.

✓ **Donations payable to another charity.** A church member may place a check in the offering plate of $250 or more payable to a mission organization designed for the support of a particular missionary serving with the mission. In this instance, no reporting is required by your church. Since the check was payable to the mission agency, that entity will need to issue the acknowledgment to entitle the donor to claim the gift as a charitable contribution.

✓ **Donations in support of a missionary.** Donations may be received, payable to your church, for the support of a particular missionary. These gifts generally qualify for a charitable deduction and the church should include the amounts in acknowledgments issued to donors. However, the funds should be remitted to the missionary-sending organization for their disbursement in relation to the individual missionary.

✓ **Donor's out-of-pocket expenses.** You may have volunteers that incur out-of-pocket expenses on behalf of your church. Substantiation from your charity is required if a volunteer claims a deduction for unreimbursed expenses of $250 or more. However, the IRS acknowledges that you may be unaware of the details of the expenses or the dates on which they were incurred. Therefore, the charity must substantiate only types of services performed by the volunteer.

✓ **Individuals.** Gifts made to poor or needy individuals ordinarily do not qualify as charitable contributions. Gifts made personally to employees of a charity are not charitable contributions.

✓ **Foreign organizations.** Donations must be made to domestic organizations to qualify for a charitable deduction.

Example 1: A gift made directly to a missionary group organized and operating in Israel does not qualify for a charitable deduction.

Sample Letter to Noncash Donors

Charitable Gift Receipt
(Receipts should be numbered consecutively for control and accounting purposes.)
RETAIN FOR INCOME TAX PURPOSES

Donor's Name
Address

Thank you for your noncash gift as follows:
Date of gift:
Description of gift:
(*Note:* No value is shown for the gift. Valuation is the responsibility of the donor.)

To substantiate your gift for IRS purposes, the tax law requires that this acknowledgment state whether you have received any goods or services in exchange for the gift. You have received no goods or services. (Note: If goods or services were provided to the donor, replace the previous sentence with: In return for your contribution, you have received the following goods or services (description) which we value at (good-faith estimate). The value of the goods and services you received must be deducted from the value of your contribution to determine your charitable deduction.)

You must follow the IRS's reporting rules to assure your charitable deduction. We have enclosed a copy of IRS Form 8283 (Noncash Charitable Contributions) and its instructions.

If your noncash gifts for the year total more than $500, you must include Form 8283 with your income tax return. Section A is used to report gifts valued at $5,000 or under. You can complete Section A on your own. When the value of the gift is more than $5,000, you will need to have the property appraised. The appraiser's findings are reported in Section B of Form 8283. The rules also apply if you give "similar items of property" with a total value above $5,000—even if you gave the items to different charities. Section B of Form 8283 must be signed by the appraiser. As the donee, we have already signed the form. It is essential to attach the form to your tax return.

You might want an appraisal (even if your gift does not require one) in case you have to convince the IRS of the property's worth. You never need an appraisal or an appraisal summary for gifts of publicly traded securities, even if their total value exceeds $5,000. You must report those gifts (when the value is more than $500) by completing Section A of Form 8283 and attaching it to your return.

For gifts of closely held stock, an appraisal is not required if the value of the stock is under $10,000, but part of the appraisal summary form must be completed if the value is over $5,000. If the gift is valued over $10,000, then both an appraisal and an appraisal summary form are required.

If we receive a gift of property subject to the appraisal summary rules, we must report to both the IRS and you if we dispose of the gift within two years. We do not have to notify the IRS or you if we dispose of a gift that did not require an appraisal summary.

Again, we are grateful for your generous contribution. Please let us know if we can give you and your advisors more information about the IRS's reporting requirements.

Your Nonprofit Organization

Example 2: A gift to a U.S.-based missionary organization with a designation that the funds be used for mission work in China may qualify for a charitable deduction.

✓ **Contingencies.** If a contribution will not be effective until the occurrence of a certain event, an income tax charitable deduction generally is not allowable until the occurrence of the event.

Example: A donor makes a gift to a college to fund a new education program that the college does not presently offer and is not contemplating. The donation would not be deductible until the college agrees to the conditions of the gift.

✓ **Charitable remainders in personal residences and farms.** The final charitable gift regulations are silent on the substantiation rules for remainder interests in personal residences and farms. It should be assumed that the $250 substantiation rules apply to those gifts unless the IRS provides other guidance.

✓ **Charitable trusts.** The $250 substantiation rules do not apply to charitable remainder annuity trusts, charitable remainder unitrusts, and charitable lead trusts.

✓ **Gift annuities.** When the gift portion of a gift annuity or a deferred payment gift annuity is $250 or more, a donor must have an acknowledgment from the charity stating whether any goods or services—in addition to the annuity—were provided to the donor. If no goods or services were provided, the acknowledgment must so state. The acknowledgment need not include a good faith estimate of the annuity's value.

✓ **Pooled income funds.** The substantiation rules apply to pooled income funds. To deduct a gift of a remainder interest of $250 or more, a donor must have an acknowledgment from the charity.

Gifts That May Not Qualify as Contributions

Some types of gifts do not result in a tax deduction and no contribution acknowledgment should be provided by the church:

CAUTION

✓ **Beyond due diligence.** Some donors to your charity may want to make sure their gifts are put to good use. As long as your charity clearly owns the gift, and the donor and charity agree that it will further the charity's purposes, the IRS approves. But they draw the line when the donor demands too much control, intending to benefit a private class of people rather than the public at large. For example, a gift made to a church with the requirement that the funds be used to provide scholarships to students from the church with the donor's last name. The IRS would undoubtedly reject an income tax deduction for this type of gift.

✓ **Passing gifts through to pastors or other employees.** A church member may donate a car, a personal computer, or some other asset and specify that the property be given to one of the church pastors. The member expects a charitable contribution receipt and wants the pastor to have the gift without incurring any taxes on the gift. Should the church accept the gift and what are the consequences of the gift?

Before accepting such a gift, the church must determine if it can exercise adequate control over the gift and if the specified use of the gift would result in appropriate compensation for services rendered to the church. If the church does not feel comfortable with these issues, the gift should be declined. If the church feels that it can properly accept the gift, the fair market value of the assets distributed to staff members must be included on Form W-2.

✓ **Strings attached.** A gift must generally be complete and irrevocable to qualify for a charitable deduction. There is usually no gift if the donor leaves "strings attached" that can be pulled later to bring the gift back to the donor or remove it from the control of the church.

Example: A donor makes a "gift" of $10,000 to a church. The "gift" is followed or preceded by the sale from the church to the donor of an asset valued at $25,000 for $15,000. In this instance, the $10,000 gift does not qualify as a charitable contribution. It also raises the issue of private inurement relating to the sale by the church.

✓ **Services.** No deduction is allowed for the contribution of services to a church.

Example: A carpenter donates two months of labor on the construction of a new facility built by your church. The carpenter is not eligible for a charitable deduction for the donation of his time. The carpenter is entitled to a charitable deduction for any out-of-pocket expenses including mileage (14 cents per mile for 1999) for driving to and from the project. If out-of-pocket expenses are $250 or more in a calendar year, the carpenter will need an acknowledgment from the church. See the out-of-pocket discussion later.

✓ **Use of property.** The gift to a church of the right to use property does not yield a tax deduction to the donor.

Example: A donor provides a church with the rent-free use of an automobile for a year. There is no charitable deduction available to the donor for the value of that use. If the donor paid the taxes, insurance, repairs, gas or oil for the vehicle while it is used by the church, these items are deductible as a charitable contribution based on their cost.

Reporting to the IRS

CAUTION

Most gifts do not require any reporting by the charity to the IRS. However, some gifts do require IRS reporting, or execution of a form that the donor files with the IRS and the rules are complicated:

✓ **Gifts of property in excess of $5,000.** Substantiation requirements apply to contributions of property (other than money and publicly traded securities), if the total claimed or reported value of the property is more than $5,000. For these gifts, the donor must obtain a qualified appraisal and attach an appraisal summary to the return on which the deduction is claimed. There is an exception for nonpublicly traded stock. If the claimed value of the stock does not exceed $10,000 but is greater than $5,000, the donor does not have to obtain an appraisal by a qualified appraiser.

The appraisal summary must be on Form 8283, signed and dated by the charity and the appraiser, and attached to the donor's return on which a deduction is claimed. The signature by the charity does not represent concurrence in the appraised value of the contributed property.

If Form 8283 is required, it is the donor's responsibility to file it. The charity is under no responsibility to see that donors file this form nor that it is properly completed. However, advising donors of their obligations and providing them with the form can produce donor goodwill.

✓ **Gifts of property in excess of $500.** Gifts of property valued at $500 or more require the completion of certain information on page one of Form 8283. For gifts between $500 and $5,000 in value, there is not a requirement of an appraisal or signature of the charity.

✓ **Charity reporting for contributed property.** If property received as a charitable contribution requiring an appraisal summary on Form 8283 is sold, exchanged, or otherwise disposed of by the charity within two years after the date of its contribution, the charity must file Form 8282 with the IRS within 125 days of the disposition.

This form provides detailed information on the gift and the disposal of the property. A copy of this information return must be provided to the donor and retained by the charity. A charity that receives a charitable contribution valued at more than $5,000 from a corporation generally does not have to file Form 8283.

A letter or other written communication from a charity acknowledging receipt of the property and showing the name of the donor, the date and location of the contribution, and a detailed description of the property is an

Form **8282** (Rev. September 1998) Department of the Treasury Internal Revenue Service

Donee Information Return

(Sale, Exchange, or Other Disposition of Donated Property)

▶ See instructions on back.

OMB No. 1545-0908

Give a Copy to Donor

Please Print or Type

Name of charitable organization (donee): Oneonta First Church

Employer identification number: 35 : 4829942

Address (number, street, and room or suite no.): 292 River Street

City or town, state, and ZIP code: Oneonta, NY 13820

Part I **Information on ORIGINAL DONOR and DONEE Receiving the Property**

1a Name(s) of the original donor of the property: Keith E. Chapman

1b Identifying number: 512-40-8076

Note: *Complete lines 2a–2d only if you gave this property to another charitable organization (successor donee).*

2a Name of charitable organization

2b Employer identification number

2c Address (number, street, and room or suite no.)

2d City or town, state, and ZIP code

Note: *If you are the original donee, skip Part II and go to Part III now.*

Part II **Information on PREVIOUS DONEES—Complete this part only if you were not the first donee to receive the property.** If you were the second donee, leave lines 4a–4d blank. If you were a third or later donee, complete lines 3a–4d. On lines 4a–4d, give information on the preceding donee (the one who gave you the property)

3a Name of original donee

3b Employer identification number

3c Address (number, street, and room or suite no.)

3d City or town, state, and ZIP code

4a Name of preceding donee

4b Employer identification number

4c Address (number, street, and room or suite no.)

4d City or town, state, and ZIP code

Part III **Information on DONATED PROPERTY—**If you are the original donee, leave column (c) blank.

(a) Description of donated property sold, exchanged, or otherwise disposed of (if you need more space, attach a separate statement)	**(b)** Date you received the item(s)	**(c)** Date the first donee received the item(s)	**(d)** Date item(s) sold, exchanged, or otherwise disposed of	**(e)** Amount received upon disposition
Real estate/vacant lot, 82 White Street Oneonta, NY	9/04/99		11/10/99	3780

For Paperwork Reduction Act Notice, see back of form. Cat. No. 62307Y Form **8282** (Rev. 9-98)

Note: The donee must file this form with the IRS if property received as a charitable contribution is sold, exchanged, or otherwise disposed of within two years after the date of its contribution.

Form **8283** (Rev. October 1998)
Department of the Treasury Internal Revenue Service

Noncash Charitable Contributions

▶ **Attach to your tax return if you claimed a total deduction of over $500 for all contributed property.**

▶ **See separate instructions.**

OMB No. 1545-0908
Attachment Sequence No. **55**

Name(s) shown on your income tax return: Mark A. and Joan E. Murphy

Identifying number: 392-83-1982

Note: *Figure the amount of your contribution deduction before completing this form. See your tax return instructions.*

Section A—List in this section **only** items (or groups of similar items) for which you claimed a deduction of $5,000 or less. Also, list certain publicly traded securities even if the deduction is over $5,000 (see instructions).

Part I **Information on Donated Property**—If you need more space, attach a statement.

1	(a) Name and address of the donee organization	(b) Description of donated property
A	Endless Mountain Church, 561 Maple, Rochester, NY 14623	Used bedroom furniture
B		
C		
D		
E		

Note: *If the amount you claimed as a deduction for an item is $500 or less, you do not have to complete columns (d), (e), and (f).*

	(c) Date of the contribution	(d) Date acquired by donor (mo., yr.)	(e) How acquired by donor	(f) Donor's cost or adjusted basis	(g) Fair market value	(h) Method used to determine the fair market value
A	10/1/99	6/91	Purchased	3,400	750	Sale of comparable used furniture
B						
C						
D						
E						

Part II **Other Information**—Complete line 2 if you gave less than an entire interest in property listed in Part I. Complete line 3 if conditions were attached to a contribution listed in Part I.

2 If, during the year, you contributed less than the entire interest in the property, complete lines a–e.

a Enter the letter from Part I that identifies the property ▶ ________. If Part II applies to more than one property, attach a separate statement.

b Total amount claimed as a deduction for the property listed in Part I: **(1)** For this tax year ▶ ________.
(2) For any prior tax years ▶ ________.

c Name and address of each organization to which any such contribution was made in a prior year (complete only if different from the donee organization above):

Name of charitable organization (donee)

Address (number, street, and room or suite no.)

City or town, state, and ZIP code

d For tangible property, enter the place where the property is located or kept ▶ ________

e Name of any person, other than the donee organization, having actual possession of the property ▶ ________

3 If conditions were attached to any contribution listed in Part I, answer questions a – c and attach the required statement (see instructions).

	Yes	No
a Is there a restriction, either temporary or permanent, on the donee's right to use or dispose of the donated property?		
b Did you give to anyone (other than the donee organization or another organization participating with the donee organization in cooperative fundraising) the right to the income from the donated property or to the possession of the property, including the right to vote donated securities, to acquire the property by purchase or otherwise, or to designate the person having such income, possession, or right to acquire?		
c Is there a restriction limiting the donated property for a particular use?		

For Paperwork Reduction Act Notice, see page 4 of separate instructions. Cat. No. 62299J Form **8283** (Rev. 10-98)

Note: This form must be completed and filed with the donor's income tax return for gifts of property valued at $500 or more.

There is no requirement of an appraisal or signature of the donee organization for gifts valued between $500 and $5,000.

Form 8283 (Rev. 10-98) Page **2**

Name(s) shown on your income tax return	Identifying number
Mark A. and Joan E. Murphy	392-83-1982

Section B—Appraisal Summary—List in this section only items (or groups of similar items) for which you claimed a deduction of more than $5,000 per item or group. **Exception.** Report contributions of certain publicly traded securities only in Section A.

If you donated art, you may have to attach the complete appraisal. See the **Note** in Part I below.

Part I **Information on Donated Property**—To be completed by the taxpayer and/or appraiser.

4 Check type of property:

☐ Art* (contribution of $20,000 or more) ☒ Real Estate ☐ Gems/Jewelry ☐ Stamp Collections
☐ Art* (contribution of less than $20,000) ☐ Coin Collections ☐ Books ☐ Other

*Art includes paintings, sculptures, watercolors, prints, drawings, ceramics, antique furniture, decorative arts, textiles, carpets, silver, rare manuscripts, historical memorabilia, and other similar objects.

Note: *If your total art contribution deduction was $20,000 or more, you must attach a complete copy of the signed appraisal. See instructions.*

5	(a) Description of donated property (if you need more space, attach a separate statement)	(b) If tangible property was donated, give a brief summary of the overall physical condition at the time of the gift	(c) Appraised fair market value
A	Residence and two lots:	Good repair	42,500
B	2080 Long Pond road		
C	Syracuse, New York		
D			

	(d) Date acquired by donor (mo., yr.)	(e) How acquired by donor	(f) Donor's cost or adjusted basis	(g) For bargain sales, enter amount received	See instructions: (h) Amount claimed as a deduction	(i) Average trading price of securities
A	7/20/91	Purchased	36,900		42,500	
B						
C						
D						

Part II **Taxpayer (Donor) Statement**—List each item included in Part I above that the appraisal identifies as having a value of $500 or less. See instructions

I declare that the following item(s) included in Part I above has to the best of my knowledge and belief an appraised value of not more than $500 (per item). Enter identifying letter from Part I and describe the specific item. See instructions. ▶ ____________

Signature of taxpayer (donor) ▶ *Mark A. Murphy* Date ▶

Part III **Declaration of Appraiser**

I declare that I am not the donor, the donee, a party to the transaction in which the donor acquired the property, employed by, or related to any of the foregoing persons, or married to any person who is related to any of the foregoing persons. And, if regularly used by the donor, donee, or party to the transaction, I performed the majority of my appraisals during my tax year for other persons.

Also, I declare that I hold myself out to the public as an appraiser or perform appraisals on a regular basis; and that because of my qualifications as described in the appraisal, I am qualified to make appraisals of the type of property being valued. I certify that the appraisal fees were not based on a percentage of the appraised property value. Furthermore, I understand that a false or fraudulent overstatement of the property value as described in the qualified appraisal or this appraisal summary may subject me to the penalty under section 6701(a) (aiding and abetting the understatement of tax liability). I affirm that I have not been barred from presenting evidence or testimony by the Director of Practice.

Sign Here Signature ▶ *Andrew J. Noble* Title ▶ President Date of appraisal ▶ 9/15/99

Business address (including room or suite no.)	Identifying number
1100 North Adams Street	541-90-9796

City or town, state, and ZIP code
Elmira, NY 14904

Part IV **Donee Acknowledgment**—To be completed by the charitable organization.

This charitable organization acknowledges that it is a qualified organization under section 170(c) and that it received the donated property as described in Section B, Part I, above on ▶ 9/25/99 (Date)

Furthermore, this organization affirms that in the event it sells, exchanges, or otherwise disposes of the property described in Section B, Part I (or any portion thereof) within 2 years after the date of receipt, it will file **Form 8282,** Donee Information Return, with the IRS and give the donor a copy of that form. This acknowledgment does not represent agreement with the claimed fair market value.

Does the organization intend to use the property for an unrelated use? . . . . ▶ ☐ Yes ☐ No

Name of charitable organization (donee)	Employer identification number	
Fairlawn Heights Church	35-4029876	
Address (number, street, and room or suite no.)	**City or town, state, and ZIP code**	
P.O. Box 829	Oswego, NY 13126	
Authorized signature	**Title**	**Date**
James A. Black	Excecutive Pastor	10/31/99

acceptable contribution receipt for a gift of property.

There is no requirement to include the value of contributed property on the receipt. Most charities are not prepared to value gifts of property. A tension often surrounds a significant gift of property because the donor may request the charity to include an excessively high value on the charitable receipt. It is wise for the charity to remain impartial in the matter and simply acknowledge the property by description with the exclusion of a dollar amount.

Example 1: A charity receives the gift of an automobile. The charitable contribution receipt should reflect the make, model, vehicle number, options, mileage, and condition with no indication of dollar value.

Example 2: A charity receives a gift of real estate. The receipt should include the legal description of the real property and a description of the improvements with no indication of the dollar value.

Quid Pro Quo Disclosure Requirements

A quid pro quo contribution is a payment made partly as a contribution and partly for goods or services provided to the donor by the charity. A donor may deduct only the amount of the contribution above what the goods or services are worth.

The charity is required to provide a receipt for all transactions where the donor makes a payment of more than $75 to the charity and receives goods or services (other than intangible religious benefits or items of token value).

Form of the receipt

The receipt must

- ✓ inform the donor that the amount of the contribution that is deductible for federal income tax purposes is limited to the excess of the amount of any money and the value of any property other than money contributed by the donor *over* the value of the goods or services provided by the organization, and

- ✓ provide the donor with a good-faith estimate of the value of goods or services that the charity is providing in exchange for the contribution.

Only single payments of more than $75 are subject to the rules. Payments are not cumulative. It is not a difference of $75 between the amount given by the donor and the value of the object received by the donor that triggers the disclosure requirements, but the amount actually paid by the donor.

Calculating the gift portion

It is not a requirement for the donee organization to actually complete the subtraction of the benefit from a cash payment, showing the net charitable deduction. However, providing the net amount available for a charitable deduction is a good approach for clear communication with your donors.

When to make the required disclosures

The disclosure of the value of goods or services provided to a donor may be made in the donor solicitation as well as in the subsequent receipt. However, sufficient information will generally not be available to make proper disclosure upon solicitation. For example, the value of a dinner may not be known at the time the solicitation is made.

Goods provided to donors

A gift must be reduced by the fair market value of any premium, incentive, or other benefit received by the donor in exchange for the gift to determine the net charitable contribution. Common examples of premiums are books, tapes, and Bibles. Organizations must advise the donor of the fair market value of the premium or incentive and that the value is not deductible for tax purposes.

Donors must reduce their charitable deduction by the fair market value of goods or services they receive even when the goods or services were donated to the charity for use as premiums or gifts or when they were bought by the charity at wholesale. Therefore, charities cannot pass along to donors the savings realized by receiving products at no cost or buying products at a discount.

If donors receive benefits of insubstantial value, they are allowed a full tax deduction for the donation:

- ✓ **Low-cost items.** If an item has a cost (not retail value) of less than $7.20 and an item that bears the name or logo of your organization is given in return for a donation of more than $36.00 (1999 inflation-adjusted amount), the donor may claim a charitable deduction for the full amount of the donation. Examples of items that often qualify as tokens are coffee mugs, key chains, bookmarks, and calendars.

- ✓ **De minimis benefits.** A donor can take a full deduction if the fair market value of the benefits received in connection with a gift does not exceed 2% of the donation or $72.00 (1999 inflation-adjusted amount), whichever is less.

Examples of the quid pro quo rules

Here are various examples of how the quid pro quo rules apply:

- ✓ **Admission to events.** Many organizations sponsor banquets, concerts, or other events to which donors and prospective donors are invited in exchange for a contribution or other payment. Often, the donor receives a benefit equivalent to the payment and there is no charitable deduction available.

CAUTION

But if the amount paid is more than the value received, the amount in excess of the fair market value is deductible if there was intent to make a contribution.

✓ **Auctions.** The IRS generally takes the position that the fair market value of an item purchased at a charity auction is set by the bidders. The winning bidder, therefore, cannot pay more than the item is worth. That means there is no charitable contribution in the IRS's eyes, no deduction, and no need for the charity to provide any charitable gift substantiation document to the bidder.

However, many tax professionals take the position that when the payment (the purchase price) exceeds the fair market value of the items, the amount that exceeds the fair market value is deductible as a charitable contribution. This position also creates a reporting requirement under the quid pro quo rules. Most charities set the value of every object sold and provide receipts to buyers.

Example: Your church youth group auctions goods to raise funds for a mission trip. An individual bought a quilt for $200. The church takes the position that the quilt had a fair market value of $50 even though the bidder paid $200. Since the payment of $200 exceeded the $75 limit, the church is required to provide a written statement indicating that only $150 of the $200 payment is eligible for a charitable contribution.

✓ **Bazaars.** Payments for items sold at bazaars and bake sales are not tax deductible to donors since the purchase price generally equals the fair market value of the item.

✓ **Banquets.** Whether your organization incurs reporting requirements in connection with banquets where funds are raised depends on the specifics of each event.

Example 1: Your church sponsors a banquet for missions charging $50 per person. The meal costs the church $15 per person. There is no disclosure requirement since the amount charged was less than $75. However, the amount deductible by each donor is only $35.

Example 2: Your church invites individuals to attend a missions banquet without charge. Attendees are invited to make contributions or pledges at the end of the banquet. These payments probably do not require disclosure even if the amount given is $75 or more because there is only an indirect relationship between the meal and the gift.

✓ **Deduction timing.** Goods or services received in consideration for a donor's payment include goods and services received in a different year. Thus, a donor's deduction for the year of the payment is limited to the amount, if any, by which the payment exceeds the value of the goods and services.

✓ **Good faith estimates.** A donor is not required to use the estimate provided by

Charitable Contribution Substantiation Requirements

	Not more than $75	Over $75 and under $250	At least $250 and under $500	At least $500 and under $5,000	$5,000 and over
Canceled check acceptable for donor's deduction?	Yes	Yes	No	No	No
Contribution receipt required for deduction?	No	No	Yes	Yes	Yes
Charity's statement on donor's receipt of goods or services required?	No	Yes*	Yes*	Yes*	Yes*

*May be avoided if the charity meets the low-cost items or de minimis benefits exceptions described on page 151.

a donee organization in calculating the deductible amount. When a taxpayer knows or has reason to know that an estimate is inaccurate, the taxpayer may not treat the donee organization's estimate as the fair market value.

✓ **Rights of refusal.** A donor can claim a full deduction if he or she refuses a benefit from the charity. However, this must be done affirmatively. Simply not taking advantage of a benefit is not enough. For example, a donor who chooses not to make use of tickets that you made available by your organization must deduct the value of the tickets from his or her contribution before claiming a deduction. However, a donor who rejects the right to a benefit at the time the contribution is made (e.g., by checking off a refusal box on a form supplied by your charity) can take a full deduction.

CAUTION

✓ **Sale of products or a service at fair market value.** When an individual purchases products or receives services at fair market value, no part of the payment is a gift.

Example 1: An individual purchases tapes of a series of Sunday morning worship services for $80. The sales price represents fair market value. Even though the amount paid exceeds the $75 threshold, the church is not required to provide a disclosure statement to the purchaser.

Example 2: The Brown family uses the fellowship hall of the church for a family reunion. The normal rental fee is $300. The Browns give a check to the church for $300 marked "Contribution." No

Sample Charitable Gift Receipt

Received from: Nancy L. Wilson

Cash received:
Received on April 1, 1999 $100.00

Property received on June 30, 1999 and is described as follows:
(***Note:*** If property was given instead of cash or check, describe the property here. No value is shown for the property. Valuation of property is the responsibility of the donor.)

In return for your gift described above, we provided you with a study Bible with an estimated value of $30.00. *(**Note:** Insert the description of goods and/or services provided in exchange for the gift.)* You may have also received goods or services consisting solely of intangible benefits, but these benefits do not need to be valued for tax purposes.

The deductible portion of your contribution for federal income tax purposes is limited to the excess of your contribution over the value of goods and services we provided to you. The $30.00 value of benefits you received must be subtracted from your cash contribution and the value of the property you donated to determine your net charitable contribution. *(**Note:** For receipting purposes, do not calculate the net contribution for gifts of property to the charity because the charity does not place a value on the property received.)*

This document is necessary for any available federal income tax deduction for your contribution. Please retain it for your records.

Receipt issued on: January 10, 2000
Receipt issued by: Harold Morrison, Treasurer
Castleview Church
1008 High Drive
Dover, DE 19901

Note: 1. This sample receipt is based on the following assumptions:
A. Goods or services were provided in exchange for the gifts.
B. The receipt is issued for a single gift (versus one receipt for multiple gifts).
2. Receipts should be numbered consecutively for control and accounting purposes.

Sample Charitable Gift Receipt

Received from: Charles K. Vandell

Cash received as an absolute gift:

Date Cash Received	Gross Amount Received	Value of Goods or Services	Net Charitable Contribution
1/23/99	$80.00	$25.00 (1)	$ 55.00
3/20/99	300.00		300.00
4/24/99	60.00		60.00
6/19/99	500.00	100.00 (2)	400.00
9/04/99	275.00		275.00
10/30/99	200.00		200.00
12/18/99	1,000.00		1,000.00
			$2,900.00

Property received described as follows:
Received on October 22, 1999, 12 brown Samsonite folding chairs.

In return for certain gifts listed above, we provided you with the following goods or services:

(1) Christian music tapes $25.00
(2) Limited edition art print $100.00

You may have also received goods or services consisting solely of intangible religious benefits, but these benefits do not need to be valued for tax purposes.

The deductible portion of your contribution for federal income tax purposes is limited to the excess of your contribution over the value of goods and services we provided to you.

This document is necessary for any available federal income tax deduction for your contribution. Please retain it for your records.

Receipt issued on: January 15, 2000
Receipt issued by: Harold Morrison, Treasurer
Castleview Church
1008 High Drive
Dover, DE 19901

Note: 1. This sample receipt is based on the following assumptions:
A. Goods or services were provided in exchange for the gifts.
B. The receipt is issued on a periodic or annual basis for all gifts whether over or under $250.
2. Receipts should be numbered consecutively for control and accounting purposes.

receipt should be given because no charitable contribution was made.

Example 3: The Brown family uses the church sanctuary and fellowship hall for a wedding and the reception. The church does not have a stated use fee but asks for a donation from those who use the facility. The comparable fee to rent similar facilities is $250. The Browns give a check to the church for $250 marked "Contribution." No receipt should be given because no charitable contribution was made.

Example 4: Your church operates a Christian school. The parent of a student at the school writes a check payable to the church for his child's tuition. No receipt should be given because no charitable contribution was made.

Special Charitable Contribution Issues

Gifts of real estate

Gifts of real estate to a charity can bring incredible opportunities and headaches—opportunities because of the potential dollars that may be realized for ministry and headaches because of the administrative effort required to process many of these gifts.

When drafting a real estate gift policy, consider these issues:

✓ **Inspection of the property.** A charity should not accept a gift of real estate without first inspecting the property. A cursory inspection will make sure there are no visible environmental hazards on the property and determine if there are any obvious marketability issues.

✓ **Information about the property.** The prospective donor should provide the following information about the property:

- A survey.
- A legal description.
- The names of any co-owners and their ownership shares.
- A copy of recent tax statements.
- A copy of any recent appraisals.
- Information on any current leases or contracts outstanding on the property.
- A brief description of the current use of the property.

✓ **Debt on the property.** The charity needs to know the details of any debt on the property, and should decide in advance how much debt is acceptable. If the charity assumes a mortgage, it will usually pay unrelated business income tax on the income from either the rental or sale of the property.

✓ **The property's use.** A charity can either use a real estate gift for ministry purposes, hold it for investment, or turn around and sell it. Real property that's not used in connection with your charity's exempt purpose is usually subject to property tax.

✓ **Disposing of the property.** Will it be the charity's policy to sell the property as soon as possible? If so, the charity must have full authority to decide the buyer and the sales price. Too often, donor's have prearranged a sale and expect the property to be immediately sold to the buyer of their choice at a price agreed upon before the donation. This situation places the charity in a very awkward position.

If the sale is prearranged, the IRS may attribute the gain on the sale by the charity to the donor. In this instance, the donor would have to pay tax on the difference between what the donor originally paid for the property and the sales price the charity receives. Also, an immediate resale could fix the value of the donor's gift to an amount lower than the donor would like to claim as a tax deduction.

✓ **Environmental issues.** Avoid property that has signs of environmental problems. Your charity will probably be liable for any clean-up costs—even if the property was contaminated before your charity received it. Your charity should generally not accept gifts of real estate that could result in liability for environmental contamination. It is wise to perform a Level I Environmental Site Assessment before accepting a gift of real estate.

Gifts of inventory

Donors may give some of their business inventory to a charity and ask for a charitable contribution receipt for the retail value of the merchandise. A charity should never provide such a receipt.

Example: Bill owns a lumber yard. The charity is constructing a building and Bill donates some lumber for the project. Bill's company purchased the lumber during his current business year for $10,000. The retail price on the lumber is $17,000 and it would have generated a $7,000 profit if Bill's company sold it. What is the tax impact for Bill's company? Since Bill's company acquired the item in the same business year that the lumber was donated, there is no charitable contribution for his company. The cost of the lumber, $10,000, is deducted as part of the cost of goods sold on the company books.

CAUTION

What is the bottom line of inventory contributions? An inventory item can only be deducted once—there is no contribution deduction and also a deduction as a part of cost of goods sold. The tax benefit to the donor is generally equal to the donor's cost of the items, not their retail value. Acknowledgements issued by a charity for inventory contributions should not state the value of the gift—only the date of the gift and a description of the items donated should be noted.

Gifts of church bonds

Individuals who purchase church bonds often keep the bonds for several years and then donate them back to the church. The charitable tax deduction for a gift of bonds is based on the face of the bond plus any accumulated interest on the date of donation. The church should issue a gift acknowledgment that simply identifies the bond(s) donated by bond number and face value.

Gifts of a partial interest

A contribution of less than the donor's entire interest in property is a gift of a partial interest. Generally, there is no charitable deduction for gifts of partial interest in property, including the right to use the property. Gifts of a partial interest which qualify for charitable deductions are

- ✓ gifts made in qualified trust form (using a so-called "split-interest trust," such as pooled income funds, charitable remainder trusts, and charitable lead trusts),
- ✓ outright gifts of a future remainder interest (also called a life estate) in a personal residence or farm,
- ✓ gifts of an undivided portion of one's entire interest in property,
- ✓ gifts of a lease on, option to purchase, or easement with respect to real property granted in perpetuity to a public charity exclusively for conservation purposes, or
- ✓ a remainder interest in real property granted to a public charity exclusively for conservation purposes.

Membership fees

Sometimes a membership fee may be partially or fully deductible. If the member receives benefits from the membership, a monetary value must be assigned to the benefits as the nondeductible portion of the payment.

Example 1: An individual pays a $100 membership fee to a nonprofit organization. In exchange, the individual receives publications and admission privileges to certain events. The value of the benefits received approximates the membership amount. Therefore, the membership fee is nondeductible as a charitable contribution.

Example 2: A nonprofit organization solicits funds for a particular program based on membership in a fund-raising "club." The donors do not receive any benefits from the membership. In this instance, membership fees are fully deductible as contributions.

Payments to private schools

Tuition payments to private schools are generally nondeductible since they correspond to value received. The IRS has ruled that payments to private schools are not deductible as charitable contributions

- ✓ if there is the existence of a contract under which a parent agrees to make a "contribution" and that contains provisions ensuring the admission of the child;
- ✓ if there is a plan allowing a parent either to pay tuition or to make "contributions" in exchange for schooling;
- ✓ if there is the earmarking of a contribution for the direct benefit of a particular individual; or
- ✓ if there is the otherwise unexplained denial of admission or readmission to a school for children of individuals who are financially able, but who do not contribute.

The IRS also will take into consideration other factors to decide deductibility such as

- ✓ no significant tuition charge;
- ✓ the parents of children attending a school receive substantial or unusual pressure to contribute;
- ✓ contribution appeals made as part of the admissions or enrollment process;
- ✓ no significant potential sources of revenue for operating the school other than contributions by parents or children attending the school; and
- ✓ other factors suggesting that a contribution policy was created to avoid the characterization of payments as tuition.

Payments to a church that operates a private school

Some churches operate related private schools on a "tuition-free" basis. These churches typically request that families with children in the school increase their contributions by the amount that they would otherwise have paid as tuition.

In reviewing "tuition-free" situations, the IRS often questions the deductibility of gifts to the church if

- ✓ contributions of several families increased or decreased markedly as the number of their children enrolled in the school changed;
- ✓ the contributions of parents of students drop off significantly in the summer months when the school is not in session; and
- ✓ the parents are not required to pay tuition out of their pockets.

Generally, contributions by parents are not deductible as charitable contributions to the extent that the church pays the parent's tuition liabilities.

Contributions to organizations to support specific individual workers

Many charitable organizations raise funds to support the ministry of specific individual workers. The individuals may be missionaries, youth workers, or employees of the organization.

Contributions to support the ministry of specific individual workers of a nonprofit organization may be deductible if

- ✓ the organization controls and administers the funds following its board-approved policies and procedures, and the work it supports is in the furtherance of its exempt purpose;
- ✓ the amounts distributed to the recipient missionary/staff members are in salary payments for services rendered for the organization or in payment for business expenses related to the work of the missionary/staff member;
- ✓ the amounts distributed to the recipient missionary/staff members are properly included for information reporting purposes (such as on Forms W-2 or 1099-MISC); and
- ✓ the organization clearly distinguishes the funds given to the organization for the support of a missionary/staff member from funds that are nondeductible personal gifts passed on directly to the individual.

Contributions that benefit specific individuals other than staff members and other than the needy

Occasionally individuals give money to a church but request that it be sent to a particular recipient who is not on the staff of the organization, not a missionary related to the organization, and does not qualify as a "needy" individual. When told that this "conduit" role is improper, the donor usually responds, "But I can't get a tax deduction otherwise!" The donor is absolutely correct.

The general rule in a conduit situation is that the donor is making a gift to the ultimate beneficiary. The IRS will look to the ultimate beneficiary to decide whether the gift qualifies for a charitable contribution deduction.

There are certain limited circumstances in which an organization may serve as an intermediary with respect to a gift that will be transferred to another organization or to a specific individual. In such circumstances, it is essential that the organization first receiving the monies have the right to control the ultimate destination of the funds.

Example: Frank Lee makes a gift of $5,000 to Shady Lane Church. Mr. Lee stipulates that the gift must go to a particular music group of which his son is a member. The money will be used to purchase sound equipment. The group will go on tour to present religious music in churches. The group is not an approved ministry of Shady Lane Church. This gift would generally be termed a personal gift to the music group and would not be deductible as a charitable contribution. It is best if the church returns the gift to Mr. Lee. If the church accepts the gift and passes the money on to the music group, the church should advise Mr. Lee that the gift is not deductible and should not provide a charitable receipt.

Donor intent is also a key factor. If the donor intends for a gift to benefit a specific individual instead of supporting the ministry of the charity, the gift is generally not deductible.

Contributions to needy individuals and benevolence funds

Contributions made directly by a donor to needy individuals are not deductible. To qualify for a charitable deduction, contributions must be made to a qualified organization.

Benevolence should be paid from the general fund of an organization. Contributions to benevolence funds may be claimed as charitable deductions if they are not earmarked for particular recipients.

A gift to a charitable organization involved in helping needy people marked "to aid the unemployed" is generally deductible. Yet if the gift is designated or restricted for the "Brown family" and the organization passes the money on to the Browns, the gift is generally not tax-deductible.

If a donor makes a suggestion about the beneficiary of a benevolent contribution, it may be deductible if the recipient organization exercises proper control over the benevolence fund. The suggestion must only be advisory in nature and the charity may accept or reject the gift. However, if every "suggestion" is honored by the organization, the earmarking could be challenged by the IRS.

A church or nonprofit organization may want to help a particular individual or family that has unusually high medical bills or other valid personal financial needs. To announce that funds will be received for the individual or family and receipt the monies through the church or nonprofit organization makes the gifts personal and not deductible as charitable contributions. An option is for the church to set up a trust fund at a local bank. Contributions to the trust fund would not be deductible for tax purposes. Payments from the trust fund would not represent taxable income to a needy individual or family. This method of helping the needy person or family is clearly a legal approach and would represent personal gifts from one individual to another.

Suggested Benevolence Fund Policy

Whereas, New Haven Church has a ministry to needy individuals; and

Whereas, The church desires to establish a Benevolence Fund through which funds for the support of needy individuals may be administered;

Resolved, That New Haven Church establish a Benevolence Fund to help individuals in financial need and will develop written procedures to document the need, establish reasonable limitations of support per person during a specified time period and obtain external verification of the need; and

Resolved, That the church will accept only contributions to the Benevolence Fund that are "to or for the use" of the church and their use must be subject to the control and discretion of the church board. Donors may make suggestions but not designations or restrictions concerning the identity of the needy individuals; and

Resolved, That the church will provide a charitable contribution receipt for gifts that meet the test outlined in the previous resolution. The church reserves the right to return any gifts that do not meet the test.

Payments to retirement homes

The IRS generally treats payments to nonprofit retirement homes and communities (often referred to as "founders' gifts" or "sustainers' gifts") as nondeductible transfers when the payment is made at or near the time of entry.

If the benefit provided by the home is out of proportion to the benefit, the payment is part nondeductible purchase and part deductible contribution. The burden is on the donor to prove that the contribution is not the purchase price of the benefit and that part of the payment does qualify as a contribution.

If an individual pays a tax-exempt retirement home for the right to choose an apartment and live there, the payment is not a deductible charitable gift.

Gifts designated for missionaries

Charitable contributions must be made "to or for the use of" a qualified charitable organization. The IRS has interpreted "for the use of" to mean "in trust for," implying the use of a trust or similar legal arrangement for the benefit of the organization.

Generally, gifts made by an individual directly to a missionary are not deductible as charitable contributions. The funds need to be given to a missionary organization designated for the ministry of a particular missionary to be deductible.

Donated travel and out-of-pocket expenses

Unreimbursed out-of-pocket expenses of a volunteer performing services for a charity are generally deductible. The expenses must be directly connected with and solely attributable to the providing of the volunteer services.

The type of expenses that are deductible include transportation; travel (mileage at 14 cents per mile for 1999), meals, and lodging while away from home if there is no significant element of personal pleasure, recreation, or vacation associated with the travel; postage; phone calls; printing and photocopying; expenses in entertaining prospective donors; and required uniforms without general utility.

It is generally inappropriate to provide a volunteer with a standard charitable receipt because the charity is usually unable to confirm the actual amount of a volunteer's expenses. But a letter of appreciation may be sent to the volunteer thanking the individual for the specific services provided. The burden is on the volunteer to prove the amount of the expense.

Volunteers who incur $250 or more in out-of-pocket expenses in connection with a charitable activity are subject to the acknowledgment rules. The acknowledgment should identify the type of services or expenses provided by the volunteer and state that no goods or services were provided by the charity to the donor in consideration of the volunteer efforts (see page 168 for a sample letter to volunteers).

Gifts to domestic organizations for foreign use

Gifts must be made to recognized U.S. charities to qualify for an income tax deduction. Some taxpayers have attempted to avoid this rule by funnelling gifts for a foreign-organized entity through a U.S. charity.

There are some acceptable situations where a U.S. charity may receive gifts for which a deduction is allowed with the money used abroad:

- ✓ The money may be used by the U.S. charity directly for projects that it selects to carry out its own exempt purposes. In this instance, the domestic organization would generally have operations in one or more foreign countries functioning directly under the U.S. entity. The responsibility of the donee organization ends when the purpose of the gift is fulfilled. A system of narrative and financial reports is necessary to document what was accomplished by the gift.

- ✓ It may create a subsidiary organization in a foreign country to facilitate its exempt operations there, with certain of its funds transmitted directly to the subsidiary. In this instance, the foreign organization is merely an administrative arm of the U.S. organization, with the U.S. organization considered the

Sample Letter to Volunteers

Dear Volunteer:

We appreciate the time, energy, and out-of-pocket costs you devote to our cause as follows:

Description of Services/Expenses Provided

____

____

____

No goods or services were provided to you by our church, except intangible religious benefits, in consideration of your volunteer efforts.

You may deduct unreimbursed expenses that you incur incidental to your volunteer work. So transportation costs (travel from home to our church or other places where you render services), phone calls, postage stamps, stationery, and similar out-of-pocket costs are deductible.

You can deduct 14 cents per mile (1999 rate) in computing the costs of operating your car while doing volunteer work as well as unreimbursed parking and toll costs. Instead of using the cents-per-mile method, you can deduct your actual auto expenses, provided you keep proper records. However, insurance and depreciation on your car are not deductible.

If you travel as a volunteer and must be away from home overnight, reasonable payments for meals and lodging as well as your travel costs are deductible. Your out-of-pocket costs at a convention connected with your volunteer work are deductible if you were duly chosen as a representative of our church.

You cannot deduct travel expenses as charitable gifts if there's a significant element of personal pleasure, recreation, or vacation in the travel.

You cannot deduct the value of your services themselves. If you devote 100 hours during the year to typing for us and the prevailing rate for these services is $8.00 per hour, you can't deduct the $800 value of your services. Although deductions are allowed for property gifts, the IRS doesn't consider your services "property." Nor is the use of your home for meetings a "property contribution."

Finally, you may be required to substantiate your deduction to the IRS. Be prepared to prove your costs with cancelled checks, receipted bills, and diary entries. If your expenses total $250 or more for the calendar year, you must have this acknowledgment in hand before you file your income tax return (including any extensions).

Again, thank you for furthering our cause with that most precious commodity: your time.

Castleview Church

real recipient of the contributions. The responsibility of the U.S. organization ends when the purpose of the gift is fulfilled by the foreign subsidiary.

✓ It may make grants to charities in a foreign country in furtherance of its exempt purposes, following review and approval of the uses to which the funds are to be put. The responsibility of the U.S. organization ends when the purpose of the gift is fulfilled by the foreign organization. A narrative and financial report from the foreign organization will usually be necessary to document the fulfillment of the gift.

✓ It may transfer monies to another domestic entity with the second organization fulfilling the purpose of the gift. The responsibility of the first entity usually ends when the funds are transferred to the second organization.

Charity-sponsored tours

Many religious and charitable organizations sponsor cruises and tours. The location is often a resort or tourist area. Can individuals take a charitable deduction for tour expenses? Should the organization give a charitable receipt to tour participants? If tour expenses cannot be deducted as charitable expenses, what about taking a business or education expense deduction? Are work trips to mission fields deductible as charitable contributions?

Tours sponsored by nonprofit organizations rarely provide a tax deduction to the participant. In instances where a tax deduction is available, the deduction is almost always in the business or education expense category. Even these expense deductions are denied if there is a significant element of personal pleasure, recreation, or vacation.

The general rule is that there is no charitable contribution deduction for the cost of a travel or study tour. The only exception is where individuals are actually paying for their expenses and doing work for the organization. Then there is a limited deduction available, subject to a restriction on the amount of pleasure and recreation involved in a particular trip.

Discounts provided charity by a vendor

A business donor may provide a charitable discount for goods or services purchased by a nonprofit organization and denote the discount as a "charitable contribution."

A charitable discount is generally not deductible as a charitable contribution. The donor should not receive a standard receipt, but may receive an appropriately worded acknowledgment.

Interest on restricted gifts

There is often a time period between the receipt of restricted donations and the expenditure of the funds for the specified purpose. If investment income is earned

TIP

on the monies before their expenditure, do the investment earnings accrue to the gift or may the earnings be used for the general budget of the organization? Unless there are donor or other legal restrictions on the earnings on the funds, state law controls the use of the earnings. Often, the interest earned on restricted funds held for a temporary period prior to expenditure is considered to be unrestricted.

Refunding contributions to donors

Charitable contributions generally should not be returned to donors. However, there are a few instances where donors must be given the option of receiving their contributions back and in some cases the refund should actually occur.

CAUTION

Since contributions must be irrevocable to qualify for a charitable deduction, there is no basis to return an undesignated gift to a donor. Requests from donors to return undesignated gifts should be denied under nearly any circumstances. A practice of refunding such gifts would be an extremely dangerous precedent.

Donors often contribute funds based on the anticipation that a certain event will occur. Their intent is to make an irrevocable gift. For example, a church raises money to buy new pews. However, an insufficient amount is raised and the church board abandons the project. What happens to the money that was designated by donors for the pews? If the donors can be identified, they should be asked whether they would like to remove the designation related to their gift. Otherwise, the money should be returned to the donor. If the donors cannot be identified (as in the case of cash contributions), the congregation could re-direct use of the funds.

If contributions are returned to donors, a written communication should accompany the refund advising donors of their responsibility to file amended tax returns if a charitable deduction was claimed. A written notice should be filed with the IRS to document the initial date of the gift, the date of the refund, the amount, and name and address of the taxpayer.

Key Concepts

- Since 1917, Congress has provided favored tax treatment to charitable contributions by individuals.
- Most nonprofit organizations qualify to receive tax-deductible contributions.
- Not all gifts to your organization are tax-deductible such as gifts of services or the use of property.
- Certain gifts of property may require you to file reports with the IRS.
- Gifts that are designated for the benefit of individuals may be inappropriate for your organization to receive or at least receipt as charitable contributions.

CHAPTER EIGHT

Risk Management

In This Chapter

- The risk management process
- Steps to avoid sexual abuse
- Insuring for risks
- Complying with applicable laws

Too often, nonprofits are not fully aware of their responsibilities for knowing and taking action to reduce or manage the many risks their organizations face. Some risks, such as fire, can seriously impair or even destroy an organization's ability to operate for an extended time. Other risks, such as liability claims, actually can destroy the organization itself and, in extreme cases, can leave board members personally responsible for paying out large sums. Even if a nonprofit successfully defends itself against such suits, it can cost countless hours and tens of thousands of dollars in legal fees that could otherwise have gone toward the ministry of the organization.

Some types of risk arise from the activities of employees. But risk management must also consider the involvement of volunteers. As Peter F. Drucker has said, volunteers should be considered "unpaid staff." Volunteers perform jobs to help carry out many of the nonprofit's basic functions, including stuffing envelopes, working in the church nursery, supervising youth group activities, assisting in short-term missions trips, serving as board members, and much more.

The Risk Management Process

While management of certain kinds of risk may just involve purchasing insurance coverage, overall, risk management requires much more analysis and attention than that. The risk management process involves four interrelated steps:

✓ **Identifying potential risks.** Any nonprofit can face a number of potential risks, including:

- Being held legally responsible for inadequate supervision, poor selection procedures, or not preventing harmful actions by an employee (e.g., discrimination, sexual misconduct, physical assault, or accidents);
- Having a terminated employee sue for wrongful dismissal or violation of various rights;
- Violations of a wide variety of laws that apply to nonprofits (see pages 182-89 for more on this topic);
- Environmental claims; and
- Loss of computerized or paper records whose true worth to the organization cannot be insured.

To identify other potential risks, nonprofits should engage in a thorough, systematic assessment of what might happen. Do not try to assess the odds of something happening, just identify as many possibilities as you can. Ask questions such as the following:

- Which of our current activities could cause a loss?
- What property could cause a loss (or be lost)?
- What past insurance claims have been made against us?

✓ **Studying ways to avoid or reduce risks and choosing the best way for each risk.** The first two questions to ask when analyzing each specific risk are "If this does occur, how much can we expect to lose?" and "If this does occur, can we afford the loss?" A third question is, "Is it likely to happen more than once?" The answers to these questions begin to identify the potential risk in terms of total dollar amount.

Next, study various steps that can be taken to eliminate or reduce the risk. Some common ones include:

- **Avoiding the risk by eliminating its source.** A board can take action to eliminate the source of a risk. Usually, this strategy is a last resort because it generally means not engaging in some activity. In effect, it often means a reduction in services or access (e.g., locking playgrounds of a Christian school during off-hours or dropping uninsurable sports activities of the church youth group).
- **Controlling potential losses by reducing the risk.** Nonprofits can control potential losses by reducing the degree and frequency of risk. Running background checks on people hired into potentially sensitive positions or providing training in physical risk identification and safety

can help reduce the change of certain risks and increase the organization's ability to defend itself legally.

- **Deciding to live with the risk.** Keeping some risks may be the best way to handle them. Usually this only applies to risks that represent potentially small dollar amounts that the board determines the nonprofit can pay for relatively easily if they occur. The potential dollar amount is the key to deciding to live with a risk, not the likelihood of the risk occurring. For instance, the odds of being sued for wrongful termination should not determine whether or not management provides relevant personnel policies, performance reviews, and recordkeeping, since even one successful suit can result in hundreds of thousands of dollars in damages. The board must make sure such potentially large losses are controlled, rather than assuming that they would not happen at all.

- **Transferring risk to someone else.** There are a number of ways to transfer potential risks to other parties. Buying insurance is perhaps the most common method. Others include:

  - Making sure other organizations that provide services under contract with your nonprofit have adequate insurance;

  - Having participants (or their parents) in activities (e.g., church sports leagues, youth, or adults) sign waivers and releases as a condition of participating; and

  - Having an individual or organization contracting for services from your nonprofit (e.g., an outside group rents the church fellowship hall for a meeting) hold your nonprofit harmless by agreeing to pay any claims resulting from your nonprofit's providing the services.

✓ **Putting the choice into action.** After deciding how to manage a specific risk, the board must make sure that the nonprofit's managers and staff plan and take coordinated action to ensure that everyone in the organization (employees and volunteers)

- Know the potential risk;

- Make plans for managing the risk; and

- Carry out the risk management activities on a regular basis.

Key elements of implementing any risk management program include making sure that various policy and procedure manuals exist, that they are complete and up-to-date, and that they actually are consulted and followed by managers, staff, and volunteers on a daily basis. Examples include accounting manuals that clearly explain computer backup and security procedures to help reduce the risk of losing records, and personnel manuals that clearly spell out employee rights, responsibilities, and procedures to help manage the plethora of risks that exist in personnel relations.

✓ **Monitoring the results and making needed changes.** The only way to make sure that management and staff follow through with risk management efforts is for the board to require regular monitoring and reporting in relevant areas. At the same time, the steps in the risk management process must be repeated regularly. External legal requirements and internal circumstances are both continually changing, so the board must ensure that the ongoing process of identifying, assessing, managing, and monitoring new potential risks takes place as a regular part of organizational growth and change.

Steps to Avoid Sexual Abuse

TIP

Screening can alert your organization to potentially harmful employee and volunteer applicants. Volunteers are involved with children in virtually every church. And many other nonprofit organizations work with children (and other vulnerable individuals, like the elderly or people with physical or emotional conditions).

The key elements in developing a program to avoid sexual abuse include:

✓ **Obtaining legal advice.** State laws regarding screening procedures vary. So it is important to check with an attorney knowledgeable in this area before implementing a screening system. Ask your attorney to explain your state's law regarding the mandatory reporting of instances of sexual abuse.

✓ **Use an application form.** All applicants for employee or volunteer positions should complete an application. In addition to basic contact and history information, include a statement which the applicant should acknowledge in writing, certifying that statements provided in the application are true and complete, and that any misrepresentation or omission may be grounds for rejection of the applicant or for dismissal if employed. Also ask about pending criminal charges, unless prohibited by law.

✓ **Develop guidelines for people who work with children.** Have a comprehensive written policy or handbook that delineates specific policies applicable to all employees and volunteers who work with children. For example, (1) designate a "confidential counselor" to whom any child may go at any time, to discuss any problem, (2) require that activities be done in an open area or room, and not in a private office, (3) require that more than one adult accompany children on field trips, and (4) install windows in classrooms and keep doors open except where excessive noise prohibits it.

Insuring for Risks

Most nonprofit entities need full insurance coverage similar to for-profit organizations. A frequent review of insurance requirements and a good relationship with an insurance agent or broker is important to provide a complete insurance program at competitive cost.

Setting deductible limits is a very important decision. Generally, the higher the deductible, the lower the premium will be. If the organization is financially strong enough to assume a certain degree of risk, the choice of high deductibles will often save in overall insurance costs.

Abuse or molestation insurance

All churches and many other nonprofit organizations should purchase a general liability policy that includes an abuse or molestation endorsement or separate coverage. This coverage should apply to the actual or threatened abuse or molestation by anyone of any person while in the care, custody, or control of your organization. It would also extend to the negligent employment, investigation, supervision, reporting to the proper authorities or failure to so report, or retention of an individual for whom your organization was legally responsible and who was involved in actual or threatened abuse.

Automobile insurance

Automobile insurance is required if your organization owns one or more automobiles, buses, or other vehicles. If an employee runs an errand for an organization using the employer's car and is in an auto accident, this coverage protects the organization. Even if no vehicles are owned by your organization, hired and non-owned automobile insurance is usually needed.

A commercial auto policy is generally more narrow in coverage than a personal auto policy. For example, personal auto policy coverage usually transfers to other cars that you may drive. This is generally not true with a commercial auto policy.

Medical payments provide a goodwill type of coverage. If someone is injured in your auto, the person may be treated up to the medical payment limit of the policy. Often this helps avoid a lawsuit.

Typical policy coverages are $100,000/$300,000 bodily injury, $100,000 property damage, $50,000 uninsured motorist, and $2,000 or $5,000 for medical payments. Endorsements may be added for towing or road service and for rental car reimbursement. Liability coverage should be at least $100,000. If you only purchase the minimum required by your state, you may be inadequately insured.

In the U.S., auto coverages generally follow the car and any driver who operates the vehicle with permission of the insured is covered. If an employer-provided auto is the only vehicle used by the employee—e.g., there is not a personal auto—it is important to add a "broadform drive other car" endorsement.

Crime insurance

Employee dishonesty coverage is usually essential for nonprofit organizations because of the handling of donations. The coverage usually relates to employees but may be extended to volunteers such as a church treasurer.

Protection against robbery inside and outside is often a desirable part of the crime insurance coverage. A high deductible will lower premium cost.

Director's and officer's liability insurance

When it comes to lawsuits, one of the most vulnerable positions in any nonprofit is that of a board member or officer. Employment-related claims and monetary awards are increasing, especially in the areas of wrongful discharge and employment discrimination.

Such claims are especially worrisome for individual board members and smaller nonprofits because of the amount of damages that could be involved. A successful defense against a lawsuit can be very expensive, while losing a suit can totally exhaust an organization's resources, as well as those of the individual board members involved.

The two primary options for nonprofits to provide protection to board members against individual liability are:

TIP

- ✓ **Insurance.** Director's and officer's (D&O) liability insurance is designed to protect board members and officers against certain liabilities they may incur while acting in their official capacities. D&O policies usually cover legal fees and other expenses involved in defending against a claim.
- ✓ **State law protection.** More than 30 states have legislation limiting the liability of individuals who serve as volunteer directors or officers on nonprofit boards. Generally, these laws provide that a director or officer can be held liable only for willful or wanton behavior, not just for simple negligence. Some states require an affirmative act by the organization in order for the exempting state law to apply. This means that specific language must be included in the articles of incorporation or bylaws describing the essence of the statute and clearly stating that it applies to the organization. Without the required language, directors are not covered by the law.

Even if protection is provided under state laws, it may be wise for the organization to purchase D&O insurance to cover the acts of negligence not covered under the state law.

Disability insurance

Disability insurance may be provided for nonprofit organization employees. Coverage is usually limited to 60% to 75% of the annual salary of each individual.

Social security and pension benefits are often offset against disability insurance benefits. Disability insurance premiums may be paid through a flexible benefit plan to obtain income tax and social security tax (FICA) savings.

If the organization pays the disability insurance premiums, the premiums are excluded from the employee's income. If the organization pays the premiums (and the employee is the beneficiary) as a part of the compensation package, any disability policy proceeds are fully taxable to the employee. This is based on who paid the premiums for the policy covering the year when the disability started. If the premiums are shared between the church and the minister, then the benefits are taxable in the same proportion as the payment of the premiums.

The benefit waiting period is generally in the 90-to-120-day range. Coverage may be extended to age 65 or even life.

General liability insurance

General liability insurance provides for the avoidance of unforeseeable payments and also protects against the catastrophic hazards when large groups of individuals gather under the sponsorship of an organization. Endorsements to the liability policy may cover such additional hazards as product liability, premises medical payments, real property fire legal liability, advertising injury, contractual liability, and personal injury.

Coverage is usually written for at least \$500,000 for each occurrence, \$500,000 aggregate, \$500,000 products and completed operations, \$500,000 personal and advertising, \$50,000 fire damage, and \$5,000 medical.

If an umbrella liability policy is not purchased, the \$500,000 limits listed above probably should be raised to \$1,000,000. If umbrella liability coverage is purchased, the insurance company may require that the general liability limit be \$1,000,000.

General liability insurance may be purchased with limits higher than \$1,000,000. It is usually more cost-effective to use a \$500,000 or \$1,000,000 limit for the general liability policy and then purchase an umbrella policy with higher limits.

Many churches and nonprofits need liability insurance for special events such as summer camps, skiing, beach activities, softball, basketball, and other sports. Coverage for these events should be provided with a specific endorsement under a general liability policy.

Group life insurance

Group life insurance may be written to provide a minimum amount of insurance for each employee. The first \$50,000 of coverage is a tax-free benefit for employees. Premiums may be paid wholly or partially by the employer.

Health and dental insurance

In recent years there has been a shift to managed care—prepaid health- and dental-insurance programs that stress preventive care. But for most churches and other small-to-medium charities, an indemnity plan may be the only avenue available.

Health insurance

TIP

Health insurance purchased through a group policy is usually more expensive than individual policies if the individual can qualify for coverage. Insurers often require that 75% of the full-time employees be enrolled to qualify for a group plan. This enrollment requirement is necessary to avoid adverse selection. Adverse selection occurs when a disproportionate number of employees with very high-cost medical problems are enrolled in a plan.

The basic offerings in employer-provided health-insurance plans include the following:

- ✓ **Health Maintenance Organization (HMO).** Medical treatment is prepaid and delivered by the HMO provider organization.
- ✓ **Preferred Provider Organization (PPO).** Medical treatment is supplied through a designated network of physicians and hospitals at discounted rates.
- ✓ **Indemnity plan.** These plans may include cost containment features such as prehospital authorization and a second opinion before surgery, while also offering incentives for outpatient treatment. Indemnity plans typically feature a per-person, per-year deductible and co-insurance factors and a limit on total lifetime claims covered.

  Traditional indemnity plans offer little flexibility of employer design. The partially self-funded concept allows the employer to design the exact coverage and build in customized cost-containment features. The two basic indemnity plan concepts are as follows:

  - **Fully insured through a carrier.** This is the traditional approach for health insurance with most of the risk borne by the insurance carrier.
  - **Partially self-funded by organization.** This method is a shared-risk approach. This concept may make sense if there are 25 or more employees and the maximum annual liability is only slightly higher than the premium under a fully insured plan.

    An employee group primarily composed of nonsmokers and nondrinkers and without the incidence of AIDS also may provide an incentive to consider the partially self-funded approach. Traditional fully insured plans must factor the possibility of all types of illness into their rates.

    The principles of a partially self-funded plan include payment by the organization of the first-dollar medical costs. The organization buys a high deductible medical plan. For example, the deductible may be $10,000 or $20,000 per person per year. Expenses over the $10,000 or $20,000 are covered by the insurance carrier. This is commonly called a "specific deductible."

An "aggregate stop-loss" policy is also purchased. This policy will provide that annual medical expenses exceeding a total of a certain amount will be paid by the insurance carrier. This is a type of overall stop-loss for the employer.

✓ **Traditional fully insured plan with HMO option.** Under this concept the employer gives the employee the choice of being covered under a traditional indemnity plan or using an HMO.

HMOs are typically more expensive than indemnity plans. Therefore, if the employee chooses the HMO plan, the difference between the cost of the HMO and the fully insured plan usually is paid by the employee.

Preexisting conditions waiting period

For plan years beginning after July 1, 1997, health care plans cannot apply preexisting condition limits for periods greater than 12 months (18 months for late enrollees). No limits can be applied in cases involving pregnancy, newborns, or newly adopted children. Furthermore, the 12-month limit for preexisting conditions must be reduced month-for-month by any previous health insurance coverage that a worker had, unless he or she had a break in coverage of more than 63 days.

Medical plan continuation features

Securing medical coverage while an individual is between jobs is often a concern. Churches and small nonprofit employers are exempt from the coverage continuation requirements of COBRA (see page 184) but they may voluntarily comply. Also, some state laws require continued insurance coverage for spouses and children after a divorce.

Some health plans have a conversion feature that allows conversion of group coverage to an individual policy after employment ends. The conversion policy is usually expensive and the benefits are very limited. Still, conversion may be the best alternative for someone with health problems and unable to obtain other insurance.

Flexible benefit plans

Many employers have shifted to a flexible benefit plan (often referred to as a cafeteria plan) to provide health coverage and to allow employees to choose between taxable and nontaxable benefits. In the simplest plans, employees might be offered an opportunity to choose and pay for additional medical benefits or for health benefits to cover family members.

More complex plans offer a full menu of benefits: additional vacation time, disability insurance, child-care allowances or emergency child-care service, life and disability insurance, and legal insurance (long-term care insurance does not qualify). Premiums for a private health insurance plan or for a spouse's plan are not chargeable to a flexible benefit plan. Each benefit has a price. Each employee selects the package of benefits that best meets the employee's needs and ability to pay.

The expense money employees choose to keep in their flexible benefit plan is deducted before taxes. The money is held in reserve, and the employee is reimbursed for expenses as they are incurred.

Depending on the state of employment, employee savings may apply to both federal and state income taxes and social security taxes. This may amount to a discount of around 40% (28% federal tax, 7.65% FICA, 3%-5% state tax) on what was formerly paid personally for health care insurance or child-care expense.

The flexible benefit plan offers some distinct advantages to employers. The organization does not have to pay social security taxes on money that is being withheld from employees under the plan. In some states, lower Workers' Compensation and unemployment insurance payments also result.

Some potential drawbacks for employees are

- ✓ employees must use the money they have set aside within the plan year or forfeit that money to their employer, and
- ✓ there might be a slight reduction in some of their social security benefits.

Dental Insurance

An insured dental care program is among the most popular of benefit options. It is a benefit that employees want to take advantage of and can use regularly.

In the traditional approach, a dental plan is similar to medical insurance in that the employer pays a premium to an insurer who acts as the administrator. Covered employees submit claims and the insurer pays according to a "usual and customary" schedule. Employees are typically free to select their dentists.

Similar to the HMO concept in medical insurance, "managed care" dental programs usually work with a list of contracted care providers who provide service to members in the covered group.

Reimbursed self-insurance represents an alternative approach for dental benefits. This concept allows covered employees to select their dentists, have all work done without exclusion, pay for services themselves, and file for reimbursement from the employer.

For example, an organization might choose to pay 100% of the first $200 per employee family and a decreasing percentage up to a ceiling limit of their determination. A plan can be structured flexibly to allow employers to predetermine their maximum costs for budget purposes.

Key Employee Insurance

Key employee insurance reimburses the organization for financial loss resulting from the death of a key employee of the organization. It may be used to build up a fund to be available upon the individual's retirement should death not be a factor.

Long-Term Care Insurance

Long-term care or nursing home insurance provided by the nonprofit is tax-free to the employee effective January 1, 1997. However, long-term care premiums are not excluded from an employee's income if provided through a cafeteria or other flexible spending arrangement.

Professional Liability Insurance

Pastoral counseling is rarely covered in standard policies. Each church should purchase a pastor's professional liability policy to cover any act or omission in the furnishing of pastoral counseling services. The coverage protects both pastor and church. Your pastor will feel more comfortable handling delicate matters because adequate insurance coverage is provided.

Property Insurance

A multi-peril policy provides comprehensive property and general liability insurance tailored to the needs of the insured. Endorsements may be added to provide earthquake, employee dishonesty, and money loss coverages. A general property policy provides fire insurance coverage for structures and fixtures that are a part of the structures. Machinery used in building service, air conditioning systems, boilers, and elevators are covered under a boiler policy.

Endorsements may be added to the general property policy to cover replacement cost, loss caused by windstorm, hail, explosion, riot, aircraft, vehicles and smoke, vandalism and malicious mischief, flood, sprinkler leakage, and earthquake. It may be desirable to eliminate the co-insurance provision by using an agreed amount endorsement. Be sure there is coverage on equipment, such as personal computers and video equipment, that you may take off-premises to conventions or other meetings.

Many church policies do not cover the pastor's personal property located on church premises. Even when some coverage is provided, the limit may be too low, considering the value of books, sermons, and computers.

Try to use your property insurance as catastrophic coverage and not a maintenance policy. Your organization should take care of the small property damage losses.

Travel and Accident Insurance

Travel and accident insurance is often purchased for nonprofit organization executives or perhaps all the employees. It covers injury occurring during travel authorized by the employer. The coverage also may be written on a 24-hour basis.

When purchasing insurance relating to international travel, coverage for emergency medical evacuation and assistance services are additional considerations.

Travel and accident insurance usually does not apply to certain "war zones" unless a special rider is purchased.

Umbrella Liability Insurance

Through an umbrella liability insurance policy, you may purchase liability coverage with higher limits. The particular liabilities covered do not get broader. For example, if your underlying general liability policy has a $500,000 limit and you purchase an umbrella liability policy with a $2,000,000 limit, your total liability coverage will be $2,500,000.

Umbrella policies are usually more liberal in their coverages but tend to be higher priced than excess liability policies (which are only extensions of policy limits).

Workers' Compensation

Workers' Compensation insurance coverage compensates workers for losses caused by work-related injuries. It also limits the potential liability of the organization for injury to the employee related to his job.

Workers' Compensation insurance is required by law in all states to be carried by the employer. A few states exempt churches from Workers' Compensation coverage, and several states exempt all nonprofit employers. Still, churches and nonprofit organizations are covered in most states. Most states also consider ministers to be employees regardless of the income tax filing method used by the minister and therefore they must be covered under Workers' Compensation policy. Contact your state department of labor to find out how your state applies Workers' Compensation rules to churches.

TIP

Even if a church or nonprofit organization is exempt from Workers' Compensation, the voluntary purchase of the coverage or the securing of additional general liability coverage may be prudent. This is because other types of insurance typically exclude work-related accidents: health, accident, disability, auto and general liability insurance policies are some examples.

Workers' Compensation premiums are based on the payroll of the organization with a minimum premium charge to issue the policy. An audit is done later to determine the actual charge for the policy.

Most Workers' Compensation insurance is purchased through private insurance carriers. A few states provide the coverage and charge the covered organizations.

Complying with Applicable Laws

The non-payroll laws and regulations governing nonprofits, at best, can be confusing, and at worst, very intimidating. Legal assistance may be required to provide interpretation of the laws and regulations for your organization.

This chapter is designed to provide you a very basic explanation of some key laws that may impact your organization. Complying with these laws will often result in good stewardship. There is generally a financial risk if they are ignored.

Age discrimination

The Age Discrimination in Employment Act of 1967 (ADEA) applies to employers in any industry affecting commerce with 20 or more employees. Churches with 20 or more employees may be exempt from the ADEA because of a lack of involvement in commercial activities.

The ADEA prohibits employment discrimination on the basis of age against applicants for employment and employees who are age 40 and older. The top age limit for mandatory retirement has generally been eliminated. Compulsory retirement is still permissible for certain executives or tenured college faculty members who have reached age 65. Ministers are subject to compulsory retirement.

Americans With Disabilities Act

The employment provisions of the American With Disabilities Act (ADA) cover employers with 15 or more workers in 20 or more weeks a year. For ADA questions, you can call a special information line at the Justice Department: 202–514–0301.

The ADA requirements relate to two areas:

✓ **Employment.** Hiring must be without regard to disabilities and also make reasonable accommodation for disabled individuals.

There are limited exceptions to the employment provisions of the ADA for churches and religious employers. Preferential treatment may be given in hiring individuals of a particular religion. Additionally, churches and religious organizations may require employees to conform to their religious tenets.

Example: Two applicants are members of the United Methodist denomination. A Methodist church or Methodist religious organization cannot refuse to hire the disabled applicant simply because of a disability, but it may give preference to a Methodist applicant over a Baptist.

✓ **Public accommodations.** Facilities open to the public must be accessible to the disabled. The primary focus is on facilities like restaurants, museums, hotels, retail stores, and banks.

Religious organizations or entities controlled by religious organizations (including places of worship) are exempt from the public accommodation requirements of the ADA. Caution: Although a church is exempt under the public accommodations provisions, it may still be covered under similar provisions of local building codes.

Canadian Goods and Services Tax

The Canadian Goods and Services Tax (GST) applies to all goods and services introduced into Canada. The GST applies to imports and may have impact on U.S. nonprofit organizations that have even minimal contact in Canada.

The 7% tax may be assessed on all membership dues, publication sales, magazine subscriptions, group insurance sales, advertising revenues, classified ad sales, seminar and training course revenues, and any other product or service offered by a U.S. nonprofit to a Canadian consumer.

There are certain exemptions for membership dues and educational services. Certain products and services offered by U.S. nonprofits to Canadian consumers may be covered under the GST.

For more information on the GST, write the Canadian Society of Association Executives, 45 Charles Street East, Toronto, Ontario, M4Y 1S2 and request the *Goods and Services Tax Booklet.*

Charitable solicitation

Federal, state, and local governments have enacted laws regulating the solicitation of contributions by nonprofit organizations. These laws are known as "charitable solicitation acts." They have resulted from greater interest in accountability on the part of nonprofit organizations. The laws are designed to assure contributors that funds solicited for a specified charitable purpose will be used for the intended purpose. Many states require the filing of annual registration and reports to comply with the solicitation laws (42 states have some form of solicitation laws). (See Recent Developments.)

COBRA

The Consolidated Omnibus Budget Reconciliation Act of 1985 (COBRA) requires covered employers to offer 18 months of group health coverage beyond the time the coverage would have ended because of certain "qualifying events." Premiums are reimbursable by the former employee to the former employer.

A "qualifying event" includes any termination of the employer-employee relationship, whether voluntary or involuntary, unless the termination is caused by the employee's gross misconduct. COBRA coverage applies even if the employee retires, quits, is fired, or laid off.

Churches are excluded from the COBRA requirements. However, churches may provide continuation benefits similar to COBRA. Other nonprofits are generally subject to COBRA if 20 or more employees are employed during a typical working day.

Equal pay

The Equal Pay Act prohibits employers from paying employees of one sex at a lower rate than employees of the opposite sex for equal work for positions that require the same skill, effort, and responsibility and that are performed under similar working conditions.

Environmental issues

Environmental risks are a major concern for nonprofit organizations purchasing or receiving charitable gifts of real estate. Nonprofits must exercise "due diligence" in conducting an environmental investigation prior to purchasing or accepting donated real estate. These due diligence investigations are usually called "Preliminary Environmental Site Assessments" or "Phase I Environmental Site Assessments." These assessments are performed by qualified environmental consultants.

Environmental laws that may apply to gifts or the purchase of real estate include:

- ✓ Comprehensive Environmental Response, Compensation, and Liability Act (CERCLA/Superfund, 1980)
- ✓ Resource Conservation and Recovery Act (RCRA, 1976)
- ✓ RCRA Underground Storage Tank Regulations (RCRA UST, 1984)
- ✓ Indoor Radon Abatement Act (IRAA, 1988)
- ✓ Clean Water Act (CWA, 1977)
- ✓ Clean Air Act (CAA, 1983)

Fair Labor Standards Act

The Fair Labor Standards Act (FLSA) provides protection for employees engaged in interstate commerce concerning minimum wages, equal pay, overtime pay, recordkeeping, and child labor. (Some states even have more restrictive versions of the FSLA.) Commerce is defined by the FLSA as "trade, commerce, transportation, transmission, or communication among the several states or between any state and any place outside thereof."

The employees of nonprofit organizations involved in commerce or in the production of goods for commerce are generally considered covered by the provisions of the FLSA. Conversely, nonprofits that are not engaged in commerce or fall below the $500,000 annual gross sales volume requirement are generally exempt from the Act.

The FLSA clearly applies to schools regardless of whether they are nonprofit entities operated by religious organizations. Church-operated day care centers and elementary and secondary schools are generally considered subject to the FLSA.

Most local churches would not meet the definition of being involved in commerce. However, many churches and nonprofits voluntarily choose to follow the FLSA regulations as an equitable guide and as a precaution against possible litigation.

The overtime compensation requirements of the FLSA do not apply to certain employees in executive, administrative, or professional positions. Ministers are gen-

What the FLSA Does Not Regulate

While the Fair Labor Standards Act does set basic minimum wage and overtime pay standards and regulates the employment of minors, there are a number of employment practices which the Act does not regulate. For example, the Act does not require

- ✓ vacation, holiday, severance, or sick pay;
- ✓ meal or rest periods, holidays or vacations off;
- ✓ premium pay for weekend or holiday work;
- ✓ pay raises or fringe benefits;
- ✓ a discharge notice, reason for discharge, or immediate payment of final wages to terminated employees; or
- ✓ any limit on the number of hours of work for persons 16 years of age and over.

erally exempt under the professional provisions of this exemption. Minors under age 14 generally cannot be hired.

The FLSA minimum wage became $5.15 per hour on September 1, 1997. Teenagers may be paid a training wage of $4.25 per hour for the first 90 days of employment.

The minimum wage rates of 13 states and the District of Columbia are tied to the federal minimum wage rate in some way. For example, the minimum wage rates in Alaska and the District of Columbia are generally $0.50 and $1.00 over the federal rate, respectively.

Family and Medical Leave Act

The Family and Medical Leave Act (FMLA) requires certain employers to provide up to twelve weeks of unpaid leave to eligible employees. The FMLA does not override more generous state entitlements. The law only applies to organizations with fifty or more employees. There is no exemption for religious employers.

While only large churches and nonprofit organizations may be subject to the Act, some employers will choose to comply with the provisions of the law in an effort to improve employee morale. Even though an organization is not subject to the Act, they may have legal responsibilities to pregnant or ill employees under other federal laws (see other sections of this chapter).

To be eligible under this law, a person must be employed at least twelve

U.S. Department of Justice
Immigration and Naturalization Service

OMB No. 1115-0136
Employment Eligibility Verification

Please read instructions carefully before completing this form. The instructions must be available during completion of this form. ANTI-DISCRIMINATION NOTICE. It is illegal to discriminate against work eligible individuals. Employers CANNOT specify which document(s) they will accept from an employee. The refusal to hire an individual because of a future expiration date may also constitute illegal discrimination.

Section 1. Employee Information and Verification. To be completed and signed by employee at the time employment begins

Print Name: Last	First	Middle Initial	Maiden Name
Hendricks	Fred	W.	
Address (Street Name and Number)		Apt. #	Date of Birth (month/day/year)
406 Forest Avenue			6/12/49
City	State	Zip Code	Social Security #
Cincinnati	OH	45960	514-42-9087

I am aware that federal law provides for imprisonment and/or fines for false statements or use of false documents in connection with the completion of this form.

I attest, under penalty of perjury, that I am (check one of the following):
A citizen or national of the United States
A Lawful Permanent Resident (Alien # A____________
An alien authorized to work until___/___/___
(Alien # or Admission #____________________

Employee's Signature	Date (month/day/year)
Fred W. Hendricks	1/20/00

Preparer and/or Translator Certification. *(To be completed and signed if Section 1 is prepared by a person other than the employee.) I attest, under penalty of perjury, that I have assisted in the completion of this form and that to the best of my knowledge the information is true and correct.*

Preparer's/Translator's Signature	Print Name
Address *(Street Name and Number, City, State, Zip Code)*	Date *(month/day/year)*

Section 2. Employer Review and Verification. To be completed and signed by employer. **Examine one document from List A OR examine one document from List B and one from List C as listed on the reverse of this form and record the title, number and expiration date, if any, of the document(s)**

	List A	OR	List B	AND	List C
Document title:	_____________		Driver's License		Birth Certificate
Issuing authority:	____________		Ohio		Ohio
Document #:	_____________		514-42-9087		_________________
Expiration Date (if any):	__/__/__		6 30 00		__/__/__
Document #:	_____________				
Expiration Date (if any):	__/__/__				

CERTIFICATION - I attest, under penalty of perjury, that I have examined the document(s) presented by the above-named employee, that the above-listed document(s) appear to be genuine and to relate to the employee named, that the employee began employment on *(month/day/year)* ___/___/___**and that to the best of my knowledge the employee is eligible to work in the United States. (State employment agencies may omit the date the employee began employment).**

Signature of Employer or Authorized Representative	Print Name	Title
David L. Brown	David L. Brown	Business Manager

Business or Organization Name	Address *(Street Name and Number, City, State, Zip Code)*	Date *(month/day/year)*
Fairfield Church,	110 Harding Ave., Cincinnati, OH 45960	1/31/00

Section 3. Updating and Reverification. To be completed and signed by employer

A. New Name *(if applicable)*	B. Date of rehire *(month/day/year) (if applicable)*

C. If employee's previous grant of work authorization has expired, provide the information below for the document that establishes current employment eligibility.
Document Title:___________Document #:___________Expiration Date (if any):__/__/__

I attest, under penalty of perjury, that to the best of my knowledge, this employee is eligible to work in the United States, and if the employee presented document(s), the document(s) I have examined appear to be genuine and to relate to the individual.

Signature of Employer or Authorized Representative	Date *(month/day/year)*

Form I-9 (Rev. 11-21-91) N

Note: This form must be completed and retained on file by all employers for employees hired after November 6, 1986. (For more information on completing this form, contact the Immigration and Naturalization Service office in your area for a free copy of the Handbook for Employers/Form M-274.)

months and have worked at least 1,250 hours during the twelve months. Eligible employees are entitled to a total of twelve weeks of unpaid leave for the birth of a child and certain other reasons.

Immigration control

The Immigration Reform and Control Act (IRCA) prohibits all employers from hiring unauthorized aliens, imposes documentation verification requirements on all employers, and provides an "amnesty" program for certain illegal aliens. The law also prohibits employers with three or more employees from discriminating because of national origin. An I-9 Form (see page 187) must be completed and retained on file by all employers for each employee. The form must be available for inspection at any time. Form I-9 may be obtained by calling 800–375–5283 or at www.usdoj.gov/-graphics/formsfee/forms/files/i-9.

The Form I-551 Alien Registration Receipt Card issued after August 1, 1989, is the exclusive registration card issued to lawful permanent residents as definitive evidence of identity and U.S. residence status.

National Child Care Act

Under the National Child Care Act (NCCA), later amended by the Violent Crime Control and Enforcement Act (VCCEA), states may designate organizations that will be permitted to obtain a nationwide criminal records check on child care workers. If your state designates churches, this will enable you to quickly check on prospective child care workers by asking a state agency to conduct a criminal records check.

If your state does not designate churches as eligible under the NCCA, you should rely on other methods of screening child care workers in your church.

Occupational Safety and Health Act

The Occupational Safety and Health Act (OSHA) was designed to protect workers from unsafe conditions in the workplace. OSHA generally applies to all employers engaged in commerce who have employees.

States are permitted to adopt standards of their own. Some 23 jurisdictions now have an approved state plan in place.

Churches and other nonprofit employers are not specifically exempt from OSHA. A church must employ at least one person in "secular activities" to be covered. A person who performs or participates in religious services is not considered to be involved in secular activities.

Pregnancy discrimination

Under the Pregnancy Discrimination Act, women affected by pregnancy, childbirth, or related medical conditions must be treated the same for all employment-related purposes as other workers who have a similar ability or inability to work.

Racial discrimination

Form 5578, Annual Certification of Racial Nondiscrimination for a Private School Exempt from Federal Income Tax, must be filed by churches that operate, supervise, or control a private school (see page 47). The form must be filed by the 15th day of the fifth month following the end of the organization's fiscal year. For organizations that must file Form 990, there is no requirement to file Form 5578 since the information is included in Part V of Schedule A.

The "private school" definition includes preschools, primary, secondary, preparatory, or high schools, and colleges and universities, whether operated as a separate legal entity or an activity of a church.

Religious discrimination

Title VII of the Civil Rights Act of 1964 prohibits discrimination in employment with respect to compensation, terms, conditions, or privileges of employment because of an individual's race, color, religion, sex, or national origin. The law applies to organizations with 15 or more employees.

Title VII does permit religious organizations to discriminate on the basis of religion for all positions. However, religious employers may not discriminate on the basis of race, sex, or national origin.

Sexual harassment

Under Title VII of the Civil Rights Act of 1964 two types of conduct that can constitute unlawful sexual harassment are: harassment in which concrete employment benefits are conditioned upon acquiescence to sexual advances; and harassment that does not affect economic benefits but creates a hostile working environment.

While the standards in this area are not entirely clear, certain basic precautionary steps still serve to reduce the potential for employer liability:

- ✓ Establish a comprehensive policy against sexual harassment.
- ✓ Conduct supervisory training on a regular basis.
- ✓ Implement a meaningful complaint procedure taking into account both the perspective of the aggrieved employee and the rights of the alleged harasser.
- ✓ Investigate complaints promptly, thoroughly, and tactfully, and document the investigation.
- ✓ Take appropriate remedial action in cases of proven harassment.

Key Concepts

- Risk management is much more than simply purchasing insurance. It requires a much broader analysis.
- A comprehensive program to avoid sexual abuse is a must for organizations working with children, the elderly, or people with physical or emotional conditions.
- Many organizations overlook the legal requirment to provide Workers' Compensation insurance.
- Some churches that operate day-care centers, elementary, or secondary schools are unaware that they are generally subject to the Fair Labor Standards Act.
- The immigration control forms are required to be completed by all nonprofit organizations.
- Many nonprofits are subject to the payment of sales or use taxes on purchases and the collection of sales taxes on sales.

Citations

Internal Revenue Code (Code): The Code is the "tax law" as enacted and amended by Congress and is the highest authority in all tax matters.

Federal Tax Regulations (Reg.): These are regulations published by the Department of the Treasury (it oversees the IRS) that seek to explain the sometimes vague language of the Internal Revenue Code. The Regulations give definitions, examples, and more plain-language explanations.

Treasury Decisions (T.D.): These are instructions and interpretations issued by the IRS Commissioner with the approval of the Treasury Secretary.

Private Letter Rulings (Ltr. Rul.): A private letter ruling is issued by the IRS at the request of a taxpayer. It is requested for the purpose of getting the IRS's opinion on a specific transaction or issue facing a taxpayer. Although it cannot be used as precedent by anyone else, it usually reflects the IRS's current attitude toward a particular tax matter.

Field Service Advice (F.S.A.): IRS national office personnel prepare FSAs in response to tax law questions from agents in the field. While they can only be relied upon by the recipient of the ruling, they may provide insights into the IRS view of matters that have not been decided by the courts.

Revenue Rulings (Rev. Rul.): A revenue ruling is issued by the IRS and is similar to a letter ruling, but it is not directed to a specific taxpayer. It is designed to give the public the IRS's opinion concerning how the tax law applies to some type of transaction, giving examples and explanations. It also gives the tax consequences of specific transactions.

Revenue Procedures (Rev. Proc.): A revenue procedure is similar to a revenue ruling, but it gives more general guidelines and procedural information. It usually does not give tax consequences of specific transactions.

Technical Advice Memoranda (T.A.M.): These consist of written counsel or guidance furnished by the IRS National Office on the interpretation and proper application of the tax law to a specific set of facts.

Court cases: Taxpayer disputes with the IRS may end up in court if a taxpayer is issued an unfavorable ruling by the IRS and is hit with back taxes. There are two routes to take if the taxpayer wants to take the IRS to court. The taxpayer can elect not to pay the back taxes and petition the Tax Court to find that the proposed back tax assessment is incorrect. Or, the taxpayer can pay the disputed amount and sue the IRS for a refund in a district court. A taxpayer can appeal an adverse court decision in an appellate court, and if unsuccessful, can take it to the U.S. Supreme Court.

The IRS is bound by decisions of the Supreme Court for all taxpayers. It is bound by the decisions of the other courts only for the particular taxpayer involved and only for the years involved in the litigation.

Chapter 2, Tax Exemption

- Criteria for qualifying as a church
  Spiritual Outreach Society v. Commissioner, T.C.M. 41 (1990)

  Joseph Edward Hardy v. Commissioner, T.C.M. 557 (1990)

- Exemption from filing Form 990 for certain missions organizations
  Treas. Reg. 1.6033-2(g)(1)(iv)

- General
  501(c)(3) organization established for religious purposes

  Treas. Reg. 1.511-2(a)(3)(ii)

- Private benefit/private inurement
  Treas. Reg. 1.501(a)-1(c)

  G.C.M. 37789

- Public Disclosure of Information Returns
  P.L. 100-203

- Tax-exempt status revoked for excessive UBI
  United Missionary Aviation, Inc. v. Commissioner, T.C.M. 566 (1990)

  Frazee v. Illinois Department of Employment, 57 U.S.L.W. 4397, 108 S. Ct. 1514 (1989)

  Hernandez v. Commissioner, 819 F.2d 1212, 109 S. Ct. 2136 (1989)

- Unrelated business income: general
  Code Sec. 511-13

- Unrelated business income: affinity credit card programs
  T.C.M. 34 (1996)

  T.C.M. 63 (1996)

- Unrelated business income: jeopardy to exempt status
  Ltr. Rul. 7849003

- Unrelated business income: organization's tour programs
  Ltr. Rul. 9027003

- Unrelated business income: affinity card programs
  Ltr. Rul. 9029047

  G.C.M. 39827, July 27, 1990

- Unrelated business income: mailing list profits
  Disabled American Veterans v. U.S., 94 TC No. 6 (1990)

  American Bar Endowment v. U.S., 477 U.S. 105 (1986)

- Unrelated business income: other
  Hope School v. U.S., 612 F.2d 298 (7th Cir. 1980)

  Rev. Rul. 64-182

Chapter 3, Compensation Planning

- Accountable expense reimbursement plans
  Treas. Reg. 1.62-2

  Treas. Reg. 1.274-5(e)

  Ltr. Rul. 9317003

- Medical expense reimbursement plans
  Code Sec. 125 (b), (e)

- Moving expense exclusion
  Code Sec. 132(g)

- Tax-sheltered annuities
  Code Sec. 403(b)

  Code Sec. 1402(a)

  Code Sec. 3121(a)(5)(D)

  Rev. Rul. 78-6

  Rev. Rul. 68-395

Azad v. Commissioner, 388 F.2d 74 (8th Cir. 1968)

Rev. Rul. 66-274

Chapter 4, Employer Reporting

- Classification of workers
  Rev. Proc. 85-18

  Sec. 530 of the Revenue Act of 1978
- Employee v. self-employed for income tax purposes
  Rev. Rul. 87-41
- Moving expenses
  Code Sec. 82

  Code Sec. 3401(a)(15)
- Noncash remuneration
  Code Sec. 3401(a)
- Payment of payroll taxes
  Triplett 115 B.R. 955 (N.D. Ill. 1990)

  Carter v. U.S., 717 F. Supp. 188 (S.D. N.Y. 1989)
- Per diem allowances
  Rev. Proc. 97-59
- Personal use of employer-provided auto
  Temp. Reg. Sec. 1.61-2T

  IRS Notice 91-41
- Rabbi trusts
  Rev. Proc. 92-64
- Reasonable compensation
  Truth Tabernacle, Inc. v. Commissioner of Internal Revenue, T.C.M. 451 (1989)

  Heritage Village Church and Missionary Fellowship, Inc., 92 B.R. 1000 (D.S.C. 1988)
- Taxability of benefits paid under cafeteria plans
  Ltr. Rul. 8839072

  Ltr. Rul. 8839085
- Temporary travel
  Rev. Rul. 93-86

  Comprehensive National Energy Policy Act of 1992
- Unemployment taxes
  Code Sec. 3309(b)

  St. Martin Evangelical Lutheran Church v. South Dakota, 451 U.S. 772 (1981)

  Employment Division v. Rogue Valley Youth for Christ, 770 F.2d 588 (Ore. 1989)
- Voluntary withholding for ministers
  Rev. Rul. 68-507

Chapter 5, Information Reporting Requirements

- Backup withholding
  Code Sec. 3406
- Cash reporting rules for charities
  T.D. 8373

  G.C.M. 39840
- Issuing Form 1099-MISCs
  Rev. Rul. 84-151

  Rev. Rul. 81-232
- Medical expense reimbursements to employees
  Ltr. Rul. 9112022
- Moving expense reporting
  IRS Announcement 94-2
- Nonresident alien payments
  Code Sec. 1441

  Code Sec. 7701(b)
- Volunteer fringe benefits
  Prop. Reg. 1.132-5(r)
- Withholding of tax on nonresident aliens
  Pub. 515

Chapter 7, Charitable Gifts

- Church school gifts
  Rev. Rul. 83-104

- Contributions denied/indirectly related school
  Ltr. Rul. 9004030

- Contributions earmarked for a specific individual
  Ltr. Rul. 9405003

  IRS Announcement 92-128

  Ltr. Rul. 8752031

  Rev. Rul. 79-81

- Contributions sent to children who are missionaries
  Davis v. U.S., 110 S. Ct. 2014 (1990)

- Contribution of church bonds
  Rev. Rul. 58-262

- Contribution of promissory note
  Allen v. Commissioner, U.S. of Appeals, 89-70252 (9th Cir. 1991)

- Contributions designated for specific missionaries
  Hubert v. Commissioner, T.C.M. 482 (1993)

- Contribution of unreimbursed travel expenses
  Vahan Tafralian v. Commissioner, T.C.M. 33 (1991)

  Rev. Rul. 84-61

  Rev. Rul. 76-89

- Contributions of services
  Rev. Rul 67-236

  Grant v. Commissioner, 84 T.C.M. 809 (1986)

- Contributions to needy individuals
  Stjernholm v. Commissioner, T.C.M. 563 (1989)

  Ltr. Rul. 8752031

  Rev. Rul. 62-113

- Contributions that refer to donor's name
  IR-92-4

- Criteria used to determine deductibility of payments to private schools
  Rev. Rul. 83-104

  Rev. Rul. 79-99

- Deduction of out-of-pocket transportation expenses
  Treas. Reg. 1.170A-1(g)

  Rev. Rul. 76-89

- Deductibility of membership fees as contributions
  Rev. Rul. 70-47

  Rev. Rul. 68-432

- Deductibility of payments relating to fund-raising events
  Pub. 1391

  Rev. Rul. 74-348

- Deductibility of gifts to domestic organizations for foreign use
  Ltr. Rul. 9211002

  Ltr. Rul. 9131052

  Ltr. Rul. 9129040

  Rev. Rul. 75-65

  Rev. Rul. 63-252

- Determining the value of donated property
  IRS Pub. 561

  Rochin v. Commissioner, T.C.M. 262 (1992)

- Gifts of inventory
  Code Sec. 170(e)

  Reg. 1.161-1

  Reg. 1.170A-1(c)(2), (3), (4)

Reg. 1.170A-4A(c)(3)

Rev. Rul. 85-8, superseding

- Gifts of life insurance
  Ltr. Rul. 9147040

  Ltr. Rul. 9110016

- Incentives and premiums
  IRS. Pub. 1391

  Rev. Proc. 96-59

  Rev. Proc. 92-102

  Rev. Proc. 92-49

  Rev. Proc. 90-12

- Payments in connection with use of ministry services
  Rev. Rul. 76-232

- Payments to a retirement home
  T.A.M. 9423001

  U.S. v. American Bar Endowment, 477 U.S.105 (S. Ct. 1986)

  Rev. Rul. 72-506

  Rev. Rul. 67-246

- Scholarship gifts
  Ltr. Rul. 9338014

  Rev. Rul. 83-104

  Rev. Rul. 62-113

- Substantiation rules
  Omnibus Budget Reconciliation Act of 1993

  T.D. 8690

- Travel tours
  Ltr. Rul. 9027003

- Unitrusts
  IRS Notice 94-78

Chapter 8, Risk Management

- Americans With Disabilities Act
  Public Law 101-336. 42 U.S.C. 12101 et sec.

- Child care and Development Block Grant Act of 1990, 42 U.S.C. 9801

- Equal Pay Act
  EEOC v. First Baptist Church of Mishawaka, N.D. Ind., S91-179M (1991)

  EEOC v. First Baptist Church N.D. Ind., S89-338 (1990)

- Fair Labor Standards Act
  DeArment v. Harvey, No. 90-2346 (8th Cir. 1991)

  U.S. Department of Labor v. Shenandoah Baptist Church, 899 F.2d 1389 (4th Cir.) cert. denied, 111 S. Ct. 131 (1990)

- Local sales taxes
  Thayer v. South Carolina Tax Commission, 413 S.E. 2d 810 (S.C. 1992)

  Quill Corp. v. North Dakota, S. Ct. No. 91-194

  Jimmy Swaggart Ministries v. Board of Equalization of California, 110 S. Ct. 688 (1990)

- Political activity
  Treas. Reg. 1.501(c)(3)-1(c)(1)(iii)

  IR-92-57

- Property taxes
  Trinity Episcopal Church v. County of Sherburne, 1991 WL 95745 (Minn. Tax 1991)

Index

10 Biggest Tax Mistakes Made By Churches And Nonprofit Organizations

1. Not setting up an accountable expense reimbursement plan for employees. Chapter 3.

2. Improperly classifying employees as self-employed. Chapter 4.

3. Not reporting taxable fringe benefits and social security reimbursements as additional compensation to employees. Chapter 4.

4. Deducting FICA tax from the salary of qualified ministers. Chapter 4.

5. Failing to file Form 1099-MISC for independent contractors. Chapter 5.

6. Failing to have offerings controlled by two individuals until the funds are counted. Chapter 6.

7. Failure to issue a receipt for all transactions where the donor makes a payment of more than $75 and receives goods or services. Chapter 7.

8. Providing receipts for the donation of services and the rent-free use of property. Receipting contributions designated for individuals without proper control by the donee organization. Placing a value on noncash gifts. Chapter 7.

9. Not providing Workers' Compensation coverage where required by law and not coordinating Workers' Compensation with health insurance coverages. Chapter 8.

10. Failure to comply with the Fair Labor Standards Act for church-operated schools, including day-cares, preschool, elementary, and secondary. Chapter 8.